P9-CPW-204

contents

417 *more* games, puzzles & trivia challenges specially designed to **keep your brain young.**

NANCY LINDE

Introduction by Philip D. Harvey, PhD

WORKMAN PUBLISHING, NEW YORK

Copyright © 2016 by Nancy Linde

Illustration copyright © 2016 by Holly Carden

All rights reserved. No portion of this book may be reproduced—mechanically, electronically, or by any other means, including photocopying—without written permission of the publisher. Published simultaneously in Canada by Thomas Allen & Son Limited.

Library of Congress Cataloging-in-Publication Data is available.

ISBN 978-0-7611-8740-0

Design by Orlando Adiao
Cover art © Sergey Nivens/Fotolia (gears); carlosgardel/Fotolia (head)
Additional photo credits are on pages 404–405.

Workman books are available at special discounts when purchased in bulk for premiums and sales promotions as well as for fund-raising or educational use. Special editions or book excerpts also can be created to specification. For details, contact the Special Sales Director at the address below, or send an email to specialmarkets@workman.com.

Workman Publishing Co., Inc.
225 Varick Street
New York, NY 10014-4381
workman.com

WORKMAN is a registered trademark of Workman Publishing Co., Inc.

Printed in the United States of America

First printing September 2016

10 9 8 7 6 5 4 3 2 1

William Wordsworth once wrote that the "best portion" of a good person's life is not the big events but those "little nameless, unremembered acts of kindness." This book is dedicated to all of the good people who are spending the best portion of their lives lovingly looking after our senior citizens at home, in senior communities, assisted living and independent living residences, in nursing homes, hospitals, senior centers, senior day care facilities, and other senior-serving organizations. Thank you for all you do.

acknowledgments

My most grateful thanks go to: Faith Hamlin for her good advice and for always having my best interests at heart; Bruce Tracy and all the wonderful people at Workman who are delightful to work with and whose talents made this book so much better, especially Suzie Bolotin, Orlando Adiao, Holly Carden, Kate Karol, Anne Kerman, Bobby Walsh, and Danny Cooper; I especially want to thank George and Linda Harrar for their excellent game ideas and decades of support and friendship; Jon and Yanira Palfreman who have spent many a weekend night patiently testing out game after game with hardly a complaint; Jack and Leah Romanow for all the support and encouragement . . . and their friends at North Hill in Needham, MA—game testers extraordinaire—who outsmart me most of the time; Anne Damon, who finds (and enjoys) every mistake I make, and I'm grateful for it; all the senior organizations in the Boston area (especially Sunrise Senior Living in Arlington, MA, and, as always, Neville Place in Cambridge, MA) who welcomed me in to test games; and finally to all the activities professionals who subscribe to my website, Never2Old4Games, and take the time to send me compliments, critiques, and comments of all kinds. You help me better understand how to engage, entertain, and amuse our seniors.

introduction

Philip D. Harvey, PhD
Professor of Psychiatry and Behavioral Sciences
and Director of the Division of Psychology,
University of Miami Miller School of Medicine

Those of us who enjoyed *399 Games, Puzzles & Trivia Challenges Specially Designed to Keep Your Brain Young* are delighted that Nancy Linde has been busy making more games and puzzles. This new volume is packed with a rich mix of creative challenges that are just as fun to solve and as stimulating for your brain as her first book was.

As I thought about how to revise this introduction to brain science for the new edition, I realized the best news is that current science is still showing us that exercising your brain to think in new and challenging ways continues to be a great way to maintain your cognitive edge. And so what follows is an updated reminder for new readers as well as veterans of the previous book on how your brain works and how you can keep it in good working order, no matter what your age is.

Like its predecessor, this book is, first and foremost, a book of games—fun and engaging trivia quizzes, brainteasers, puzzles, and word games. If you bought this book because you love high-quality games, feel free to just skip this introduction, turn to page 1, and start playing. But if you are also a person who wants to improve your memory and sharpen your mind, read on. Because this is not just a book of games, it is also a rigorous exercise workout to keep your brain in tip-top shape.

Games are beneficial to us in lots of ways. They can be a fun way to spend time with the people we love. They promote social interaction. They're also an absorbing way to spend our solitary time. They challenge us intellectually, and they are rich in new learning opportunities. But what science has also shown us over the last two decades is that playing the right kinds of games can actually improve the health of your brain. In the same way that regular physical exercise makes your heart stronger and your body more limber, a daily dose of games can make your brain function better.

How is this possible? The very act of thinking in novel ways triggers a physical reaction in the brain—a cascade of events, called neurogenesis, in which proteins and enzymes and stem cells all combine to grow new brain cells that rejuvenate your brain and help it to work better and more efficiently. You will find that playing these games will not only make you a better game player, but you'll feel better and more cognitively "with it" in general.

Our ideas about exercise, for the brain and the body, have evolved a lot since the days when the brain was viewed as fixed and unchangeable. Back in the 1950s, people over the age of forty were discouraged from exercising because it might cause a heart attack. As recently as the mid-1970s, most scientists believed that the number of brain cells was set early in your life—around age twelve—and only decreased after that point. This belief led to the conclusion that the mental functions of the brain were also fixed and destined to change only for the worse as aging occurred and "brain cells were lost." Today, we know this is not the case. The brain is arguably the most flexible organ in the body, able to constantly adapt, repair, and improve throughout our lifespan. If the brain is injured, by a stroke or tumor for example, it can generate new cells and repair itself. But it doesn't require injury for new cells to form. The brain can also generate new interconnections in response to its environment. Unlike your height or hat size, you can make your brain change in volume and increase in efficiency by engaging in certain activities—including mentally challenging games and puzzles.

Of course, the opposite can also happen. The concept of "use it or lose it" has been applied for years to physical fitness, but it applies to brain fitness as well. People who are mentally active in their later years (playing games, doing crossword puzzles, learning a language, etc.) are known from clinical research to be more mentally sharp, cognitively agile, and to have better memory functions. The good news is that if you've let your brain "go flabby," you can reverse the changes. In the same way that physical exercise postpones and reduces loss of muscle mass and increases physical flexibility, mental exercise sharpens memory, concentration, and mental flexibility.

A word of caution is necessary here. Games are just one part of a healthy lifestyle for a healthy brain. Nothing beats the basics that include eating properly, getting enough sleep, getting some physical exercise every day . . . you know the drill. But one thing is certain—playing the games in this book will be one of the most fun, healthy things you can do!

A Brief Tour of the Human Brain

In the same way that it's important to understand the abdominal muscles if you want to trim your midriff, it's helpful to understand the lobes of the brain and

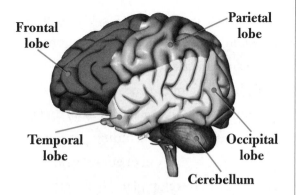

the functions they control if you want to improve your cognitive abilities.

For an overview of how it works, let's take a very abbreviated tour of the brain, the most complicated part of any living organism on earth, which is organized for conceptual convenience into several large regions called lobes. There is clear evidence from evolutionary biology that the regions of the human brain have developed in response to evolution. The earliest animal brains in, for example, worms or snails, are not much more than brain stems, where the most basic functions of the body are located: sensing pain, temperature, crude touch, sleep, and so forth. Throughout the process of evolution, the brain has grown larger, added mass, and become capable of more complex functions. The parts of the human brain that are higher and located toward the front and sides of the cerebral cortex are generally more advanced, more recent in their origin, and define more "human" qualities.

The frontal lobes (one on the right, one on the left) are the origin of all that is intrinsically human, including problem solving, the regulation of emotion, and the ability to develop plans and strategies. The frontal lobes are also critical to the most human of all abilities—language and abstraction, including the capacity to create symbolic representations such as words, letters, and numbers. These functions are more highly developed in humans than in any other species.

The temporal lobes are the home of multiple forms of memory, as well as auditory processing—and the functions are a bit different on each side of the brain. On the left side, the temporal lobes code and store verbal information for later recall; on the right side, they store similar spatial memories.

The parietal lobes are primarily responsible for spatial information, including cognitive skills such as figuring out routes, organizing complex visual materials, or putting together a puzzle.

The occipital lobes, located at the back of the brain, process visual information.

They perform basic perceptual processes such as stimulus detection and maintenance of visual perceptual processing.

The cerebellum is responsible largely for motor coordination including functions such as gait and balance, although it is becoming increasingly understood that cognitive activities require an intact cerebellum.

The limbic region is the oldest area of the brain. It generates emotional responses, and it originates and controls attentional functions, such as maintaining focus on information until it can be processed and transitioning information that has been processed recently into memory storage so that it can be used later. The classic memory region of the limbic system is the hippocampus, which is critical to being able to learn new information. The hippocampus is also

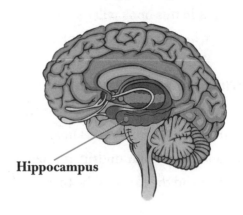

Hippocampus

the region of the brain most likely to change and respond to stimulation, which is good news for all of us who are getting older and feeling as though our memory is not aging gracefully.

But no brain region works alone. There are also a number of important connections between regions that need regular exercise to perform at top level. Consider this scenario (a good example of the importance of communication among brain regions and the circuits that facilitate them): Let's say you go to a five-star restaurant with a group of good friends and order the chef's best dish. It's a feast for the senses. It smells wonderful, looks perfect, tastes delicious, and the dinner conversation with your companions is delightful. To fully appreciate the whole dinner experience, your brain is working overtime, making important connections. The sensory cortex has the job of detecting information from the five senses (taste, touch, sight, smell, and hearing). But it doesn't interpret that information. Instead, it transfers the information along to the "association cortex" that in turn combines the input from multiple sensation systems and integrates it into a single event that can be

experienced in real time, in a multifaceted way, and recalled later upon demand. The association cortex is not located in a single lobe: it is spread among regions of several lobes, including frontal, temporal, and parietal regions. These regions are "multi-modal," meaning that they integrate information from all five senses.

Without the association among those different sensations, the restaurant dinner would not be a coherent event. If your brain perceived the taste of the meal, the smell of the food, or the sound of the restaurant, the experience would not be complete. But that's not all the association systems of the brain do. In addition to integrating the sensory information into a coherent whole, they also have the job of retrieving memories ("The last time I had paella was in New York"), making comparisons with those older memories ("I like this paella because it has more saffron"), preparing the information for later recall ("I won't forget this meal"), and making plans for the future ("When I go to Barcelona next year, I have to see what paella is like there").

All of the brain regions mentioned previously function best when they are interconnected and operating in synchrony. One of the biggest benefits from regular challenging cognitive activity is to enhance this synchrony, which will then lead to improvements in everyday cognitive functioning. In fact, as we discuss, games that have multiple demands engage multiple regions of the brain, generating synchronized activation and keeping your brain in top shape.

Brains and Games

Of course, like many other parts of the body, the brain does change as we get older. Around the age of fifty, people often start noticing small memory lapses ("Where did I put those keys?" or "Where did I park the car?"). We might notice that we don't concentrate as well as we used to or process information as speedily. Although it might be embarrassing to forget momentarily the name of a co-worker, it's really a minor problem that happens to all of us. Many cognitive functions are unaffected by the aging process—creativity, wisdom, reasoning, and the rules of language appear to be age resistant. But learning, memory, problem solving, and especially processing speed and efficiency can be vulnerable to aging,

and these cognitive functions are the ones we concentrate on in this book.

Let's just think about this from a simple, nonscientific perspective. If you wanted to build up a muscle group by weightlifting, and you know that you can lift ten pounds already, would you lift five pounds for building exercises? Of course not. By the same token, if you want to improve mentally, in any way, and had two hours a day to do it, would you spend those hours reading a book that you've already read or studying a map of your own neighborhood? No. The idea of exercise, both physical and mental, is to select an optimum level of difficulty and gradually increase it. Supported by research from both the physical and cognitive domains, we make these suggestions on how to use this book most effectively:

• You should play the games in this book for at least fifteen minutes every day.

• For optimal impact, you should start at the beginning of the book. Each chapter is carefully organized to increase just slightly in difficulty from chapter to chapter (and within each chapter), so starting at the first page and working toward the end will be most beneficial.

• Play the games with a timer by your side—an egg timer would work just fine, or you can use your watch or the stopwatch that is built into most smartphones. One difference between this book and the previous book is that a larger percentage of the games have time limits, that is, a suggested time duration in which the game should be completed by the player. Putting time pressure on a game is a great way to boost the cognitive benefit and to exercise the speed and efficiency in which your brain solves a quiz or puzzle. In fact, you can use the time factor in a few additional ways to increase the cognitive challenge:

1. Try to beat the time limit that is given. If, for example, a game asks you to complete your answers in one minute, try forty-five seconds instead.

2. Use a timer even on games that don't already have a specific time challenge.

3. Wherever appropriate, try repeating a game after you complete it, solving it again as fast as you can.

The games you play should exercise a broad set of cognitive skills. In the same way that we cross-train (i.e., do a mix of exercises) to work more than just one muscle and build wide-ranging physical fitness (endurance, aerobic capacity, strength, and flexibility), playing the same type of game over and over will not build cognitive skills. Playing an assortment of different games each day is the best strategy for diversified brain improvement. So again, as you work through the book from the beginning toward the end, the games are strategically placed to provide a healthy mix of games that exercise the key cognitive skills that are vulnerable in normal aging (more on this in the next section).

Critical Mental Functions for Healthy Brain Aging

Living normally and independently in the world requires many different cognitive abilities. Some, such as basic perception and sensory processes, usually don't change much in normal aging. In this book, we have chosen to focus on the key mental functions that can change with age including long-term memory, working memory, executive functioning, attention to detail, multitasking, and processing speed. Even among that group, some seem more vulnerable to the aging process than others, but all of them share several critical features.

- They are complex.
- They are not performed by a single region of the brain, but by multiple regions linked by circuits.
- They are critically important for functioning well and independently in the world. If any one of these mental functions was suddenly wiped out by an injury or an illness, living independently would be a real challenge.
- They can improve with the right kind of regular brain exercise.

So let's take an in-depth look at each of the cognitive functions, the symptoms that frequently occur when age-related deterioration has taken place, and some of the games to look for that work specifically on that mental skill. You'll note that throughout the book we have labeled each game with the cognitive skill (or skills) that it primarily exercises.

1. LONG-TERM MEMORY—If you have noticed occasional memory lapses, such as forgetting the names of people, objects, or events that occurred in the distant past, you should play games that exercise your long-term memory skills. The games Run the Alphabet and Endings & Beginnings are both good examples.

2. WORKING MEMORY—Sometimes called "short-term memory," working memory is the ability to actively hold information in your mind in order to accomplish a task at hand. This includes remembering verbal information like a phone number (without needing to have it repeated over and over), a short list of grocery items, or a sequence of directions to complete a task. Games that boost your working memory skills include Order, Please! and vocabulary quizzes such as Prime-Time Rhyme.

3. EXECUTIVE FUNCTIONING—Simply put, executive functioning involves solving problems by using information you already have, either in your long-term memory or in your working memory to work out novel solutions. If, for example, you are finding it more challenging to get organized and to accomplish routine tasks such as running your weekend errands, or if you find it hard to get out the door with everything you need (keys, phone, glasses), you need to shape up

your executive functioning skills. A couple of examples of fun ways to do that include the Odd Man Out and Making Connections games.

4. **ATTENTION TO DETAIL**—The process of absorbing small details when learning new information requires the ability to concentrate and stay focused. If you're finding it hard to follow instructions when setting up or using new appliances such as a microwave oven or a Blu-Ray player, or you have to study a subway map again and again to figure out which stop you want, or you are having problems navigating a website to purchase an item or fill a prescription, you may need to play games that exercise your concentration skills. The visual games in this book, including Common Bonds, are all good examples of games that improve your attention to detail.

5. **MULTITASKING**—*Multitasking* is a modern word that basically means doing more than one thing at a time. Do you find yourself interrupting a conversation on the phone because you can't take notes at the same time? Do you have trouble operating multiple controls in the car (radio, wipers, lights) while you are driving? Or do you need complete silence around you in order to read a book or work on your computer? If so, you will benefit from games such as Follow the Rules and Trimble that focus on multitasking skills.

6. **PROCESSING SPEED**—This is the speed at which your brain processes information, which includes being mentally fast enough to keep up with conversations, follow the plot of television programs or movies, and complete tasks efficiently. Recent scientific studies have shown that processing speed is the cognitive ability that changes the most with healthy aging, more than any of the other abilities previously described. If you have noticed that it takes longer for you to get simple tasks done, or if you need people to repeat things because you could not keep up, you may need to upgrade your processing skills. Try any game that imposes a time limit, such as the One Minute Madness games and Alma's Shopping List. Or, as we mentioned earlier, add a time limit to a task that does not have one and try to work as efficiently as you can while still maintaining your high level of performance.

Multiple Demands Make for Maximum Gains

As you can see from the descriptions of the games in this book, some of the tasks require only one or two cognitive demands. Others, such as Complete the Words, require four or more cognitive demands—executive functioning, long-term memory, attention to detail, and multitasking. This is a game that will keep your whole brain humming because it activates multiple circuits. We know from research on structured brain training (much more boring than cognitively active games) that the more demands we place on the brain, the bigger and more wide ranging our beneficial results. And, after you complete it, you can come back a

week or two later and try it again, working as fast as possible to complete the task in order to buff up your processing speed as well.

Much of what I've said here is known intuitively by just about anyone over the age of forty. In my work with senior citizens, I often hear how much better they feel when they use their brain—when they play a word game, complete a crossword puzzle, take a trivia quiz, or play bridge. What's great about this book is that it is filled with hundreds of fun and engaging games that just happen to also be superb cognitive exercises. There are no boring neurological tests here. No repetitive rehabilitation exercises. Just good games with real cognitive benefits.

a word from the author

I make games. Word games, trivia quizzes, puzzles, and brainteasers—as you are about to see in just a turn of the page. So you can probably imagine how exciting it was for me to discover, not so long ago, that scientific research has shown how games are not just fun but are also a healthy habit. If you haven't read it yet, go back to page vii and take a look at Dr. Phil Harvey's introduction—an easy-to-understand explanation of how games strengthen and increase the neural connections in our brains. In fact, Stuart Brown, noted physician, author, and pioneering play researcher, has actually seen the impact of games on the human brain through modern imaging techniques.

"Nothing lights up the brain like play," Brown reported in his 2010 TED talk. ". . . Play fires up the cerebellum, puts a lot of impulses into the frontal lobe—the executive portion—helps contextual memory be developed… and so on."

I think science is just recently proving what people have known intuitively for thousands of years. Play matters . . . and not just for kids. Games are an important source of relaxation and stimulation for adults. They bring people together. They are a great way to bond with friends and family. They help people develop important social skills. Games have the power to enhance health and happiness at all of life's stages. Games bring joy. And they can play a vital role in honing problem solving skills, encouraging creative thinking, and improving human relationships.

In his 2010 book *Play*, Stuart Brown compares play to oxygen. "It's all around us," he wrote, "yet goes mostly unnoticed or unappreciated until it is missing." Indeed, Brown's research has revealed that *lack* of play was just as important as other factors in predicting criminal behavior among murderers in Texas prisons.

Okay. I don't really think that playing games will reduce the crime rate. But I do believe that games have the power to increase happiness and lead to improved communication and understanding for people of all ages. Or, as Plato described it nearly 2,500 years ago, "You can discover more about a person in an hour of play than you can in a year of conversation."

So grab a friend, your son or daughter, your grandkids, or your neighbor and dig into my games. Who knows what you might learn about each other?

RUN THE ALPHABET

One-Syllable Words

long-term memory
working memory
executive functioning
processing speed

From *Art* to *Zest*, can you come up with a one-syllable word that starts with each letter of the alphabet? If you want to make this game a little more challenging, identify only words with five letters or more. And for an extra brain boost, see if you can complete the quiz in two minutes.

A _____

B _____

C _____

D _____

E _____

F _____

G _____

H _____

I _____

J _____

K _____

L _____

M _____

N _____

O _____

P _____

Q _____

R _____

S _____

T _____

U _____

V _____

W _____

X (Obscure) _____

Y _____

Z _____

Answers on page 323

MAKiNG CONNECTiONS

Given nine words or phrases randomly placed in a grid, can you find the three groups of three connected items AND explain why they are connected? Here's a sample grid:

RED	HONEY	BLUE
VIEIRA	HARVEST	PURPLE
FULL	LAUER	COURIC

GROUP 1 WORDS:
Red, Blue, Purple

THEME:
Colors

GROUP 2 WORDS:
Vieira, Lauer, Couric

THEME:
Today show hosts

GROUP 3 WORDS:
Full, Honey, Harvest

THEME:
_____moon

SPRING	SALSA	SUMMER
TWIST	TAP	JIG
MINERAL	FALL	WINTER

GROUP 1 WORDS

_____ _____ _____

THEME:

_____

GROUP 2 WORDS

_____ _____ _____

THEME:

_____

GROUP 3 WORDS

_____ _____ _____

THEME:

_____

Answers on page 323

Group Therapy

Group Therapy is the game that proves there is more than one correct answer to a question . . . and we tell you the minimum number of answers you need to come up with. For an extra brain boost, put a one-minute limit on each question.

long-term memory
executive functioning
multitasking
processing speed

1. Name five packaged breakfast cereals.

2. Name six stringed instruments.

3. Name five things, besides books, that are read.

4. Name five brands of bar soap.

5. Name six television game shows (past or present).

6. Name four countries that have four-letter names.

7. Name ten sports that use a spherical ball.

Answers on page 323

Vivienne's Vowels

executive functioning
long-term memory
attention to detail
processing speed

Vivienne is an odd one. She has an aversion to the letters A, E, I, O, and U. Can you fix her list of animals (of any type) by putting back the missing vowels? You can make this a more strenuous brain exercise by adding some time pressure: Try to solve this puzzle in thirty seconds.

1. PRCPN _____

2. CHTH _____

3. BFFL _____

4. BRRCD _____

5. CGR _____

6. CLM _____

7. CML _____

8. HYN _____

9. LLGTR _____

10. RDVRK _____

11. SQD _____

12. LPC _____

Answers on page 324

WORD PICTURES

Put one picture together with one word part (in any order) to come up with the names of eight flowers. (*Note: Spelling might not always be correct, but the pronunciation will be right.*)

BINE	NATION	MARI	CHID
PEO	SY	PY	ONIA

Answers on page 324

long-term memory
executive functioning
attention to detail

TED'S TERRIBLE TITLES

Poor Ted. He is a connoisseur of culture but he can never remember the titles of some of his favorite books, plays, songs, magazines, television shows, etc. Can you fix Ted's mangled titles by correcting his mistakes?

1. The Peculiar Pair

2. Unable to Doze Off in a City on the Puget Sound

3. Insurrection on the Brand of Paper Towel

4. Veracity or Repercussions

5. Croonin' in the Precipitation

6. Execution, She Inscribed

7. The Extreme Suffering and the Blissful Joy

8. Mandibles

9. Demise of One Fuller Brush Employee

10. Shoeless in the Urban Recreational Area

11. The Morning Meal at an Expensive Jewelry Store

12. Deceased Fellow Strolling

Answers on page 324

fill in the letters

Fill in the blank spaces with letters to make common English words (no proper nouns allowed). For example, __ **a t** yields twelve answers: *bat, cat, eat, fat, hat, mat, oat, pat, rat, sat, tat, vat.* (*Note: The number in parentheses indicates how many common English words can be made.*)

1. **j** __ __   (16)

2. __ **c** __   (4)

3. **t o** __   (9)

4. **p l** __ __   (12)

5. __ __ **m b**   (9)

6. __ **o i** __   (10)

7. **s** __ __ **n**   (15)

8. **d** __ __ **p**   (5)

Answers on page 324

Sentence Sleuth

A true sentence sleuth can find the one word that is hidden somewhere in a sentence. In this case, can you find the name of a US city? The correct answer could be spread over one, two, or several words, and you should ignore all punctuation, capital letters, etc., when looking for the hidden US city.

long-term memory
executive functioning
attention to detail

1. Young Elise hid a forbidden version of the book *Fifty Shades of Grey* under her mattress.

2. To promote the health benefits of okra, Jim-Bob brought four types of gumbos to northern cities.

3. Mr. Bartlett saw that antique rocking chair in May, but he didn't buy it until the June auction.

4. When the fashion editor saw the bejeweled handbag, she exclaimed, "That's so chic! A gold lamé bag encrusted with emeralds and diamonds! I just love it."

5. "Mom, a hamster doesn't spread disease," said Stephanie, hoping to convince her mother to buy her a pet.

6. After the tsunami, a million people were left homeless.

7. Leo was stunned when he observed his brother rebuff a lovely woman who was clearly interested in him.

8. When Fred Simpson was broke, he thought one of his younger brothers, either Rob, Al, Tim, or Ed, would loan him $1,000. He was wrong.

Answers on page 324

DOUBLE TROUBLE

Can you find the one word that precedes each list of words to make a common two-word phrase or compound word? For example, the one word that completes *weed*, *coast*, and *sick* is *sea* (*seaweed*, *seacoast*, *seasick*). If you get stuck, we've provided the first letter of the correct answer as a hint at the bottom of the page.

1. Mine, rush, standard

_____

2. Cocktail, salad, cake

_____

3. Line, house, cord, tools

_____

4. Box, lace, shine

_____

5. Brush, horse, line, pin

_____

6. Book, up, mate, mark

_____

7. Bug, spread, rock, pan

_____

8. Flower, shine, burn

_____

9. Cap, club, gown

_____

10. Shoulder, turkey, cream, sweat

_____

Hints: 1 g; 2 f; 3 p; 4 s; 5 c; 6 c; 7 b; 8 s; 9 n; 10 c   *Answers on page 324*

mamma mia!

You don't have to be Italian to identify these pasta shapes . . . but it wouldn't hurt.

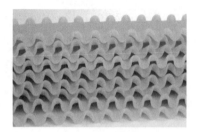

A _____

B _____

C _____

D _____

E _____

F _____

G _____   H _____

I _____   J _____

K _____   L _____

Answers on page 324

Say Cheese

How many types of cheese can you name in one minute?

long-term memory
working memory
processing speed

_____

_____

_____

_____

_____

_____

_____

_____

_____

_____

Answers on page 325

it's just grand

All of the answers in this quiz contain the word GRAND.

long-term memory
working memory

1. Republican nickname.

2. New York City transportation center.

3. Arizona landmark.

4. Vladimir Horowitz's instrument.

5. The second-largest city in Michigan.

6. This produces the maximum number of runs with one swing of the baseball bat.

7. The end of something, especially a fireworks show.

8. Important country music venue in Tennessee.

9. Famous folk artist who first took up a paintbrush at the age of 78.

10. Impressive in appearance or style, often pretentiously so.

Answers on page 325

ALPHABET TRIVIA

The only thing these trivia questions have in common is that all of the answers begin with the letter A.

1. What is the largest US city (by population) that starts with the letter A?

2. What are the three Major League Baseball teams whose names (not cities or states) begin with the letter A?

3. What are the four US states that begin with the letter A?

4. What is the only Canadian province that begins with the letter A?

5. Who are the three US presidents whose last names begin with the letter A?

6. What are the two signs of the zodiac that begin with the letter A?

7. What does Popeye have tattooed on his forearms?

8. Which two punctuation marks begin with the letter A?

9. Name one of the two men's tennis champions whose initials are AA.

10. Who wrote *Pride and Prejudice* and *Sense and Sensibility*?

11. What are the five US state capitals that begin with the letter A?

12. What do these acronyms stand for?

    AAA

    AA

    ATM

    ACLU

    AWOL

    ASAP

    AKA

    AOL

Answers on page 325

NOT TOO TAXING

For each clue below, can you put the missing letters T-A-X back in the correct order to reveal a common English word? To make this a more vigorous brain exercise, try to complete this quiz in two minutes.

1. __ __ __ i
2. E __ __ c __
3. E __ __ r _
4. L __ __ e _
5. Syn __ __ __
6. __ n __ ie __ y
7. E __ __ r __ ct
8. La __ __ __ ive
9. M __ __ chbo __
10. E __ cav __ __ e
11. E __ h __ us __ ed
12. Ju __ __ __ pose
13. In __ o __ ic __ ted
14. Rela __ __ __ ion

Answers on page 325

Scrambled Colors

Unscramble the letters in each clue below to reveal a list of colors. For an even better brain exercise, try to complete this quiz in two minutes.

1. ORBNW
2. CLABK
3. AEMRB
4. EEIGB
5. CILLA
6. GREANO
7. OWELLY
8. RULEPP
9. EIOLTV
10. IOMRNCS
11. AOORMN
12. AEEDLNRV

Answers on page 325

"QUOTATION STATION"

Move the letters in each vertical column of the top grid to the spaces in the column just below it in the bottom grid. The letters will not necessarily be moved in the order in which they appear. If you move the letters to the correct

positions, they will spell out a quotation (reading from left to right) from nineteenth-century abolitionist leader Frederick Douglass. (*Note: A black square indicates the end of a word. Words may continue from one horizontal line to the next.*)

Before attempting the big puzzle, try this example first—without looking at the answer to the right:

T	H	I	R	A	M	O	R
E		T	H	I	F	K	
I		E		E	N		

Example Answer:

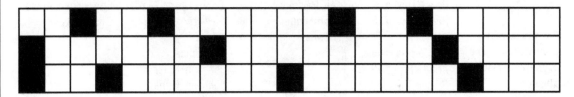

Answers on page 325

INITIAL QUIZ

All of the two-word answers in this quiz begin with the initials TP.

1. This keeps a baby's bottom dry.

2. Ultraconservative political movement that emerged in 2009.

3. A favored student.

4. Serena Williams, for example.

5. An aviator who flies and evaluates new airplane designs.

6. Collective term for Disneyland or Dollywood.

7. A semipermanent or permanent location for mobile homes.

8. He published the pro-independence pamphlet called "Common Sense" anonymously in 1776.

9. Monumental sculptures carved from large trees by the indigenous people of the Pacific Northwest coast of North America.

10. End-of-the-semester essay that often counts for a significant portion of a student's grade.

11. This 1990–91 blockbuster television series, described as both a crime drama and a psychological thriller, was created by David Lynch.

Answers on page 325

---

 trivia

NAME THEIR SPORT

long-term memory
executive functioning

Can you identify each sport by some of its winningest athletes?

❶ Oscar De La Hoya, Riddick Bowe, Ken Norton

❷ Karl Malone, Pete Maravich, Patrick Ewing

❸ Martina Hingis, Andy Murray, Althea Gibson

❹ Ryan Lochte, Missy Franklin, Ian Thorpe

❺ Shawn Johnson, Aly Raisman, Dominique Dawes

❻ Nancy Lopez, Nick Faldo, Vijay Singh

❼ Stirling Moss, Bobby Unser, Jackie Stewart

❽ Michael Johnson, Rafer Johnson, Frank Shorter

❾ Tim Howard, Abby Wambach, Diego Maradona

❿ Bonnie Blair, Eric Heiden, Apolo Ohno

Answers on page 326

WORD PARTS

The word *bather* is defined as "a person that takes a bath or goes swimming." In this game, however, we supply the definition not of a word, but of its parts. For example, given the first clue *Louisville Slugger*, plus the second clue *the opposite of him*, the answer is *bather* (*bat* + *her*).

1. Short for "hello" + scarlet

_____

2. Not against + doorway carpet

_____

3. Red or Caspian + male offspring

_____

4. To use a needle and thread + to get older, as in wine

_____

5. Sphere used in many sports + commercial

_____

6. A feline + Sony Bono's former wife

_____

7. Mr. Capone + the "loneliest" number

_____

8. Not good + where money is coined + the opposite of off

_____

9. Saloon or tavern + to put on weight, for example

_____

10. Woman's upper undergarment + fashionable or trendy

_____

11. Headwear for a swimmer + the first letter of the alphabet + a metropolitan area

_____

12. High temperature, warmth + female bird

_____

Answers on page 326

FIND THE WORDS

Find the 45 words in the picture that start with the letter W.

Answers on page 328

working memory
executive functioning
attention to detail
multitasking

THE TOP TOP

long-term memory
executive functioning
attention to detail

This is a game of repeating homonyms—words that are pronounced the same and often even spelled the same, but have different meanings. For example, given the definition *The best spinning toy ever*, your answer would be *The top top*.

1. A perfect runway walker

2. A mediocre county festival

3. A secretive young army man

4. An autumn tumble

5. A no-eating pledge that ends quickly

6. A hot dog that speaks its mind

7. A good monetary penalty

8. A de-wrinkling appliance made of metal

9. A lamp that doesn't weigh much

10. A faraway channel changer

11. A particularly fast-flying bird

12. An especially sharp-tasting pastry

13. Kindly paper money

14. A splendid thousand-dollar bill

Answers on page 326

Twiddle Your Thumbs

Can you come up with the names of the body parts that will correctly complete each of these well-known sayings? To make this a more vigorous brain exercise, try to answer all the questions in one minute.

1. Put your money _____

2. Button your _____

3. A bundle of _____

4. Joined _____

5. Have a lump _____

6. Go weak _____

7. A slap _____

8. A bleeding _____

9. Have the upper _____

10. Stick out like _____

11. A kick _____

12. The long _____

Answers on page 326

prime-time ◆ rhyme ◆

Each question in this quiz has three different answers
. . . and they all rhyme. For example:

Clues: One plus one; not false; azure color.

Answers: Two; true; blue.

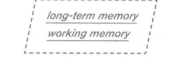

1. A short comedy routine; clever humor; to resign

2. British term for a playing field; wealthy; reason to scratch

3. A large all-terrain vehicle; Gene Krupa's occupation; the "dog days" season

4. Uncomplicated; blemish; cheek indentation

5. To tote; Diana's youngest; to wed

6. Amusing; cash; bee's output

7. A cloth bag; pretzels or cookies; a mallard's call

8. Useless stuff; confidence and audacity; dormitory bed

9. An idea or opinion; a large body of water; a thick liquid for the skin

10. One of two metals that make brass; a tattletale; hockey venue

11. A loud, deep shout; saffron or maize; an often molded dessert

12. To run away; a French cheese; a busy bug

Answers on page 326

RIDDLE
ME THIS

Riddles often require some unconventional thinking, which makes them a great brain exercise. Think outside the box as you try to solve this classic riddle.

What can you catch, but not throw?

Answer on page 326

Secret Word

How many four- and five-letter common English words can you find in the phrase below? The more words you find, the more likely you are to also get the secret word—a word that is generally a little harder to spot. (We found thirty-four 4-letter words and twelve 5-letter words.) To make this game even more challenging—and a better brain exercise—try to find at least twelve 4- or 5-letter words in one minute.

MARDI GRAS

_____ _____ _____ _____

_____ _____ _____ _____

_____ _____ _____ _____

_____ _____ _____ _____

_____ _____ _____ _____

_____ _____ _____ _____

_____ _____ _____ _____

_____ _____ _____ _____

_____ _____ _____ _____

_____ _____ _____ _____

_____ _____ _____ _____

Answers (including the secret word) on page 326

complete the words

long-term memory
executive functioning
multitasking
attention to detail

Place one letter in each blank space below to make a word of five letters or more. All twenty-six letters are used only once; and each correct answer uses at least one space on the right and one space on the left of the inserted letter. No hyphenated words, plurals, or proper nouns are allowed.

A	O	C	K	N	I		E	Q	O	R	N
B	S	K	I	N	V		T	E	M	O	N
C	I	B	L	I	Z		A	R	D	E	R
D	P	A	T	T	I		U	D	E	U	T
E	E	X	D	I	S		U	T	E	F	F
F	T	I	G	E	R		P	I	D	I	N
G	T	I	N	I	G		T	H	A	I	R
H	C	H	R	E	V		N	T	T	Y	K
I	V	E	R	V	I		I	D	A	L	Y
J	B	E	E	L	S		R	A	P	U	S
K	D	O	G	A	N		L	E	C	A	T
L	O	B	I	O	P		Y	C	K	U	M
M	A	G	O	T	R		S	T	T	E	R
N	F	R	I	F	L		U	R	U	S	T
O	V	U	L	N	E		A	B	L	E	X
P	W	G	A	L	A		Y	M	O	R	E
Q	G	R	I	N	B		A	C	K	U	D
R	B	L	O	R	E		O	N	Y	E	C
S	R	A	U	M	A		U	A	L	I	F
T	B	A	R	B	E		U	E	A	H	T
U	D	A	Y	Z	A		E	S	O	M	E
V	O	S	H	R	E		D	I	N	G	Y
W	T	N	A	P	A		A	M	A	S	H
X	B	R	A	S	Q		A	S	H	T	T
Y	U	N	U	S	U		M	E	R	V	E
Z	H	E	D	I	N		Y	E	L	L	Y

Answers on page 327

pump it up!

All of the answers in this quiz contain the consecutive letters UMP.

1. Irritable or cranky.

2. Childhood disease that causes painful swelling of the salivary glands.

3. A coarse, dark rye bread.

4. A great victory or achievement.

5. A run of bad luck and poor playing, especially for an athlete.

6. Old-fashioned name for tuberculosis.

7. Louis Armstrong's and Miles Davis's instrument.

8. A little overweight.

9. Dowdy, drab, or unattractively dressed.

10. German fairy tale character who helps the miller's daughter spin straw into gold.

11. A type of whale.

12. Common prison garb.

Answers on page 327

ODD MAN OUT

All of the items in each list have something in common—with one exception. Your job is to find which item doesn't fit and to explain why it is the "odd man out."

1. Snap, String, Finger, Wax

2. Drof, Yellort, Adnoh, Ovlov

3. Simon, Wilson, Newman, Hogan

4. Marriott, Greek, Garden, Potato

5. Pound, Pencil, Coffee, Fruit

6. Platypus, Dodo, Dinosaur, Passenger pigeon

7. Arial, Telegraph, Courier, Geneva

8. Golden Gate Bridge, The Alamo, Hearst Castle, Death Valley

Answers on page 327

Semordnilap

A *semordnilap* is a word that spells a different word forward and backward, such as *faced* and *decaf*. (Give yourself a pat on the back if you noticed something special about the word *semordnilap*!)

1. Forward, it means got married; backward, it's early-morning moisture.

2. Forward, it's a jewel; backward, it's the oldest sister in the novel *Little Women*.

3. Forward, it's a quick look; backward, it means to retain possession of something.

4. Forward, it's useful hints; backward, it means to expectorate.

5. Forward, they're eating utensils; backward, they're people who pry in sneaky ways.

6. Forward, it means crazy and irrational; backward, it's a water barrier.

7. Forward, it's Beelzebub; backward, it's the opposite of died.

8. Forward, it's a drain stopper; backward, it's a big swallow.

9. Forward, it's another word for friends; backward, it's a strike with an open palm.

10. Forward, they're the outer parts of some fruits; backward, it's a nighttime activity.

11. Forward, it's a hospital unit; backward, it means to create pictures using a pencil or crayon.

Answers on page 327

---

 trivia

FRUITS & VEGGIES

long-term memory

executive functioning

Eat all your fruits and vegetables and try answering these questions.

❶ When this vegetable is added to corned beef hash, it's called red flannel hash.

❷ These are the two vegetables most commonly used to make traditional cole slaw.

❸ Currants and sultanas are dried forms of this fruit.

❹ Can you name one of several fruits that are not recommended in Jello-O recipes because they have an enzyme that prevents jelling?

Answers on page 327

wacky wordies

egg egg egg
easy

LANG4UAGE

1 _____

2 _____

cent cent cent cent
cent cent cent
cent cent cent
DANCE

pudproofding

3 _____

4 _____

To solve these fun puzzles, look carefully at each frame, because the arrangement of the letters is a key clue to the familiar phrase contained within. For example, if the word *school* were placed high up in the frame, the answer would be *high school*. Or, if the words *easy pieces* occurred five times in the frame, the answer would be *five easy pieces*.

Answers on page 327

talk

nefriended
is
defriended

5 _____

6 _____

BAN   ANA

alarm
alarm
alarm
FIRE

7 _____

8 _____

Vivienne's Vowels

Vivienne is an odd one. She has an aversion to the letters A, E, I, O, and U. Can you fix her list of food and beverages by putting back the missing vowels? *Note: Anything that is consumable (i.e., brand names, generic names, restaurant dishes, etc.) is acceptable.* You can make this a more strenuous brain exercise by adding some time pressure: Try to solve this puzzle in thirty seconds.

1. PPPR _____

2. PNT BTTR _____

3. CSR SLD _____

4. BF TCS _____

5. SLMN _____

6. CNTLP _____

7. BLD PTT _____

8. BL CHS _____

9. RT BR _____

10. PCHD GG _____

11. LSGN _____

Answers on page 330

ALPHABET TRIVIA

The only thing these trivia questions have in common is that all of the answers begin with the letter B.

long-term memory
executive functioning

1. What are the six countries in the Western Hemisphere whose names begin with the letter B?

2. Name the three main characters in *The Flintstones* whose names begin with the letter B.

3. How many of the six Olympic sports (summer and winter) that begin with the letter B can you name?

4. Which two boroughs of New York City begin with the letter B?

5. Which two properties and one railroad in the classic version of Monopoly begin with the letter B?

6. What two US cities with populations greater than 500,000 begin with the letter B?

7. What is the name of the Old English epic poem in which the title character defeats the monster Grendel?

8. What is the last name of the character played by Sylvester Stallone in the *Rocky* movies?

9. Can you name the three US presidents whose last names begin with the letter B?

10. This "B" couple starred in several movies together, including *The Big Sleep* and *Key Largo*.

11. He is the title character in J.R.R. Tolkien's 1937 novel *The Hobbit* and a secondary character in *The Lord of the Rings*.

12. What do these acronyms and abbreviations stand for?
BYOB
BBB
BMOC
BYU
BLT
BBC

Answers on page 330

alphabetically speaking

long-term memory
executive functioning
attention to detail

Everyone knows that January is the first month of the year. But "alphabetically speaking," April is the first month because it begins with the letters AP. In this game, can you figure out what comes first, last, or next . . . alphabetically speaking?

1. Alphabetically speaking, who is the first US president?

2. Alphabetically speaking, what is the first continent?

3. Alphabetically speaking, what is the first planet in our solar system?

4. Alphabetically speaking, what is the first playing card suit?

5. Alphabetically speaking, what is the first day of the week?

6. Alphabetically speaking, who is the first Marx brother?

7. Alphabetically speaking, what is the last state in New England?

8. Alphabetically speaking, what is the first mammal?

9. Alphabetically speaking, who is the first *Brady Bunch* child?

10. Alphabetically speaking, what is the first color in the color spectrum?

11. Alphabetically speaking, what is the first of Christopher Columbus's three ships?

12. Alphabetically speaking, what is the first Great Lake?

Answers on page 330

THE NAME GAME

This is a two-part game. First answer the clues. Then put the answers in the correct order to reveal the name of a famous person (living or dead, real or fictional). Example question: *The sound of a growl + men's neckwear + the forest.* Answer: *Grrr + tie + woods (Tiger Woods).*

1. Sound a crow makes + out of money + male cat

2. To iron fabric + snake sound + one of Santa's helpers + brand of jeans since 1889

3. Oolong and Pekoe + half a pair of knitted footwear + city-loving rodent

4. Sports sphere + snake-like fish + not tight

5. The twelfth letter of the alphabet + vehicle that is smaller than a truck and bigger than a car + to signal by quickly opening and closing one's eye + tear or shred

6. To attempt + what a law student has to pass + what dunes are made of + women's upper undergarments

7. Thanksgiving main dish + public transportation vehicle + 2,000 pounds

8. Bus rider Ms. Parks + candid, forthright + fabric atop a pool table + not dirty

9. Head of a college + hirsute + what an owl says + leg joint

Answers on page 330

Anagrams

The letters of each word in this list can be rearranged in multiple ways to form other words. We provide the word and the number of anagrams that are possible to make. (*Remember, you must use ALL the letters in the given word.*) You should give your brain a rest if you can solve all of these anagrams in two minutes.

1. Tap (2) _____ _____

2. Arm (2) _____ _____

3. Guts (2) _____ _____

4. Opts (5) _____ _____ _____ _____ _____ _____

5. Mean (3) _____ _____ _____

6. Meats (4) _____ _____ _____ _____

7. Voles (2) _____ _____

8. Serve (3) _____ _____ _____

Answers on page 330

---

trivia

ON YOUR MARK

long-term memory

executive functioning

Mark my words, this quiz is all about people named Mark.

❶ Michael Phelps beat the seven-gold-medal record set by this Mark at the 1972 Olympics.

❷ This Mark was a Roman general, a loyal friend to Julius Caesar, and a lover to Cleopatra, with whom he had three children.

❸ This Mark's father won a Heisman Trophy, and his wife played Mindy in the TV series *Mork and Mindy*.

❹ After becoming born again, this Mark said he killed John Lennon because it was "God's will."

Answers on page 330

Triplets

Larry, Curly, and Moe. Ready, aim, fire. Those are well-known "triplets." Can you fill in the two missing items that complete each of these triplets?

1. Blood, _____ , and _____

2. Lock, _____ , and _____

3. Hop, _____ , and a _____

4. The butcher, _____ ,

   _____

5. Life, _____ , and _____

6. Planes, _____ , and _____

7. Lather, _____ , _____

8. Id, _____ , and _____

9. Eat, _____ , and be _____

10. Cool, _____ , and _____

11. Healthy, _____ , and

    _____

12. Here, _____ , and _____

13. Hook, _____ , and _____

14. Rock, _____ , _____

Answers on page 330

What's the Nationality?

long-term memory
executive functioning
attention to detail

There are, of course, French and Dutch people. But things are often connected to nationalities too—such as a *French twist* or a *Dutch uncle*. In this game, we provide the "thing" and you need to come up with its nationality (language group, region, etc.).

1. _____ Army Knife

2. _____ Roulette

3. _____ Numeral

4. _____ Goulash

5. _____ Chocolate Cake

6. _____ Saddle

7. _____ Cigar

8. _____ Bacon

9. _____ Waffles

10. _____ Waltz

11. _____ Jumping Beans

12. _____ Jig

13. _____ Pastry

14. _____ Checkers

Answers on page 331

RIDDLE
ME THIS

Riddles often require some unconventional thinking, which makes them a great brain exercise. Think outside the box as you try to solve this classic riddle.

What starts with E and ends with E and contains one letter?

Answer on page 331

WORD TOWER

Every word in a word tower begins with the same two letters. You build the tower by increasing the length of each word by one letter. For example, a five-word tower built on the letters FA could include: FAN, FAST, FABLE, FACTOR, FAILURE.

How far can you go before you get stumped? Using the letters ME, we made a tower twelve words high. (*Note: Proper nouns are not allowed, and you cannot just add an* s *to make a longer word. For example, if your four-letter word is* melt, *your five-letter word cannot be* melts.) For an extra brain boost, see how tall your tower of words can get in two minutes.

1. M E
2. M E __
3. M E __ __
4. M E __ __ __
5. M E __ __ __ __
6. M E __ __ __ __ __
7. M E __ __ __ __ __ __
8. M E __ __ __ __ __ __ __
9. M E __ __ __ __ __ __ __ __
10. M E __ __ __ __ __ __ __ __ __
11. M E __ __ __ __ __ __ __ __ __ __
12. M E __ __ __ __ __ __ __ __ __ __ __

Answers on page 331

MAKING CONNECTIONS

Given nine words or phrases randomly placed in a grid, can you find the three groups of three connected items AND explain why they are connected? Here's a sample grid:

RED	HONEY	BLUE
VIEIRA	HARVEST	PURPLE
FULL	LAUER	COURIC

GROUP 1 WORDS:
Red, Blue, Purple

THEME:
Colors

GROUP 2 WORDS:
Vieira, Lauer, Couric

THEME:
Today show hosts

GROUP 3 WORDS:
Full, Honey, Harvest

THEME:
_____moon

BASS	BRIDGE	CAPRI
SPADES	HEARTS	STATEN
IRELAND	SNARE	KETTLE

GROUP 1 WORDS

_____ _____ _____

THEME:

_____

GROUP 2 WORDS

_____ _____ _____

THEME:

_____

GROUP 3 WORDS

_____ _____ _____

THEME:

_____

Answers on page 331

SHARP AS A TACK

long-term memory
executive functioning
processing speed

Similes are comparative expressions that use the words *like* or *as*. In this game, we give the first half of a familiar simile and you must provide the rest. If you come up with half of these, you're "sharp as a tack"! To make this a more vigorous brain exercise, try to answer all the questions in one minute.

1. American as _____

2. Clean as _____

3. Cool as _____

4. Dead as _____

5. Dull as _____

6. Fit as _____

7. Fresh as _____

8. Guilty as _____

9. Hard as _____

10. High as _____

11. Pretty as _____

12. Right as _____

Answers on page 331

Group Therapy

long-term memory
executive functioning
multitasking
processing speed

Group Therapy is the game that proves there is more than one correct answer to a question . . . and we tell you the minimum number of answers you need to come up with. For an extra brain boost, put a one-minute limit on each question.

1. Name five famous overweight people.

2. Name six items you would find in the condiments aisle of the supermarket.

3. Name five people whose first name is James, Jim, or Jimmy.

4. Name five foreign cities or countries that begin with the letter A.

5. Name six things that are green.

6. Name six types of nuts (just the edible, culinary kind).

7. Name five board games.

8. Name five common men's first names that begin with the letter C.

Answers on page 331

Finish the Proverb

Given the first two words of a familiar proverb or saying, can you complete it?
To make this a more vigorous brain exercise, try to answer all the questions in
one minute.

1. A fool _____.

2. A picture _____.

3. An army _____.

4. The apple _____.

5. The end _____.

6. The grass _____.

7. The pen _____.

8. The squeaky _____.

9. Money doesn't _____.

10. Make hay _____.

11. Laughter is _____.

12. Good things _____.

13. God helps _____.

Answers on page 332

DOUBLE TROUBLE

Can you find the one word that follows each list of words to make a common two-word phrase or compound word? For example, the one word that completes *honey*, *polar*, and *teddy* is *bear* (*honey bear*, *polar bear*, *teddy bear*). If you get stuck, we've provided the first letter of the correct answer as a hint at the bottom of the page.

1. Bed, fry, dead

_____

2. Air, carpet, sand

_____

3. Candy, handle, side

_____

4. Time, score, flash

_____

5. Bird, green, clearing

_____

6. Bat, gentle, fresh

_____

7. Cotton, loud, blabber

_____

8. Snow, butter, meat

_____

9. Buck, eye, saber

_____

10. Sugar, candy, walking

_____

Hints: 1 p; 2 b; 3 b; 4 c; 5 h; 6 m; 7 m; 8 b; 9 t; 10 c

Answers on page 332

ALPHABET TRIVIA

The only thing these trivia questions have in common is that all of the answers begin with the letter C.

1. What are the three US states that begin with the letter C?

2. What are the six US state capital cities that begin with the letter C?

3. Name four US presidents whose last names begin with the letter C.

4. Which two Ivy League colleges begin with the letter C?

5. When purchasing a diamond, consumers are advised to look for quality in these four "C" factors.

6. How many of the nineteen countries that begin with the letter C can you name?

7. Name the capital city of:
   a. Egypt
   b. Australia
   c. Venezuela
   d. Denmark

8. What are the two signs of the zodiac that begin with the letter C?

9. What are the two baseball fielding positions that begin with the letter C?

10. Which two of the eight vegetables in V-8 vegetable juice begin with the letter C?

11. Name these one-word movie titles that begin with the letter C:
   a. 1967 movie that starred Richard Harris as King Arthur.
   b. 1942 film starring Humphrey Bogart and Ingrid Bergman.
   c. 1972 musical starring Liza Minnelli and Joel Grey.
   d. 1956 musical film starring Gordon MacRae and Shirley Jones that features the song "You'll Never Walk Alone."

12. What do these acronyms or abbreviations stand for?
CV
CNN
CST
CEO
CDC
CPA
CPR
CIA

Answers on page 332

Two . . .

Can you finish these familiar sayings, idioms, and titles that contain the word *Two*?

1. It takes two . . .

2. One, two . . .

3. Two heads . . .

4. Two and a half . . .

5. Two-car . . .

6. Two cents' . . .

7. Two sides of . . .

8. Two shakes . . .

9. Two can play . . .

10. Two-piece . . .

11. Two for the . . .

12. Two-liter . . .

Answers on page 333

Three . . .

Can you finish these familiar sayings, idioms, and titles that begin with the word *Three*?

1. *Three Coins* . . .

2. Three French . . .

3. *Three Days of* . . .

4. Three sheets . . .

5. *Three Faces* . . .

6. Three Mile . . .

7. *Three Men* . . .

8. *Three on a* . . .

9. *Threepenny* . . .

10. Three bean . . .

11. Three-point . . .

12. Three-card . . .

13. Three-toed . . .

14. Three-prong . . .

15. Three Rivers . . .

16. Three Dog . . .

Answers on page 333

INITIAL QUIZ

All of the two-word answers in this quiz begin with the initials RB.

1. Shaving necessity.

2. Mr. Elizabeth Taylor . . . twice.

3. This beverage, based on the sassafras plant, is almost exclusive to North America.

4. The life of boxer Jake LaMotta was explored in this 1980 film.

5. Popular breakfast cereal.

6. A dictionary, encyclopedia, or almanac, for example.

7. This annual sports event occurs every New Year's Day in Pasadena, California.

8. Pressing this is one way to reboot your computer.

9. English athlete who is still widely remembered as the first person to run a mile in less than four minutes.

10. This seventeenth-century Scottish poet wrote "(My Love Is Like) A Red, Red, Rose."

11. In a Mexican restaurant they're called "refritos."

12. Prolific author of science fiction stories such as *Fahrenheit 451* and *Something Wicked This Way Comes.*

13. An unflattering, but not necessarily inaccurate, term for certain late-nineteenth-/ early-twentieth-century titans of industry, including Andrew Carnegie and J. P. Morgan.

Answers on page 333

Word Rebus

long-term memory
executive functioning
attention to detail

In this game, each rebus represents one word. If you get the right word or sound for each image, you should be able to sound out the answer. Here's an example of a one-word rebus—and be sure to pay attention to the plus sign (+) or minus sign (-) to know whether to add or subtract a sound:

The answer is LOVEBIRD (glove – G = love + bird)

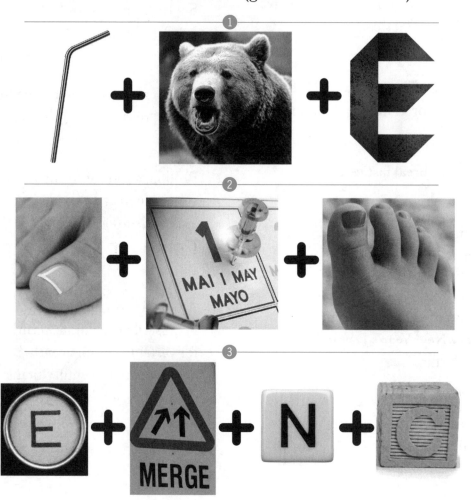

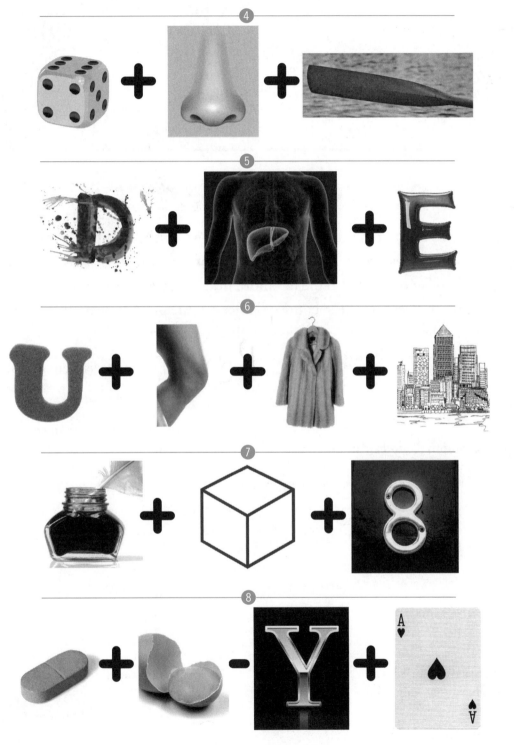

Answers on page 333

HETERONYMS

long-term memory
working memory

Heteronyms are words that are spelled the same, but have different meanings and are sometimes pronounced differently. For example, the word *number* can be a numeral and it can also mean "more numb." *Entrance* can be a doorway and, with the stress on the second syllable, can mean "to charm or delight." Given two definitions, can you identify the heteronym?

1. To continue on . . . and a *curriculum vitae*.

2. To abandon . . . and an arid region.

3. A tied ribbon decoration . . . and to bend the upper body as a sign of respect.

4. Nearby . . . and to shut.

5. Not easy to understand . . . and a group of apartment buildings.

6. Behavior . . . and to lead an orchestra.

7. A legal agreement . . . and the opposite of expand.

8. What Greg Louganis did at the Olympics . . . and the bird of peace.

9. Fruits and vegetables . . . and to create or make something.

10. To decline something . . . and trash or garbage.

Answers on page 333

Common Bonds

The pictures in this puzzle may seem like they have nothing in common. But if you look carefully, you'll see a theme emerge. What is the common bond among these three images?

Answer on page 333

MAGAZINE MATTERS

long-term memory
executive functioning

The more time you spend in your dentist's waiting room, the better you'll do on this quiz.

❶ This magazine's first "Person of the Year" was Charles Lindbergh, in 1927.

❷ This magazine's first "Sexiest Man Alive" was Mel Gibson, who was 29 years old at the time.

❸ The name of this magazine is a phrase often said before dining.

❹ In 2011, she said, "I realized . . . that there really was nothing for women to read that was controlled by women." So she founded *Ms.* magazine in 1971.

❺ This magazine has been chronicling music, liberal politics, and popular culture since 1967.

Answers on page 334

"QUOTATION STATION"

Move the letters in each vertical column of the top grid to the spaces in the column just below it in the bottom grid. The letters will not necessarily be moved in the order in which they appear. If you move the letters to the correct positions, they will spell out a wise Jewish proverb (reading from left to right). (*Note: A black square indicates the end of a word. Words may continue from one horizontal line to the next.*)

long-term memory
executive functioning
multitasking
attention to detail

Before attempting the big puzzle, try this example first—without looking at the answer to the right:

T	H	I	R	A	M	O	R
E		T	H	I	F	K	
I		E		E	N		

Example Answer:

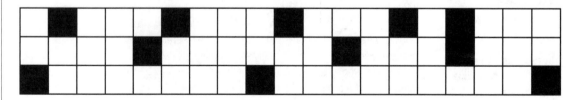

Answer on page 334

What a Pair

Harvard and Yale, Thunder and Lightning, Coke and Pepsi are all common pairs . . . but what about *Wonder and Perrier*? If you redefine *Wonder and Perrier* correctly, you'll come up with the more familiar pairing *Bread and Water*. How many familiar pairs can you make from the clues below?

1. Hemoglobin . . . and Clinton's vice president.

   _____

2. Mr. Hope . . . and to use a loom.

   _____

3. The staff of life . . . and a three-ring show.

   _____

4. Demise . . . and tariffs.

   _____

5. Eider feathers . . . and filthy.

   _____

6. Liberated . . . and transparent.

   _____

7. Gherkins . . . and gelato.

   _____

8. Under the weather . . . and weary.

   _____

9. Epidermis . . . and skeletal units.

   _____

10. Activity on Google . . . and to save someone.

   _____

11. Diminutive . . . and sugary.

   _____

Answers on page 334

Vivienne's Vowels

executive functioning
long-term memory
attention to detail
processing speed

Vivienne is an odd one. She has an aversion to the letters A, E, I, O, and U. Can you fix her list of famous people by putting back the missing vowels? *Note: All well-known people, male or female, living or dead, and those who are known by one name, two names, or more are all acceptable.* You can make this a more strenuous brain exercise by adding some time pressure: Try to solve it in one minute.

1. BRCK BM _____

2. WDY LLN _____

3. RSN WLLS_____

4. JHN LNNN_____

5. LS PSTR _____

6. LCLL BLL_____

7. J DMGG _____

8. BDDH _____

9. NPLN _____

10. BB RTH_____

11. CNN BRN _____

12. JN BZ _____

Answers on page 334

endings & beginnings

In this game, we provide the first half of a two-word phrase or compound word and the second half of another. For example, given *Credit* _____ *trick*, the one word that completes both clues is *Card*, i.e., *Credit card* and *Card trick*. (If you get stuck, the first letter of the answer is provided in a hint below.)

1. Miniature _____ ball

2. Rubber _____ collector

3. Rain _____ floor

4. Quick _____ bag

5. Skeleton _____ board

6. Ski _____ rope

7. Spelling _____ sting

8. Picture _____ shade

9. Wrapping _____ clip

10. Turtle _____ tie

Hints: 1 g; 2 s; 3 d; 4 s; 5 k; 6 j; 7 b; 8 w; 9 p; 10 n

Answers on page 334

Human Anatomy

From *Aorta* to *Windpipe*, can you come up with a human body part that starts with each letter of the alphabet? And for an extra brain boost, see how many you can get in three minutes.

A _____

B _____

C _____

D _____

E _____

F _____

G _____

H _____

I _____

J _____

K _____

L _____

M _____

N _____

O _____

P _____

Q _____

R _____

S _____

T _____

U _____

V _____

W _____

X (Obscure) _____

Y (Obscure) _____

Z (Obscure) _____

Answers on page 334

Alma's Shopping List

Alma is a great shopper but a bad speller. Every word on her shopping list is misspelled by one letter. Can you fix Alma's list? Remember, you should not move any letters; just change one to reveal the correct word. (*Note: All of the items are common brand names or generic names for food and other products that are usually sold in a grocery store.*) For an extra brain boost, see how many correct answers you can get in two minutes.

1. Basic
2. Belly
3. Cooties
4. Demons
5. Hot Boast
6. Pot Dot

7. Sale
8. Saloon
9. Tickles
10. Tuba Dish
11. Mental Flops
12. Pager Towers

Answers on page 334

looking for love

Each word in this list is missing all of its letters except L-O-V-E. Can you fill the bank spaces with letters that make a common English word? For a more vigorous brain exercise, try to solve this quiz in three minutes.

1. OL _ VE
2. _ OLVE
3. VO _ EL
4. _ OVEL
5. _ _ OLVE
6. LO _ VE _
7. _ _ OVEL
8. _ EVOL _

9. _ _ VELO _
10. V _ OLE _ _
11. _ OVEL _ _
12. EL _ V _ _ O _
13. LOVE _ _ _ _
14. _ O _ LEV _ _ _
15. _ _ _ VELO _ _
16. VO _ _ E _ _ _ L

Answers on page 334

long-term memory
executive functioning
attention to detail
processing speed

Sentence Sleuth

A true sentence sleuth can find the one word that is hidden somewhere in a sentence. In this case, can you find the name of a flower? The correct answer could be spread over one, two, or several words, and you should ignore all punctuation, capital letters, etc., when looking for the hidden flower.

long-term memory
executive functioning
attention to detail

1. A real hero seldom runs away from danger.

2. Linda told the sitter not to let the baby's nap drag on into the afternoon or he'd be awake all night.

3. "Aunt Lil, your potatoes are boiling over!" said Eric excitedly.

4. Little Christina loved her dance recital because she got to wear a tutu, lipstick, and eye makeup.

5. When I lived in Boston, I risked my life every day just crossing the busy streets.

6. "When I plant my garden, I always add fertilizer and peat moss," advised expert botanist Neville Bowdridge.

7. George said that *The Silence of the Lambs* was as terrifying a movie as both *Psycho* and *The Shining*.

8. "In England," said the vicar, "national pride in our health care system is very important to its success."

Answers on page 335

WORD PICTURES

Each picture represents one part of a word or common two-word phrase. For example, if you combined a picture of a *key* and a picture of a *hole*, you would get the word *keyhole*. How many of the eight words or two-word phrases can you find?

Answers on page 335

Two-Letter Words

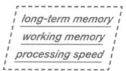

long-term memory
working memory
processing speed

How many of the twenty-four most frequently used two-letter English words (according to the *Oxford English Dictionary*) can you come up with in one minute?

_____ _____ _____ _____ _____ _____

_____ _____ _____ _____ _____ _____

_____ _____ _____ _____ _____ _____

_____ _____ _____ _____ _____ _____

Answers on page 335

house work

long-term memory
working memory

All of the answers in this quiz contain the word HOUSE.

1. Dwellings for people who shouldn't throw stones.

2. 1600 Pennsylvania Avenue

3. Where ferns and philodendrons flourish.

4. Classic PBS nonfiction series.

5. Property made famous by Nathaniel Hawthorne.

6. Tip O'Neill and Newt Gingrich have both held this job.

7. Series of books by Laura Ingalls Wilder.

8. Where no husband likes to be.

9. Where beatniks often gathered in the 1950s.

10. An organization or a plan that is very weak and can easily be destroyed.

11. A highly valued cut of beef.

12. Virginia Woolf's classic novel, *To the* _____.

Answers on page 335

ALPHABET TRIVIA

The only thing these trivia questions have in common is that all of the answers begin with the letter D.

long-term memory
executive functioning

1. What is the only US state that begins with the letter D?

2. Name the three US state capitals that begin with the letter D.

3. What is the only European country that begins with the letter D?

4. What is the largest US city (by population) that begins with the letter D?

5. Which three of Santa's reindeer have names beginning with the letter D?

6. Name three of the four breeds of dogs registered by the American Kennel Club that begin with the letter D.

7. Can you identify these famous "D" authors by their equally famous works?
   a. *David Copperfield* and *A Tale of Two Cities*
   b. *Crime and Punishment* and *The Brothers Karamazov*
   c. *The Adventures of Sherlock Holmes* and *The Hound of the Baskervilles*

8. Can you name the European river that begins in Germany and empties into the Black Sea in Romania?

9. Can you identify these famous people with the initials DD?
   a. This actress's first film with Rock Hudson was 1959's *Pillow Talk*.
   b. The 4' 10" actor who co-starred in the television series *Taxi*.
   c. Hall of Fame pitcher for the Los Angeles Dodgers in the 1960s.
   d. Actor who played Fox Mulder on the science fiction series *The X-Files*.

10. What do the following acronyms and abbreviations stand for?
   DOB
   DBA
   DIY
   DNA
   DH
   DUI

Answers on page 335

DROP A LETTER AND SCRAMBLE

long-term memory
working memory
multitasking

This game starts with a word. Your job is to drop one letter, then rearrange the remaining letters to form another word. A brief hint for the new word is provided.

1. CATER — What sprinters do.

2. STEAM — Beef or chicken.

3. HEARS — Skin malady.

4. BREAD — Shakespeare was one.

5. ASTER — Betelgeuse . . . or the sun.

6. FALSE — An umpire's call.

7. CLEAT — A tall story.

8. TASTE — One way to go.

9. WHEAT — What spring brings after a cold winter.

10. MAPLE — What some fortune tellers read.

11. BEARD — Undressed.

12. FRIEND — Roadside restaurant.

13. YACHTS — Done with excessive speed and insufficient consideration.

14. MUTATES — *The Thinker . . . or Lady Liberty.*

Answers on page 335

change a letter

long-term memory
executive functioning
multitasking
attention to detail

Change the first letter of the three words in each list to create three new words that all start with the same letter. For example, given the words *whine, plant,* and *reason,* what one letter can replace the first letter of each word to make three new words? The answer is S—*shine, slant,* and *season.*

1. Bell, Fable, Pamper

2. Mail, Mingle, Racket

3. Cookie, Peach, Thyme

4. Snarled, Blue, Terms

5. Flight, Dense, Boot

6. Guest, Suite, Built

7. Aimed, Pouch, Swine

8. Irate, Wolf, Coal

9. Leaf, Brain, Crafty

10. Gasp, Traps, Shopper

Answers on page 335

Signature Songs

Sometimes a song is associated with a particular performer no matter how many others record it. In this quiz, we give the song title. Can you name the singer or group most closely identified with it?

1. "Everybody Loves Somebody Sometime" _____

2. "Stand By Your Man" _____

3. "I Got You Babe" _____

4. "Thanks for the Memory" _____

5. "It Was a Very Good Year" _____

6. "(I Can't Get No) Satisfaction" _____

7. "Over the Rainbow" _____

8. "I Left My Heart in San Francisco" _____

9. "People" _____

10. "It's Not Unusual" _____

11. "This Land Is Your Land" _____

12. "Hello, Dolly" _____

13. "Coal Miner's Daughter" _____

14. "Tiptoe Through the Tulips" _____

Answers on page 336

Rivals

We provide one half of a famous feuding pair (it could be a decades-long rivalry or a one-time face-off). Can you provide the name of the opposition?

1. PC and _____

2. The Sharks and _____

3. Cain and _____

4. Ford and _____

5. The Red Sox and _____

6. Dr. Jekyll and _____

7. The Hatfields and _____

8. Burger King and _____

9. Batman and _____

10. Joe Frazier and _____

11. John F. Kennedy and _____

12. Captain Hook and _____

Answers on page 336

RIDDLE
ME THIS

Riddles often require some unconventional thinking, which makes them a great brain exercise. Think outside the box as you try to solve this classic riddle.

I'm the beginning of eternity; the end of time and space; the beginning of every end; and the end of every place. What am I?

Answer on page 336

Follow the Rules

If you follow each instruction precisely, you will discover the second half of this quotation often attributed to Elizabeth Taylor: "Big girls need . . ." We've provided the first line, and the rest is up to you. A gold star to the solver who gets it right on the first try. (This game is harder than you might think.)

1. Without spaces between the letters, write down the phrase: B I G   G I R L S   N E E D

2. Double the last letter.

3. Replace the R with an A.

4. Place an M in the seventh position.

5. Place the first letter of the last name of the forty-fifth president of the United States after the S.

6. Swap the fourth and the last letters.

7. Remove the ninth letter and place it in the last position.

8. Remove the eighth, eleventh, twelfth, and fourteenth letters.

1 _____ B I G G I R L S N E E D _____

2 _____

3 _____

4 _____

5 _____

6 _____

7 _____

8 _____

Did you get the right answer?

Answers on page 336

whoopee!

All of the answers in this quiz end with the letters EE.

1. To run away or escape.

_____

2. Species most closely related to humans.

_____

3. Disc used in catching games.

_____

4. To contradict, oppose, or quarrel.

_____

5. An elastic cord used in a modern sport that involves leaping from tall heights.

_____

6. Delicate ornamental work of fine silver, gold, or other metal wires made into lacy designs.

_____

7. Large, slow-moving, aquatic mammal often found in warm, shallow coastal waters.

_____

8. What a tourist does.

_____

9. A group of people charged with a particular task.

_____

10. An order that is usually backed up by a court of law.

_____

11. A heavy fabric used especially for jeans.

_____

12. The family history of a dog or horse, for example.

_____

Answers on page 336

alphabetically speaking

Everyone knows that January is the first month of the year. But "alphabetically speaking," April is the first month because it begins with the letters AP. In this game, can you figure out what comes first, last, or next . . . alphabetically speaking?

1. Alphabetically speaking, this is the first of the three branches of the US government.

2. Alphabetically speaking, this is the first cardinal direction on a compass.

3. Alphabetically speaking, he is the first of Donald Duck's three nephews.

4. Alphabetically speaking, this is the first US state.

5. Alphabetically speaking, this is the last of the common vegetables.

6. Alphabetically speaking, he is Snow White's first dwarf.

7. Alphabetically speaking, he is the first person inducted into the Baseball Hall of Fame.

8. Alphabetically speaking, this is the first official US public holiday.

9. Alphabetically speaking, this is the first sign of the zodiac.

10. Alphabetically speaking, this is the last of the five branches of the US Armed Services.

11. Alphabetically speaking, this is the first country of South America.

12. Alphabetically speaking, this is the last planet in our solar system.

Answers on page 336

A Penny for Your Thoughts

Can you finish these idioms and sayings that all relate to money? To make this a more vigorous brain exercise, try to answer all the questions in one minute.

1. A day late _____.

2. All that glitters _____.

3. Penny wise _____.

4. Worth its _____.

5. You get what _____.

6. From rags _____.

7. You bet your _____.

8. Don't take _____.

9. A dime _____.

10. It's not worth _____.

11. One man's trash _____.

12. Two sides _____.

13. You pays your _____.

Answers on page 336

WORD PARTS

The word *bather* is defined as "a person that takes a bath or goes swimming." In this game, however, we supply the definition not of a word, but of its parts. For example, given the first clue *Louisville Slugger*, plus the second clue *the opposite of him*, the answer is *bather* (*bat* + *her*).

1. Not on + the final part

2. The hearing organ + a bird's home

3. The red planet + a corridor

4. Highest or uppermost + postal code for Phoenix's state

5. Dove or pigeon sound + the highest face card

6. Taxi + first person singular pronoun + tennis court separator

7. One sheet of a book + picnic pest

8. Advice giver Landers + one-sixteenth of a pound

9. To prohibit + a queen's husband

10. To make a wager + a shaft of light

11. Tin container + past tense of do + consumed

12. Not against + to make an offer at an auction + a lion's lair

Answers on page 337

Secret Word

long-term memory
executive functioning
attention to detail
processing speed

How many four- and five-letter common English words can you find in the letters of the phrase below? The more words you find, the more likely you are to also get the secret word—a word that is generally a little harder to spot. (We found fifty-two 4-letter words and thirty-six 5-letter words.) To make this game even more challenging—and a better brain exercise—try to find at least twenty 4- and 5-letter words in one minute.

BASEBALL GAME

_____ _____ _____ _____

_____ _____ _____ _____

_____ _____ _____ _____

_____ _____ _____ _____

_____ _____ _____ _____

_____ _____ _____ _____

_____ _____ _____ _____

_____ _____ _____ _____

_____ _____ _____ _____

_____ _____ _____ _____

_____ _____ _____ _____

Answers (including the secret word) on page 337

How Much Is...?

This game involves simple addition ... but you have to figure out which numbers to add up. For example: *How much is ... the number of Dalmatians in the Disney movie + the number of items in a half dozen?* The answer: *107 (101 + 6).*

1. How much is ... the number of words a picture is worth + the number of stitches a stitch in time saves?

2. How much is ... a foot + a yard (in inches)?

3. How much is ... the number of legs on a spider + the number of arms on an octopus?

4. How much is ... the original area code for New York City + the phone number for directory assistance?

5. How much is ... the number of "sheets to the wind" you are if you are *very* drunk + the number of heads that are better than one?

6. How much is ... the value of an X in Scrabble + the number of Michael Jordan's Chicago Bulls jersey?

7. How much is ... the number of ounces in a pound + the number of pints in a quart?

8. How much is ... the amount of money you get for passing GO in the original Monopoly game + the number of karats in pure gold?

9. How much is ... the sum of the Spanish numbers *nueve* + *diez*?

10. How much is ... the number of countries that share a land border with the United States + the number of countries that share a land border with Canada + the number of countries that share a land border with Australia?

Answers on page 337

Find the Quotation

Cross out words in the grid below according to the instructions, then rearrange the remaining words to reveal a quotation.

shark	thanks	identical	Peru	turkey
Monroe	Alabama	sit	Miller	fig
is	Molson	maximum	giving	first
eat	utopia	robin	orange	then
Chile	extra	bud	January	Ford
Hoover	jinx	Thanksgiving	Heineken	Brazil
mouse	Atlantic	Lincoln	Coors	Mexico

INSTRUCTIONS:

1. Cross out all three-letter words.

2. Cross out all words that are names of animals.

3. Cross out all four-syllable words.

4. Cross out all names of South American countries.

5. Cross out all words that contain the letter X.

6. Cross out all surnames of US presidents.

7. Cross out all names of oceans.

8. Cross out all brands of beer.

9. Cross out all names of colors.

_____ _____ _____ _____ _____

Answers on page 338

MUSICAL ANATOMY

Can you identify the body parts mentioned in these songs?

❶ According to the traditional American spiritual, God "has the whole world" here.

❷ Fred Astaire sang, "I find the happiness I seek" when he's dancing this way with Ginger Rogers.

❸ Sunshine here made John Denver happy.

❹ The first time ever Roberta Flack saw this, she thought the sun rose in your eyes.

Answers on page 338

Group Therapy

Group Therapy is the game that proves there is more than one correct answer to a question . . . and we tell you the minimum number of answers you need to come up with. For an extra brain boost, put a one-minute limit on each question.

1. Name eight airline companies, past or present.

2. Name seven female first names that begin with the letter J.

3. Name five white (or white-ish) food items.

4. Name twelve words that end in the letters OP.

5. Name seven Canadian provinces and/or territories.

6. Name all eighteen US presidents who served in the twentieth century.

7. Name five things that melt.

8. Name ten things that have wheels.

Answers on page 338

TED'S TERRIBLE TITLES

Poor Ted. He is a connoisseur of culture but he can never remember the titles of some of his favorite books, plays, songs, magazines, television shows, etc. Can you fix Ted's titles by correcting his mistakes?

1. Pharmacy Ranch Hand

2. Precipitation Guy

3. Ripped Drape

4. A Parting Word to Munitions

5. A Small Dried Fruit in the Central Body of the Solar System

6. Terror and Hatred in a Nevada City

7. Ms. Ball in the Firmament with Clear Gemstones

8. The Elderly Male and the Marine Environment

9. The Crimson Unit of the Alphabet

10. The Highest Female Singing Voices

11. The Rustic Dwelling of My Father's Brother Thomas

12. Gratitude for the Recollection

Answers on page 338

Vivienne's Vowels

Vivienne is an odd one. She has an aversion to the letters A, E, I, O, and U. Can you fix her list of geographical locations by putting back the missing vowels? *Note: Any geographical locations, from bodies of water and landmarks to cities, states, and countries, are acceptable.* You can make this a more strenuous brain exercise by adding some time pressure: Try to solve this puzzle in one minute.

1. STNBL _____
2. PNM _____
3. SPN _____
4. RM _____
5. TRNT _____

6. NNPLS _____
7. PRS _____
8. THNS _____
9. MSSR _____

10. CP CD _____
11. HNLL _____
12. CLRD _____
13. LBQRQ _____

Answers on page 339

Common Bonds

The pictures in this puzzle may seem like they have nothing in common. But if you look carefully, you'll see a theme emerge. What is the common bond among these three images?

Answer on page 339

ALPHABET TRIVIA

The only thing these trivia questions have in common is that all of the answers begin with the letter E.

long-term memory
executive functioning

1. The name of which planet begins with the letter E?

2. Name four of the seven countries that begin with the letter E.

3. What is the one deadly sin that begins with the letter E?

4. Name four animals (of any type) that begin with the letter E.

5. With a population of more than 800,000, this is the fifth-largest city in Canada, and the only large Canadian city that begins with the letter E.

6. Name three of the six books of the Bible (King James Version) that begin with the letter E.

7. Which *Seinfeld* character's name begins with the letter E?

8. What is the only gemstone (precious or semi-precious) that begins with the letter E?

9. Who is the only US president whose last name begins with the letter E?

10. Identify these people whose last names begin with the letter E:
   a. Pioneering female aviator
   b. Gambler and sometimes lawman who participated in the gunfight at the O.K. Corral
   c. Inventor of the Kodak camera
   d. Film critic
   e. Founder of the Christian Science movement
   f. Sibling musicians who sang "Wake Up, Little Susie"

11. What do these acronyms or abbreviations stand for?
EKG
EST
EMT
EPA
ESP
EU

Answers on page 339

Memorable TV Lines

Can you identify the television show from these memorable lines? And for an extra brain workout, try to remember the character (in fiction TV) or the real-life person (in nonfiction TV) who said each line.

1. "Now cut that out!"

_____

2. "No soup for you!"

_____

3. "Baby, you're the greatest!"

_____

4. "Danger, Will Robinson!"

_____

5. "Heeeere's Johnny!"

_____

6. "How *you* doin'?"

_____

7. "And that's the way it is."

_____

8. "Come on down!"

_____

9. "He's dead, Jim."

_____

10. "Sock it to me!"

_____

11. "Stifle!"

_____

12. "Good night, John-Boy."

_____

Answers on page 339

---

 trivia

BATTER UP!

long-term memory
executive functioning

This quiz is all about America's sport.

❶ What is it called when a pitcher allows no opposing player to reach base safely for any reason during a game?

❷ It should come as no surprise that this National League baseball stadium is nicknamed "The Ted."

❸ What is a "full count" in baseball?

❹ What does ERA stand for?

❺ What, precisely, is the designated hitter rule?

Answers on page 339

honorific titles

In English, words such as *Mr., Mrs., Ms., Dr., Uncle, Captain*, etc., are called "honorific titles." Can you identify the honorific title for each character in this quiz?

1. Kermit the Frog was the object of her affection.

2. This Hugh Lofting character could talk to the animals.

3. Television time traveler.

4. Pancake mix and syrup brand.

5. Sherlock Holmes's friend and assistant.

6. All-purpose household cleanser.

7. Rice brand.

8. Science officer on the *USS Enterprise*.

9. He's the tall, top-hatted personification of the United States.

10. This little girl was quite frightened of spiders.

Answers on page 339

fill in the letters

long-term memory
executive functioning
attention to detail

Fill in the blank spaces with letters to make common English words (no proper nouns allowed). For example, __ **a t** yields twelve answers: *bat, cat, eat, fat, hat, mat, oat, pat, rat, sat, tat, vat.* (*Note: The number in parentheses indicates how many common English words can be made.*)

1. __ **a y**   (15)

2. **a** __ **e**   (10)

3. __ **u n**   (8)

4. **s t** __ __   (15)

5. **p r** __ __   (12)

6. __ __ **c h**   (11)

7. **b i** __ __   (12)

8. **p** __ __ **p**   (10)

Answers on page 340

MAKING CONNECTIONS

Given nine words or phrases randomly placed in a grid, can you find the three groups of three connected items AND explain why they are connected? Here's a sample grid:

RED	HONEY	BLUE
VIEIRA	HARVEST	PURPLE
FULL	LAUER	COURIC

GROUP 1 WORDS:
Red, Blue, Purple

THEME:
Colors

GROUP 2 WORDS:
Vieira, Lauer, Couric

THEME:
Today show hosts

GROUP 3 WORDS:
Full, Honey, Harvest

THEME:
_____moon

CLOG	KISS	SHUMAI
PUMP	PIEROGI	TOAST
KREPLACH	FRIES	LOAFER

GROUP 1 WORDS

_____ _____ _____

THEME:

_____

GROUP 2 WORDS

_____ _____ _____

THEME:

_____

GROUP 3 WORDS

_____ _____ _____

THEME:

_____

Answers on page 340

Water Words

Ocean is the name of just one of the many types of water formations, both large and small, that can be found on Earth. How many can you identify in one minute? (*Note: We are not looking for specific bodies of water, such as the Atlantic Ocean, but rather names of water formations of any type.*)

Answers on page 340

long-term memory
executive functioning
attention to detail

beware of the dog

If you're a dog lover, it should be easy to identify these popular breeds.

A _____

B _____

C _____

D _____

E _____

F _____

G _____

H _____

I _____

J _____

K _____

L _____

Answers on page 340

TRIMBLE

Trimble is a trivia game and a word jumble combined. First, answer the trivia questions (all related to animals) and cross out the letters of each answer in the letter grid. Then rearrange the remaining letters (those that have not been crossed out) to reveal another word or phrase related to the same theme.

A	A	A	A	A	A	A	B	B	C	D	D	E
E	G	G	H	H	H	I	I	I	I	I	K	K
L	L	L	L	M	M	M	N	N	N	O	O	O
O	P	R	R	R	R	S	T	U	U			

1. This type of bird, some of which are less than three inches long, can hover in midair by flapping its wings very rapidly.

_____

2. Types of this marine creature include nurse and basking.

_____

3. This Australian tree-dwelling marsupial eats only one food—eucalyptus leaves.

_____

4. Dian Fossey studied this African primate for nearly twenty years until she was murdered in Rwanda in 1985.

_____

5. Three types of this marine mammal are the short-beaked, the long-beaked, and the bottlenose.

_____

6. The dugong is closely related to this large and gentle marine mammal that is found in the warm waters of Florida.

_____

Word Jumble hint: A denizen of the Arctic Circle.

Answers on page 340

nicknames

Can you identify the person, place, or thing by its nickname?

1. Horseless Carriage

_____

2. Chairman of the Board

_____

3. The Big Apple

_____

4. Jewish Penicillin

_____

5. Broadway Joe

_____

6. The Land of the Rising Sun

_____

7. The Show-Me State

_____

8. The Mile-High City

_____

9. The Eternal City

_____

10. Snake Eyes

_____

11. Big Sky Country

_____

Answers on page 340

Vivienne's Vowels

executive functioning
long-term memory
attention to detail
processing speed

Vivienne is an odd one. She has an aversion to the letters A, E, I, O, and U. Can you fix her list of book, movie, song, and television show titles by putting back the missing vowels? You can make this a more strenuous brain exercise by adding some time pressure: Try to solve this puzzle in ninety seconds.

1. WR ND PC _____

2. HY JD _____

3. ST LSWHR _____

4. TH FFC _____

5. TX _____

6. DRCL _____

7. CHRS _____

8. TH WR _____

9. SNFLD _____

10. ZRR _____

11. TH D VNC CD _____

12. LT T B _____

13. FC TH NTN _____

Answers on page 340

Anagrams

The letters of each word in this list can be rearranged in multiple ways to form other words. We provide the word and the number of anagrams that are possible to make. (*Remember, you must use ALL the letters in the given word.*) You should give your brain a rest if you can solve all of these anagrams in two minutes.

1. Posh (2)　　_____　　_____

2. Awls (2)　　_____　　_____

3. Scat (3)　　_____　　_____　　_____

4. Deus (3)　　_____　　_____　　_____

5. Fares (2)　　_____　　_____

6. Tarps (3)　　_____　　_____　　_____

7. Coats (3)　　_____　　_____　　_____

8. Poser (4)　　_____　　_____　　_____　　_____

Answers on page 340

RIDDLE **ME THIS**

Riddles often require some unconventional thinking, which makes them a great brain exercise. Think outside the box as you try to solve these classic riddles.

What is the only type of cheese that is made backward?

You will survive if I'm stolen or given away, yet you cannot live without me. What am I?

Answers on page 341

WORD TOWER

Every word in a word tower begins with the same two letters. You build the tower by increasing the length of each word by one letter. For example, a five-word tower built on the letters FA could include: FAN, FAST, FABLE, FACTOR, FAILURE.

How far can you go before you get stumped? Using the letters PA, we made a tower fourteen words high. (*Note: Proper nouns are not allowed, and you cannot just add an s to make a longer word. For example, if your four-letter word is* part, *your five-letter word cannot be* parts.) For an extra brain boost, see how tall your tower of words can get in two minutes.

1. P A
2. P A __
3. P A __ __
4. P A __ __ __
5. P A __ __ __ __
6. P A __ __ __ __ __
7. P A __ __ __ __ __ __
8. P A __ __ __ __ __ __ __
9. P A __ __ __ __ __ __ __ __
10. P A __ __ __ __ __ __ __ __ __
11. P A __ __ __ __ __ __ __ __ __ __
12. P A __ __ __ __ __ __ __ __ __ __ __
13. P A __ __ __ __ __ __ __ __ __ __ __ __
14. P A __ __ __ __ __ __ __ __ __ __ __ __ __

Answers on page 341

WORD PICTURES

In this game, you just need to combine one image with one letter to make a word. It is important to note that the "name" of the letter, not its sound, is used here. For example, if there were a picture of a can and the letter E, the answer would **not** be *cane*; rather, it would be *canny* (*can* + *E*). The letter can also precede the picture, i.e., the picture of a witch with the letter B would yield the word *bewitch* (*B* + *witch*). (*Note: Each picture and each letter will be used once.*)

BDELMNSX

Answers on page 341

ALPHABET TRIVIA

The only thing these trivia questions have in common is that all of the answers begin with the letter F.

long-term memory
executive functioning

1. What is the only US state that begins with the letter F?

2. What is the one US capital city that begins with the letter F?

3. Name two of the three countries (sovereign states only) that begin with the letter F.

4. Name a fruit or vegetable that begins with the letter F.

5. Name a US president whose last name begins with the letter F.

6. Name three animals (of any type) that begin with the letter F.

7. Who played Jill Munroe on TV's *Charlie's Angels* for only the series's first season?

8. He wrote *The Great Gatsby* and *Tender Is the Night*.

9. She starred in *Rosemary's Baby* in 1968, the same year she was divorced from her first husband, Frank Sinatra.

10. This Mississippi-born writer is the author of *Absalom! Absalom!* and *The Sound and the Fury*.

11. She played *The Flying Nun* on television and *Norma Rae* in the movies.

12. This British author wrote *Chitty Chitty Bang Bang* as well as the James Bond series of spy novels.

13. This New England poet, at age 86, read his well-known poem "The Gift Outright" at the inauguration of John F. Kennedy.

14. What do these acronyms/initials stand for?
FAQ
FBI
FDA
FDIC
FDR
FEMA
FM
FYI

Answers on page 341

Scrambled Sports

Unscramble the letters in each clue below to reveal a list of sports. For an even better brain exercise, try to complete this quiz in two minutes.

1. EINNST _____

2. EOCHKY _____

3. IOBGNX _____

4. AUHSSQ _____

5. IIDGNV _____

6. IIGKNS _____

7. IOBGLNW _____

8. IUFGNRS _____

9. AECHRRY _____

10. AAEBBLLS _____

11. IIGMMNSW _____

12. EIGLNRSTW _____

Answers on page 341

INITIAL QUIZ

All of the two-word answers in this quiz begin with the initials HH.

1. Television sitcom set in a WWII German prisoner-of-war camp.

2. A late-afternoon event designed to get patrons into bars and pubs.

3. This children's toy gained international popularity in the 1950s.

4. An employment recruiter.

5. Golfing mecca in South Carolina.

6. Classic children's toy with an equine head on a stick.

7. Term used when referring to the Pope.

8. She was known as "the First Lady of the American Theater."

9. This cheap cut of pork is mostly used for flavoring foods such as collard greens.

10. Quick to anger, quarrelsome, argumentative.

11. This 1960s pants style lowered the waistline of jeans by three or four inches.

12. A Canadian bay and a New York river are named after this seventeenth-century English explorer.

Answers on page 341

prime-time ✦ rhyme ✦

Each question in this quiz has three different answers . . . and they all rhyme. For example:

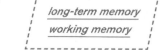
Clues: One plus one; not false; azure color.

Answers: Two; true; blue.

1. Roman title for a ruler; a hair puller; Mr. Scrooge

2. An ear part; a representation of the earth; a patient man

3. A wild member of the feline family; this brings bad luck; an Egyptian landmark

4. A type of seaweed; a short, sharp cry of pain or alarm; S.O.S.

5. Drag your body on the floor or ground; a short, intense storm; a noisy fight

6. A shrimp; reflex associated with tiredness or boredom; a young deer

7. A computer criminal; a person who avoids work; Ritz, or Graham

8. Sculpting tool; misty rain; drink stirrer

9. Himalayan country; French bread; brown-haired girl

10. Option or preference; author of Ulysses; sound uttered through the mouth

Answers on page 341

---

trivia

DANDY CANDY

long-term memory

executive functioning

This is a tasty little quiz about candy.

❶ In a 1977 film, Diane Keaton was looking for more than this chocolate-and-peanut candy.

❷ This is a tooth-destroying candy bar . . . or a wealthy older man who lavishes gifts on a young woman in return for her company.

❸ According to the advertising slogan, this is "the great American chocolate bar."

❹ This pink-and-white candy is one of the oldest candy brands in the United States.

❺ Which two candy bars are referenced in the advertising jingle "Sometimes you feel like a nut, sometimes you don't"?

Answers on page 341

"QUOTATION STATION"

Move the letters in each vertical column of the top grid to the spaces in the column just below it in the bottom grid. The letters will not necessarily be moved in the order in which they appear. If you move the letters to the correct positions, they will spell out a quote from comedian Lily Tomlin (reading from left to right). (*Note: A black square indicates the end of a word. Words may continue from one horizontal line to the next.*)

Before attempting the big puzzle, try this example first—without looking at the answer to the right:

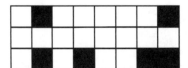

T	H	I	R	A	M	O	R
E		T	H	I	F	K	
I		E		E	N		

Example Answer:

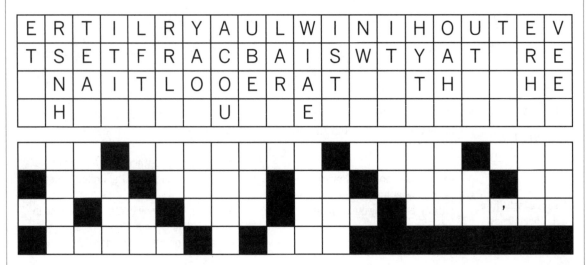

Answer on page 342

Islands

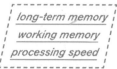

long-term memory
working memory
processing speed

Believe it or not, there are more than 180,000 islands on Earth, although many of them are too small, or too remote, to have names. How many of the islands that do have names can you come up with in one minute? (*Note: Australia is generally considered a continental landmass, not an island. Also, island countries are often made up of several islands. Therefore, we consider Japan to be a correct answer, as are any of the islands that make up Japan: Hokkaido, Honshu, Shikoku, Kyushu, etc.*)

Answers on page 342

Common Bonds

long-term memory
executive functioning
attention to detail

The pictures in the row below may seem like they have nothing in common. But if you look carefully, you'll see a theme emerge. Can you figure out the unique theme for these three pictures?

Answer on page 342

raise the bar

long-term memory
working memory

All of the answers in this quiz begin with the consecutive letters BAR.

1. Housing for soldiers.

2. Male singing voice.

3. A person who tries to attract patrons to events such as the circus.

4. An economic system that trades goods and services for goods and services.

5. She became world famous at age six as Gertie in *E.T. the Extra-Terrestrial*.

6. They're experts in making Zombies.

7. Scientific instrument that measures atmospheric pressure.

8. A tonsorial artist.

9. Some uses for this member of the grass family include animal feed and a component in soups and stews.

10. This fish, known for its ferocity and fanglike teeth, can reach six feet long.

11. A courtroom lawyer in England and Australia.

12. A marine crustacean.

Answers on page 342

Chapter Three

Fictional Occupations

You might remember these classic television characters, but do you know what their occupations were? And, for an extra memory exercise, can you name the television series that featured each character?

long-term memory
executive functioning

1. Murphy Brown

_____

2. Doogie Howser

_____

3. Frasier Crane

_____

4. Archie Bunker

_____

5. George Jefferson

_____

6. Ross Geller

_____

7. Carla Tortelli

_____

8. Ginger Grant

_____

9. Joey Tribbiani

_____

10. Grace Adler

_____

11. Robert Barone

_____

12. Carrie Bradshaw

_____

13. Walter White

_____

Answers on page 342

Sentence Sleuth

long-term memory
executive functioning
attention to detail

A true sentence sleuth can find the one word that is hidden somewhere in a sentence. In this case, can you find the name of a vegetable? The correct answer could be spread over one, two, or several words, and you should ignore all punctuation, capital letters, etc., when looking for the hidden vegetable.

1. The auto mechanic told Oscar, "Rotate and balance your tires once a year and they'll last much longer."

2. When I became pregnant with my oldest son, Brad, I shelved the idea of going to graduate school.

3. When my brother Michael ripped half my doll's hair off, he said, "Give it to Ma to fix."

4. When my youngest daughter, Fleur, insisted that Justin Bieber is really smart, I choked on my sandwich.

5. I was impressed when Laurie said she painted all the walls and that her husband, Glen, tiled the kitchen and bathroom floors.

6. "If you're afraid you'll forget to take the payment," said Mrs. Walters, "pin a check to the corkboard near the door."

7. When Catalina had her wedding shower, Amy gave her a teapot, a toaster, and a blender for her kitchen.

8. When we went to the museum in Austin, I couldn't pay the admission. I only brought five dollars, but it cost fifteen.

9. "Break a leg" actually means "good luck" to superstitious theater actors.

10. Most mystery books are predictable. Before I get to the end, I've already figured out "whodunit."

Answers on page 342

last name please

Do you ever have trouble remembering names? Try these names that double as titles of books and movies.

1. *Pippi* _____

2. *Citizen* _____

3. *Cyrano de* _____

4. *Madame* _____

5. *Moll* _____

6. *Mrs.* _____

7. *Johnny* _____

8. *Silas* _____

9. *Nicholas* _____

10. *The Brothers* _____

11. *The Secret Life of Walter* _____

12. *The Prime of Miss Jean* _____

13. *One Day in the Life of Ivan* _____

14. *McCabe and Mrs.* _____

15. *Who's Afraid of Virginia* _____?

Answers on page 343

Group Therapy

Group Therapy is the game that proves there is more than one correct answer to a question . . . and we tell you the minimum number of answers you need to come up with. For an extra brain boost, put a one-minute limit on each question.

1. Name seven countries located in South America.

2. Name six card games.

3. Name five fruits that have pits (also called stones).

4. Name six cities in California that begin with the letter S.

5. Name five Meryl Streep movies.

6. Name five candy bars.

7. Name five brands of toothpaste.

8. Name ten cable television networks.

Answers on page 343

ODD MAN OUT

All of the items in each list have something in common—with one exception. Your job is to find which item doesn't fit and to explain why it is the "odd man out."

1. Lions, Rams, Bears, Wolves

2. Tots, Shoestring, Poplin, Chips

3. Double, Teaspoon, Feather, Sofa

4. Your shoelaces, Loose ends, Cheese fondue, The knot

5. The circus, A bride and groom, A tree, A piano

6. MacDonald, Maid, O'Brien, Faithful

7. Yard, Garden, Foot, Cup

Answers on page 344

Alma's Shopping List

Alma is a great shopper but a bad speller. Every word on her shopping list is misspelled by one letter. Can you fix Alma's list? Remember, you should not move any letters; just change one to reveal the correct word. (*Note: All of the items are common brand names or generic names for food and other products that are usually sold in a grocery store.*) For an extra brain boost, see how many correct answers you can get in two minutes.

1. Felon

2. Fist

3. Jag

4. Ten

5. Beast

6. Lice

7. Handles

8. Child

9. Bumble Gym

10. Soul Dream

11. Flesh Blowers

12. Port Chap

Answers on page 344

Birds

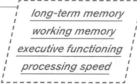

long-term memory
working memory
executive functioning
processing speed

From *Albatross* to *Zebra finch*, can you name a bird for every letter in the alphabet? And for an extra brain boost, see how many you can get in three minutes.

A _____   N _____

B _____   O _____

C _____   P _____

D _____   Q _____

E _____   R _____

F _____   S _____

G _____   T _____

H _____   **U** (Obscure) _____

I _____   V _____

J _____   W _____

K _____   **X** (Obscure) _____

L _____   Y _____

M _____   Z _____

Answers on page 344

MAKING CONNECTIONS

Given nine words or phrases randomly placed in a grid, can you find the three groups of three connected items AND explain why they are connected? Here's a sample grid:

RED	HONEY	BLUE
VIEIRA	HARVEST	PURPLE
FULL	LAUER	COURIC

GROUP 1 WORDS:
Red, Blue, Purple

THEME:
Colors

GROUP 2 WORDS:
Vieira, Lauer, Couric

THEME:
Today show hosts

GROUP 3 WORDS:
Full, Honey, Harvest

THEME:
_____moon

LID	ALL	FINGER
OIL	CHEER	LASH
PUPIL	LATEX	TIDE

GROUP 1 WORDS

_____ _____ _____

THEME:

_____

GROUP 2 WORDS

_____ _____ _____

THEME:

_____

GROUP 3 WORDS

_____ _____ _____

THEME:

_____

Answers on page 344

ALPHABET TRIVIA

The only thing these trivia questions have in common is that all of the answers begin with the letter G.

long-term memory
executive functioning

1. Name the five US presidents whose first names begin with the letter G.

2. What are the two deadly sins that begin with G?

3. What are the three European countries that begin with G?

4. Which sign of the zodiac begins with the letter G?

5. Name the major river in India that begins in the Himalayas and stretches more than 1,500 miles to the Bay of Bengal.

6. Can you identify these movies with one-word titles that begin with the letter G (not counting the word "the" in some cases)?
   a. Demi Moore is a potter, Patrick Swayze is murdered, and Whoopi Goldberg is a psychic.
   b. Russell Crowe is a slave in ancient Rome who lives to avenge the murder of his family.
   c. John Travolta and Olivia Newton-John are dancing and singing teenagers at fictional Rydell High School in the 1950s.
   d. Dustin Hoffman, who just finished college with no life goals, is seduced by Anne Bancroft and then proceeds to fall in love with her daughter.
   e. Ben Kingsley won an Oscar for his role as this lawyer and leader of India's nonviolent movement against British rule.

7. Identify these famous people whose last names begin with G:
   a. He played Rhett Butler.
   b. He is the first human to travel into outer space.
   c. He played Tony Soprano.
   d. He's Paul Simon's 1960s singing partner.

8. What do these acronyms that begin with the letter G stand for?
   GDP
   GI
   GMT
   GOP
   GPS
   GQ

Answers on page 344

in the middle

Can you identify this list of famous people by their middle names?

1. Amadeus

2. Delano

3. Graham

4. Ford

5. Christian

6. Beecher

7. Fitzgerald

8. Quincy

9. Waldo

10. Bernard

11. Earl

12. Scott

13. Harvey

Answers on page 344

Finish the Proverb

Given the first couple of words of a familiar proverb or saying, can you complete it? To make this a more vigorous brain exercise, try to answer all the questions in one minute.

1. Every cloud _____ .

2. Absence makes _____ .

3. All work and _____ .

4. Strike _____ .

5. One man's trash _____ .

6. No good deed _____ .

7. Almost only counts _____ .

8. Quitters never _____ .

9. If wishes were _____ .

10. Imitation is _____ .

Answers on page 345

time out!

All of the answers in this quiz contain the word TIME.

1. A small container of objects that is meant to be opened in the future.

2. Workers often punch this.

3. Russia has eleven, China has five, and the continental United States has four.

4. Manhattan intersection that stretches from 42nd to 47th streets.

5. Children's story opener.

6. Photographic technique that speeds up the action.

7. Scott Joplin's type of music.

8. These wait for no man.

9. "To everything there is a season, and ..." this.

10. A person who is unfaithful to a spouse.

11. H. G. Wells's 1895 novel.

12. Opening line of Charles Dickens's novel *A Tale of Two Cities*.

Answers on page 345

RIDDLE ME THIS

Riddles often require some unconventional thinking, which makes them a great brain exercise. Think outside the box as you try to solve this classic riddle.

What "room" has no door, no windows, no floor, and no roof?

Answer on page 345

A Sheepish Sheep

The phrase "sheepish sheep" is formed when a noun is turned into an adjective (*sheepish*) and is then used to modify the original noun (*sheep*). Given a brief definition, can you identify more of these kinds of phrases?

1. An impudent Worcestershire.

2. A nasty-tongued feline.

3. A cheap and tacky Emmental.

4. A cowardly poultry.

5. A flattened gourd.

6. A crazy macadamia.

7. A fine fruit from Georgia.

8. A small crustacean.

9. An excessively theatrical cut of pork.

10. A suspicious guppy.

11. A timid rodent.

12. A chattering wild ox.

13. A sexy carnivore.

Answers on page 345

Common Bonds

The pictures in this puzzle may seem like they have nothing in common. But if you look carefully, you'll see a theme emerge. What is the common bond among these three images?

Answer on page 345

they're grand!

Can you identify these grandparents?

1. If he had lived long enough, he would have welcomed his first grandchild, a daughter born to Lisa Marie, in 1989.

2. She became a grandma at age 44 when her daughter Bristol had a child out of wedlock.

3. The young actress Oona Castilla Chaplin is not only the granddaughter of silent film star Charlie Chaplin, but also the great-granddaughter of this legendary playwright.

4. She has eight grandchildren: Zara, Peter, Louise, James, Eugenie, Beatrice, Harry, and William.

Answers on page 345

sibling rivalry

long-term memory
executive functioning
attention to detail

We give you the first names of some famous siblings; can you provide their last names (which are sometimes the same and sometimes different)?

1. Warren and Shirley _____

2. Alec, Daniel, William, and Stephen _____

3. Fred and Adele _____

4. Lionel, Ethel, and John _____

5. Beau and Jeff _____

6. George and Jeb _____

7. Joan and Jackie _____

8. Olivia and Joan _____

9. Frank and Jesse _____

10. Wynonna and Ashley _____

Answers on page 345

INITIAL QUIZ

long-term memory

working memory

All of the two-word answers in this quiz begin with the initials RR.

1. Anger, sometimes violent, exhibited by automobile drivers.

2. One half of a musical duo who created *Oklahoma!*, *South Pacific*, and many other Broadway blockbusters.

3. Track and field competition.

4. Collective term for politically conservative Christians.

5. British car company.

6. A way to transport luggage on a driving vacation.

7. This largely terrestrial bird is a member of the cuckoo family.

8. In the movies, he played Jeremiah Johnson, Hubbell Gardiner, and journalist Bob Woodward.

9. Term used for solar or wind power because it will not run out.

10. An area in a house that is used for children's play and parties.

11. Nickname given to the first United States Volunteer Cavalry during the Spanish-American War—young Teddy Roosevelt's regiment.

12. A person who stirs up the passions or prejudices of a crowd of people.

13. Celebrity chef, author, and queen of the thirty-minute meal.

Answers on page 345

 **RIDDLE ME THIS**

executive functioning

attention to detail

Riddles often require some unconventional thinking, which makes them a great brain exercise. Think outside the box as you try to solve this classic riddle.

What can run but never walks; has a mouth but never talks; has a bed but never sleeps; has a head but never weeps?

Answer on page 345

complete the words

Complete the words in the grid below using the three-letter words from the list to its left. Each three-letter word will be used once.

ZOO	H	A	S				T	E	R
AIR	E	X	H				P	I	N
AGE	I	M	A				E	A	R
BOO	S	P	Y				I	D	Y
ODE	E	N	G				D	E	D
INK	O	B	A				K	A	N
FAN	A	B	E				C	H	T
GIN	S	C	A				S	E	L
HER	R	O	P				E	R	S
ILL	G	N	S				B	E	T
WIT	R	E	M				L	L	Y
CAT	A	T	R				E	T	O
RAY	S	I	N				T	S	Y
RAM	T	H	R				S	E	D

Answers on page 345

wacky wordies

GOODGOOD
BB
GOTGOTGOTGOT10

1 _____

a cut

average

2 _____

the plate
P
E
T
S

3 _____

all
―――
again

4 _____

To solve these fun puzzles, look carefully at each frame, because the arrangement of the letters is a key clue to the familiar phrase contained within. For example, if the word *school* were placed high up in the frame, the answer would be *high school*. Or, if the words *easy pieces* occurred five times in the frame, the answer would be *five easy pieces*.

Answers on page 346

PERSO   NALITY

over
over
over

5 _____

6 _____

TAKE TAKE
TAKE TAKE
TAKE

B
CLOUD CLOUD CLOUD
CLOUD CLOUD CLOUD
CLOUD CLOUD CLOUD

7 _____

8 _____

letter pairs

long-term memory
executive functioning
multitasking
attention to detail

Below is a list of six-letter words with only the first two letters revealed. To finish each word, you need to add two of the two-letter pairs in the top grid. Each two-letter pair will be used only once.

AC	CT	DN	EN	ER	ER	ER	EY	HT	HY	IC	IC
IG	KY	MP	NN	RI	RO	ST	SW	TE	TT	WY	YO

1. ST__ __ __ __   4. CO__ __ __ __   7. SH__ __ __ __   10. KI__ __ __ __

2. DI__ __ __ __   5. FR__ __ __ __   8. LA__ __ __ __   11. HE__ __ __ __

3. AN__ __ __ __   6. PE__ __ __ __   9. RO__ __ __ __   12. BI__ __ __ __

Answers on page 346

---

endings & beginnings

In this game, we provide the first half of a two-word phrase or compound word and the second half of another. For example, given *Credit* _____ *trick*, the one word that completes both clues is *Card*, i.e., *Credit card* and *Card trick*. (If you get stuck, the first letter of the answer is provided in a hint below.)

1. Plate _____ ceiling

2. Petty _____ register

3. Sweet _____ flakes

4. Club _____ fountain

5. Nest _____ noodle

6. Red _____ walk

7. Frozen _____ stamps

8. Chain _____ dust

9. Cotton _____ cane

10. String _____ bag

Hints: 1 g; 2 c; 3 c; 4 s; 5 e; 6 c; 7 f; 8 s; 9 c; 10 b

Answers on page 346

The Presidents' Jobs

Do you know what some US presidents did before they became president?

1. He was an oil executive, a sports team owner, and a governor.

_____

2. He was a community organizer, a constitutional law professor, and a US senator.

_____

3. He was a journalist, a US congressman, and a US senator.

_____

4. He was a postmaster, a lawyer, and a US congressman.

_____

5. He was an inventor, an architect, and a Secretary of State.

_____

6. He was a schoolteacher, a soldier, and a US senator.

_____

7. He was a farmer, a haberdasher, a judge, and a US senator.

_____

8. He was a lawyer, a university president, and a governor.

_____

9. He was an engineer and the US Secretary of Commerce under Warren Harding and Calvin Coolidge.

_____

Answers on page 346

On the Map

From *Alabama* to *Zanzibar*, can you come up with the name of a geographical location for each letter of the alphabet? And for an extra brain boost, see how many you can get in three minutes.

A _____

B _____

C _____

D _____

E _____

F _____

G _____

H _____

I _____

J _____

K _____

L _____

M _____

N _____

O _____

P _____

Q _____

R _____

S _____

T _____

U _____

V _____

W _____

X _____

Y _____

Z _____

Answers on page 346

Group Therapy

Group Therapy is the game that proves there is more than one correct answer to a question . . . and we tell you the minimum number of answers you need to come up with. For an extra brain boost, put a one-minute limit on each question.

1. Name six people whose first name is Joe, Joey, or Joseph (spelling can vary).

2. Name seven foods of any kind that start with the letter P.

3. Name six words that mean *angry*.

4. Name ten US states with four or more syllables in their name.

5. Name six Christmas songs.

6. Name eight metals (pure and/or alloys).

7. Name six jobs/careers that begin with the letter S.

8. Name ten words that end with the letters MP.

Answers on page 346

Vivienne's Vowels

Vivienne is an odd one. She has an aversion to the letters A, E, I, O, and U. Can you fix her list of famous people by putting back the missing vowels? *Note: All well-known people, male or female, living or dead, and those who are known by one name, two names, or more are all acceptable.* You can make this a more strenuous brain exercise by adding some time pressure: Try to solve this puzzle in ninety seconds.

1. DGR LLN P _____

2. PT SGR _____

3. HNK RN _____

4. J BDN _____

5. LBRC _____

6. LRNC LVR _____

7. MM SNHWR _____

8. TM CRS _____

9. MDNN _____

10. SC SMV _____

11. PT RS _____

12. CLPTR _____

Answers on page 347

ALPHABET TRIVIA

The only thing these trivia questions have in common is that all of the answers begin with the letter H.

long-term memory
executive functioning

1. Name two of the three countries that begin with the letter H.

2. Five world capitals begin with the letter H, but you'll be doing great if you can name two of them.

3. Which four US state capitals begin with the letter H?

4. "H" in the Table of Elements:
- **a.** What lighter-than-air element is used as a lifting gas in balloons?
- **b.** Gas that was blamed for the Hindenburg disaster.

5. How many of the five US presidents whose last names begin with the letter H can you name?

6. What do the four H's stand for in the 4-H clubs?

7. Quick-Answer Questions:
- **a.** Which of the five senses begins with the letter H?
- **b.** Which of the five Great Lakes begins with the letter H?
- **c.** Which Ivy League college begins with the letter H?
- **d.** Which of the four largest world religions begins with the letter H?

8. Famous people whose last names begin with H:
- **a.** President Nixon's Chief of Staff and key Watergate figure.
- **b.** Legendary escape artist.
- **c.** *Playboy* founder.
- **d.** Filmmaker and master of suspense.
- **e.** Star of *Forrest Gump* and *Sleepless in Seattle*.

9. What do the following acronyms and abbreviations stand for?
HBO
HD
HGTV
HMO
HOV
HQ
HUD
HVAC

Answers on page 347

WORD PICTURES

Put one picture together with one word part (in any order) to come up with the names of eight wearable items. (*Note: Spelling might not always be correct, but the pronunciation will be right.*)

RON	IGAN	ET	ERS
ENS	AFORE	GA	GERIE

Answers on page 347

Where's the Suburb?

long-term memory

Given the names of three suburbs, can you identify their closest major US city?

1. Yonkers, Hoboken, New Rochelle

2. Hialeah, Homestead, Coral Gables

3. Torrance, Redondo Beach, Pasadena

4. Newton, Quincy, Brookline

5. Daly City, Sausalito, Mill Valley

6. Bethesda, Arlington, Alexandria

7. Cicero, Skokie, Elgin

8. Slidell, Gulfport, Bay St. Louis

9. Katy, Sugar Land, Galveston

10. Golden, Aurora, Boulder

11. Camden, Bryn Mawr, Blue Bell

Answers on page 348

---

 oy!

long-term memory
working memory

All of the answers in this quiz contain the consecutive letters OY.

1. To bother or pester.

2. A person who works for, and is paid by, a company.

3. An entrance hall.

4. A carved figure projecting from the gutter of a building.

5. A mollusk.

6. 1960s band with the California sound.

7. An anchored float to mark location or aid in marine navigation.

8. A long journey, often on a ship.

9. A thick cotton fabric with soft ribs.

10. Slang term for a person who smuggles undocumented immigrants into the United States.

11. Exceedingly sweet.

12. To refuse to buy goods as a punishment or protest.

Answers on page 348

Scrambled Foods

Unscramble the letters in each clue below to reveal a list of foods. For an even better brain exercise, try to complete this quiz in two minutes.

1. AIPZZ

2. ABCNO

3. BELORST

4. AEFFLSW

5. EELPRTZ

6. AIILORV

7. DDGINPU

8. CNOOPPR

9. CCEHIKN

10. CCHIINUZ

11. AAAGLNS

12. ABERRRSTWY

Answers on page 348

WHAT'S THE WEATHER?

All of these book, movie, and song titles include a "weather" word.

1. *Inherit the* _____

2. *The Perfect* _____

3. "_____ *to the Chief*"

4. _____ *Man*

5. _____ *Falling on Cedars*

6. *House of Sand and* _____

7. *Gravity's* _____

8. _____ *with a Chance of Meatballs*

9. *It's Always_____ in Philadelphia*

Answers on page 348

PBS

long-term memory
executive functioning

How well do you know these PBS icons?

❶ Most everyone remembers Julia Child, but do you remember the title of her pioneering cooking show?

❷ *Keeping Up Appearances*, a so-called "Brit-com," featured this social-climbing snob, who insisted on "improving" the pronunciation of her husband's last name.

❸ The creator of this PBS program, which debuted in 1973, spent a year at the BBC studying how to make science documentaries.

❹ Can you name the two newsmen who originated the nightly program that is now simply called *PBS NewsHour*?

❺ This comedic genius, famous for his pioneering work in late night talk television, brought historical figures "back to life" for this 1970s PBS talk show, *Meeting of the Minds.*

Answers on page 348

complete the words

long-term memory
executive functioning
multitasking
attention to detail

Place a letter in each blank space below to make a word of five letters or more. All twenty-six letters are used only once. And each correct answer uses at least one space on the right and one space on the left of the inserted letter. No hyphenated words, plurals, or proper nouns are allowed.

A	W	A	T	E	R		E	L	O	N	E
B	I	G	O	L	L		B	R	A	R	Y
C	S	H	A	L	L		A	Y	F	E	R
D	A	U	T	O	M		B	I	L	E	T
E	O	O	P	L	I		U	O	R	Z	E
F	D	A	Y	V	O		K	A	N	G	A
G	I	T	C	R	I		K	W	E	L	D
H	U	R	B	A	N		R	U	P	T	Y
I	S	A	G	A	U		E	B	R	I	D
J	S	W	I	T	H		M	P	E	R	O
K	F	I	R	E	P		A	C	E	W	I
L	O	A	F	L	A		O	R	O	O	F
M	T	O	G	N	I		H	T	R	E	N
N	S	C	R	U	S		A	C	E	A	N
O	J	U	P	R	E		U	D	I	C	E
P	P	R	E	K	I		S	I	N	G	N
Q	U	P	E	R	O		I	D	E	N	T
R	G	R	A	S	P		E	R	R	Y	U
S	E	L	E	C	T		I	C	I	T	Y
T	R	O	B	J	E		T	Z	I	C	K
U	A	L	O	N	E		H	E	W	E	N
V	E	F	L	U	F		Y	O	U	Z	L
W	M	A	N	I	C		R	E	N	N	K
X	B	E	L	A	T		E	R	E	E	F
Y	F	R	E	E	H		D	R	A	N	T
Z	C	A	N	D	L		S	T	I	C	K

Answers on page 348

ALPHABET TRIVIA

The only thing these trivia questions have in common is that all of the answers begin with the letter I.

long-term memory
executive functioning

1. Name six of the eight world countries that begin with the letter I.

2. The two largest world cities that begin with the letter I are both in Turkey. Can you name them?

3. What are the four US states that begin with the letter I?

4. What is the only US state capital that begins with the letter I?

5. Which two colors that begin with the letter I are on opposite sides of the color spectrum?

6. Name a lizard that begins with the letter I.

7. Name a unit of length that begins with the letter I.

8. What is the Russian-language equivalent to the name John?

9. Name an ancient South American civilization that begins with the letter I.

10. Name a part of the eye that begins with the letter I.

11. Identify these people whose last names begin with the letter I:

a. Automotive executive who revived Chrysler in the 1980s.

b. Radio "shock-jock," famous for his insult humor.

c. US Senator from Hawaii who died in 2012, while still in office, at age 88.

d. British actor who starred in *The French Lieutenant's Woman*.

e. Early American author of *The Legend of Sleepy Hollow* and *Rip Van Winkle*.

f. The judge who presided over the O.J. Simpson murder trial.

12. Identify the following acronyms and abbreviations.
IBEW
IBM
i.e.
IQ
IRS
IVF

Answers on page 349

FIND THE WORDS

Find the 48 words in the picture that start with the letter L.

working memory
executive functioning
attention to detail
multitasking

Answers on page 350

Mangled Monograms

Unscramble the three letters in each clue below and you'll have the initials of a president of the United States.

long-term memory
executive functioning

1. DRF

2. EDD

3. MRN

4. BJL

5. AQJ

6. GSU

7. WBG

8. FJK

9. JCW

10. STH

11. BOH

12. WRR

13. HHC

14. VBM

15. FGR

Answers on page 349

Order, Please!

long-term memory
working memory
executive functioning
multitasking

Put the following list of people in order of when they were born, starting with the earliest.

___ Al Gore

___ Jay Leno

___ James Dean

___ Barack Obama

___ Bob Dylan

___ Bill Clinton

___ Elvis Presley

___ Vladimir Putin

___ Michael Jordan

___ Dick Van Dyke

___ John Lennon

___ Queen Elizabeth II

___ Michael Jackson

Answers on page 349

TRIMBLE

Trimble is a trivia game and a word jumble combined. First, answer the trivia questions (all related to people named David) and cross out the letters of each answer in the letter grid. Then rearrange the remaining letters (those that have not been crossed out) to reveal another word or phrase related to the same theme.

A	A	A	A	A	B	D	D	E	E	E	E	E	E
F	G	H	I	I	I	K	L	L	L	M	N	N	N
N	N	N	O	O	O	O	R	R	R	R	R	R	S
S	T	T	T	T	U	V	V	W	Y	Y			

1. Last name of the David who hosted a late-night talk show from 1982 to 2015.

2. This David conducted a series of televised interviews with Richard Nixon a couple of years after he resigned the presidency.

3. Last name of the David whose mom and dad were Ozzie and Harriet.

4. Last name of the David who co-anchored a nightly news program from 1956 through 1970, with Chet Huntley.

5. This Dave was the first host of NBC's *Today* show—and his co-host was a chimpanzee named J. Fred Muggs.

6. This Henry David wrote about the simple life on Walden Pond.

Word Jumble hint: British actor.

Answers on page 349

go for it!

All of the answers in this quiz begin with the letters GO.

1. A connoisseur of fine food.

2. Protective eyewear.

3. Eat hastily.

4. Slander, scuttlebutt, rumor.

5. Nickname for a peanut.

6. Transportation in Venice, Italy.

7. Internet search engine.

8. Magnificent-looking; resplendent.

9. A swelling in the thyroid gland—usually caused by iodine deficiency.

10. A legendary evil or mischievous creature.

11. Nonsense, gibberish, mumbo-jumbo.

12. Violent, gruesome, bloody.

Answers on page 349

Finish the Equation

These brainteasers have been around for decades. Can you complete each equation by replacing the initials with the words that make the saying correct? For example, the answer to *7 = D of the W* is 7 = Days of the Week.

1. 4 = Q in a G

2. 7 = W of the A W

3. 12 = I in a F

4. 12 = S of the Z

5. 26 = L of the A

6. 30 = D H S, A, J, and N

7. 36 = I in a Y

8. 50 = W to L Y L

9. 52 = W in a Y

10. 60 = M in an H

11. 90 = D in a R A

12. 20,000 = L U the S

Answers on page 349

like *what*?

Some similes (comparative expressions that use the words *like* or *as*) are so familiar that you only need one or two words to complete them. Try these—that all begin with the word *like*. To make this a more vigorous brain exercise, try to answer all the questions in one minute.

1. Like two _____

2. Like rats _____

3. Like a kid _____

4. Like a bat _____

5. Like a bull _____

6. Like shooting _____

7. Like a duck _____

8. Like a lamb _____

9. Like a cat _____

10. Like water _____

11. Like taking _____

Answers on page 352

Vivienne's Vowels

executive functioning
long-term memory
attention to detail
processing speed

Vivienne is an odd one. She has an aversion to the letters A, E, I, O, and U. Can you fix her list of animals (of any type) by putting back the missing vowels? You can make this a more strenuous brain exercise by adding some time pressure: Try to solve this puzzle in ninety seconds.

1. BBN _____

2. MSQT _____

3. STRCH _____

4. BLD GL _____

5. JGR _____

6. RCCN _____

7. RMDLL _____

8. CCKT _____

9. GN PG _____

10. B _____

11. CYT _____

12. YSTR _____

Answers on page 352

long-term memory
executive functioning
attention to detail

Add Some Letters

The first word in each clue below has one letter missing. Without moving the letters around, how many words can you make by placing a letter in the blank spot? For example: RE ___ TED would yield the answers RENTED and RESTED. The second word in each question has the same letters in the same order. They also follow the same rules, but this time there are two letters missing. The number in parentheses indicates the number of words we found. *Note: No proper nouns are allowed.*

1.   ___ OUND   (8) _____
     ___ ___ OUND   (3) _____
2.   ___ ITCH   (6) _____
     ___ ___ ITCH   (5) _____
3.   ___ URRY   (3) _____
     ___ ___ URRY   (4) _____
4.   ___ UNCH   (5) _____
     ___ ___ UNCH   (5) _____

Answers on page 352

Common Bonds

long-term memory
executive functioning
attention to detail

The pictures in this puzzle may seem like they have nothing in common. But if you look carefully, you'll see a theme emerge. What is the common bond among these three images?

Answer on page 352

honorific titles

long-term memory

In English, words such as *Mr., Mrs., Ms., Dr., Uncle, General*, etc., are called "honorific titles." Can you identify the honorific title for each character in this quiz?

1. Feminist publication that debuted in 1971.

2. Children's toy, introduced in 1952. (Originally, you had to supply the vegetable.)

3. Footwear and foot care products.

4. Pen name of Theodor Geisel.

5. Breakfast food.

6. Basketball Hall of Famer who played most of his career with the Philadelphia 76ers (1976–1987).

7. Morgan Freeman played her chauffeur in the movies.

8. He was TV's talking palomino.

9. Tough guy from television's *The A-Team*.

10. Captain Kangaroo's sidekick.

Answers on page 352

FOOD ON THE MAP

long-term memory

executive functioning

All of the names of foods in this quiz include geographical locations.

❶ This yellow sauce is an emulsion of egg yolk and butter seasoned with lemon juice, salt, and pepper.

❷ One of the most popular styles of sushi, this roll contains cucumber, crab, and avocado.

❸ The popover is the American version of this English dish.

❹ This drink is typically made with tequila, vodka, light rum, triple sec, and gin . . . and not a drop of tea.

Answers on page 352

DOUBLE TROUBLE

Can you find the one word that precedes each list of words to make a common two-word phrase or compound word? For example, the one word that completes *weed, coast, sick* is *sea* (*seaweed, seacoast, seasick*). If you get stuck, we've provided the first letter of the answer as a hint at the bottom of the page.

working memory
executive functioning

1. Cat, flower, life

_____

2. Cheese, puff, soda

_____

3. Place, proof, fly

_____

4. Light, bulb, back

_____

5. Coat, notch, knot

_____

6. Check, off, dirt

_____

7. Dog, tub, plate

_____

8. Plant, shell, head

_____

9. Office, spring, car

_____

10. Door, test, writer

_____

Hints: 1 w; 2 c; 3 f; 4 t; 5 t; 6 p; 7 h; 8 e; 9 b; 10 s

Answers on page 352

MAKING CONNECTIONS

Given nine words or phrases randomly placed in a grid, can you find the three groups of three connected items AND explain why they are connected?

Here's a sample grid:

RED	HONEY	BLUE
VIEIRA	HARVEST	PURPLE
FULL	LAUER	COURIC

GROUP 1 WORDS:
Red, Blue, Purple

THEME:
Colors

GROUP 2 WORDS:
Vieira, Lauer, Couric

THEME:
Today show hosts

GROUP 3 WORDS:
Full, Honey, Harvest

THEME:
_____moon

GREEN	TONY	CORAL
BEE	EM	EMMY
GRAMMY	GARTER	MAME

GROUP 1 WORDS

_____ _____ _____

THEME:

_____

GROUP 2 WORDS

_____ _____ _____

THEME:

_____

GROUP 3 WORDS

_____ _____ _____

THEME:

_____

Answers on page 352

By the Letter

long-term memory
executive functioning

In this game, players need to guess a word—one letter at a time. Place the letter called for in each question in the line below (the first answer above the number 1, the second above the number 2, and so on).

1. The first letter of the name of a large fish with a barbed tail . . . or a Corvette model.

2. The first letter of the name of the luxury automobile that was introduced in 1902 and named after the founder of Detroit.

3. The last letter of the name of the Japanese art form that uses miniature trees grown in containers.

4. Either the first or last letter of the name of the chain store that sells office supplies, from paper clips to computers.

5. The last letter of the name of the US state that has been ruled by Spain, France, Mexico, the Confederate States, and, for a short time, itself.

6. The first letter of the popular name for US Public Law 111-148, the Patient Protection and Affordable Care Act.

7. The first letter of the name of the large nation that has the greatest amount of land within the Arctic Circle.

8. The first letter of the name of the country that has two similarly named cities—Lausanne and Lucerne.

____ ____ ____ ____ ____ ____ ____ ____

   1   2   3   4   5   6   7   8

Answers on page 352

Finish the Proverb

Given the first couple of words of a familiar proverb or saying, can you complete it? In this quiz, all of the answers will include the name of an animal. To make this a more vigorous brain exercise, try to answer all the questions in one minute.

1. You can lead _____.

2. You can catch _____.

3. When the cat _____.

4. There's plenty _____.

5. There's more than one _____.

6. If you lie down _____.

7. Curiosity _____.

8. Don't count _____.

9. Don't put _____.

Answers on page 352

 **RIDDLE ME THIS**

Riddles often require some unconventional thinking and are a great brain exercise. Think outside the box as you try to solve this classic riddle.

I am basically weightless, yet the strongest man can't hold me for much more than a minute. What am I?

Answer on page 353

Follow the Rules

If you follow each instruction precisely, you will discover the second half of the phrase "God created light . . ." We've provided the first line, and the rest is up to you. A gold star to the solver who gets it right on the first try. (*This game is harder than you might think.*)

1. Without spaces between the letters, write down the phrase:
G O D C R E A T E D L I G H T

2. Remove the first D and replace it with an N.

3. Place a P at the end.

4. Remove the O and the I and replace each of them with an A.

5. Swap the first T and the D.

6. Remove the sixth letter and place it before the L.

7. Place an M in the first position.

8. Place an M before the second A and after the third A.

9. Remove the seventeenth letter and place it in the twelfth position.

10. Remove all G's

11. Remove the fourth, fifth, and next-to-last letters.

1 <u>G O D C R E A T E D L I G H T</u>

2 _____

3 _____

4 _____

5 _____

6 _____

7 _____

8 _____

9 _____

10 _____

11 _____

Did you get the right answer?

Answers on page 353

Move the letters in each vertical column of the top grid to the spaces in the column just below it in the bottom grid. The letters will not necessarily be moved in the order in which they appear. If you move the letters to the correct positions, they will spell out a quotation (reading from left to right) from President Ronald Reagan. (*Note: A black square indicates the end of a word. Words may continue from one horizontal line to the next.*)

long-term memory
executive functioning
multitasking
attention to detail

Before attempting the big puzzle, try this example first—without looking at the answer to the right:

Example Answer:

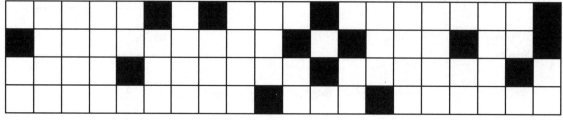

Answer on page 353

change a letter

long-term memory
executive functioning
multitasking
attention to detail

Change the first letter of the three words in each list to create three new words that all start with the same letter. For example, given the words *whine*, *plant*, and *reason*, what one letter can replace the first letter of each word to make three new words? The answer is S—*shine*, *slant*, and *season*.

1. Freak, Clock, Folder

2. Foul, Pimple, Handbag

3. Warm, Lather, Racial

4. Noodle, Swindle, Ventures

5. Haunt, Couch, Brain

6. Watch, Eighty, Yodel

7. Nagged, Head, Teach

8. Cater, Leather, Height

9. Fever, Waive, Serve

10. Pace, Moose, Father

Answers on page 353

Group Therapy

Group Therapy is the game that proves there is more than one correct answer to a question … and we tell you the minimum number of answers you need to come up with. For an extra brain boost, put a one-minute limit on each question.

1. Name five things that complete the phrase: A pair of _____.

2. Name four words that mean hungry.

3. Name eight Caribbean islands/countries.

4. Name five famous people whose first name is George.

5. Name six types of bread.

6. Name six common road signs.

7. Name four colors that begin with the letter P.

8. Name six Major League Baseball teams that do NOT have animals in their names.

Answers on page 353

WORD PICTURES

Each picture represents one part of a word or common two-word phrase. For example, if you combined a picture of a spoon and a picture of a table, you would get the word *tablespoon*. How many of the eight words or two-word phrases can you find?

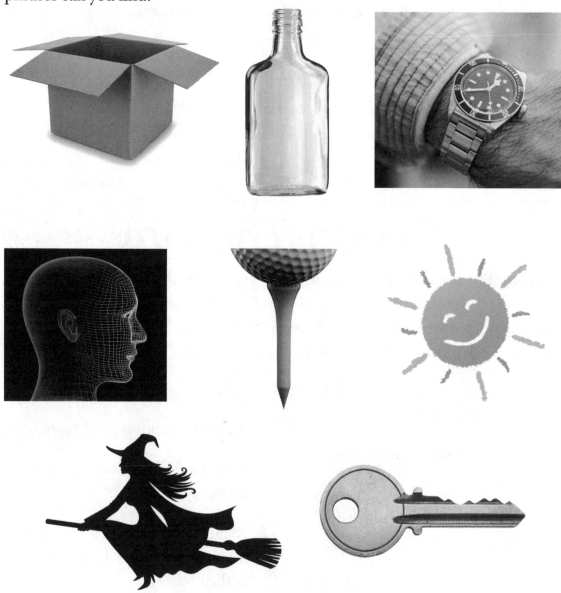

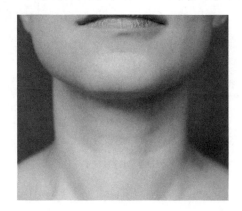

Answers on page 354

ALPHABET TRIVIA

The only thing these trivia questions have in common is that all of the answers begin with the letter J.

1. Who are the four US presidents whose last names begin with J?

2. What are the three US state capitals that begin with the letter J?

3. Name two of the three world countries that begin with the letter J.

4. Name four of the nine books of the Bible (King James Version) that begin with the letter J.

5. Name four Spanish first names that begin with J.

6. Name two articles of clothing that start with the letter J.

7. Name a game or toy that begins with the letter J.

8. Can you identify four brand names (any type of product or business) that begin with the letter J?

9. Can you name two famous people with the initials JJ?

10. Can you identify these film titles that begin with the letter J?

a. 1975 blockbuster that was shot mostly on the island of Martha's Vineyard.

b. Tom Cruise plays a sports agent.

c. 1961 film, starring Spencer Tracy and Burt Lancaster, that focuses on the Nazi war crime trials.

d. Dinosaurs come back to life in this 1993 thriller.

Answers on page 354

Secret Word

long-term memory
executive functioning
attention to detail
processing speed

How many five-letter common English words can you find in the word below? The more words you find, the more likely you are to also get the secret word—a word that is generally a little harder to spot. (We found 71 five-letter words.) To make this game even more challenging—and a better brain exercise—try to find at least 12 five-letter words in one minute.

ENCYCLOPEDIA

_____ _____ _____ _____ _____

_____ _____ _____ _____ _____

_____ _____ _____ _____ _____

_____ _____ _____ _____ _____

_____ _____ _____ _____ _____

_____ _____ _____ _____ _____

_____ _____ _____ _____ _____

_____ _____ _____ _____ _____

_____ _____ _____ _____ _____

_____ _____ _____ _____ _____

_____ _____ _____ _____ _____

_____ _____ _____ _____ _____

_____ _____ _____ _____ _____

_____

Answers (including the secret word) on page 354

president in name only

Although this is not a quiz about US presidents, every answer includes the last name of a US president.

1. Dennis the Menace's next-door neighbor.

2. TV's fictional sheriff of Mayberry, North Carolina.

3. *M*A*S*H* character from Crabapple Cove, Maine.

4. Luxury car division of the Ford Motor Company.

5. Comic strip cat that hates Mondays.

6. This actor, who starred in the *Indiana Jones* films, has two presidential names.

7. A brand of beer.

8. A brand of vacuum cleaner.

9. They "moved on up to the East Side, to a deluxe apartment in the sky."

10. Mary Richards's boss at WJM-TV.

11. Former Los Angeles Lakers basketball great and advocate for HIV/AIDS prevention.

12. He starred in *Cry Freedom* (1987) and *Malcolm X* (1992).

Answers on page 355

GONE FISHIN'

long-term memory
executive functioning

Pescatarians will definitely like this quiz.

❶ A small fish used mostly for bait; it's also the name of the boat on TV's *Gilligan's Island*.

❷ Wildlife expert Steve Irwin died in the waters off Australia when he was pierced in the chest by a foot-long barb from the tail of this large, flat fish.

❸ The name of this fish comes from the Latin *salire*, "to leap," which describes its habit of leaping over mini falls and other obstacles to get to its breeding grounds.

❹ Because this popular food fish has no scales and is a bottom-feeding food scavenger, it is not eaten by observant Jews and Muslims.

❺ The name of this fish, found in freshwater rivers in South America, comes from a native language and means "scissors"— which refers to its thin, razor-sharp teeth.

Answers on page 355

Sentence Sleuth

A true sentence sleuth can find the one word that is hidden somewhere in a sentence. In this case, can you find the name of an occupation? The correct answer could be spread over one, two, or several words, and you should ignore all punctuation, capital letters, etc., when looking for the hidden occupation.

1. Julie likes banana-berry smoothies, but I favor plum-berry or just pineapple.

2. When Thea let the giant Asian carp enter the aquarium, it ate all the goldfish.

3. Every time we go to Auntie Petra's, we have tea, cherry pie, and ice cream.

4. Mateo told Joshua that his new girlfriend Flor is the prettiest girl in school.

5. The headline said it all: Boxer suffers terrible defeat—torn eyelid, broken nose, and ruptured eardrum.

6. Grandma loved strange headgear. I remember her wearing a turban, kerchiefs, tiaras, and even a man's fez.

7. After their honeymoon in Spain, Teri and Joe moved to San Diego.

8. *The Wall Street Journal* is too conservative for Uncle Fred, a liberal from way back.

9. As soon as Jeannie and Steve got the computer hard drive repaired, the electricity went out.

10. Dad bought Mother a pistol for Christmas but she didn't want it in the house.

11. Sonny Bono was not a very good singer, but Cher is excellent.

12. As soon as the Toyota went over that big bump, I realized that the muffler had fallen off the car.

Answers on page 355

What's Their Job?

Given the names of three well-known people, what careers do they all share? *Note: While some of the individuals mentioned may hold other jobs, we're looking for the one job that the three people in the clue all have in common.*

long-term memory
attention to detail

1. Hugo Black, Abe Fortas, David Souter

2. Margot Fonteyn, Gelsey Kirkland, Agnes DeMille

3. Eero Saarinen, Walter Gropius, Frank Gehry

4. Vijay Singh, Bubba Watson, Annika Sörenstam

5. Ray Borque, Phil Esposito, Mark Messier

6. Andrew Young, Coleman Young, Ray Nagin

7. Rafael Trujillo, Augusto Pinochet, Francois Duvalier

8. David Denby, Vincent Canby, Pauline Kael

9. Christian Louboutin, Jimmy Choo, Bruno Magli

10. Henri Cartier-Bresson, Richard Avedon, Alfred Stieglitz

11. Seymour Hersh, Jimmy Breslin, Walter Winchell

12. Arthur Rubinstein, Vladimir Horowitz, Daniel Barenboim

Answers on page 355

complete the words

long-term memory
executive functioning
multitasking
attention to detail

Place a letter in each blank space below to make a word of five letters or more. All twenty-six letters are used only once. And each correct answer uses at least one space on the right and one space on the left of the inserted letter. No hyphenated words, plurals, or proper nouns are allowed.

A	O	F	I	L	I		U	S	T	E	R
B	G	O	T	R	I		G	E	R	T	H
C	E	N	D	P	O		I	T	E	C	S
D	C	O	M	F	O		T	A	B	L	E
E	H	U	C	H	E		S	E	T	A	N
F	T	R	E	A	D		U	S	T	E	D
G	C	L	I	S	P		O	N	I	R	E
H	T	A	P	E	S		R	Y	I	N	G
I	A	C	H	E	A		E	N	A	B	E
J	R	A	J	I	N		E	D	O	N	T
K	E	X	T	W	I		A	R	D	E	W
L	B	E	C	H	O		O	L	A	T	E
M	S	P	A	M	P		L	E	T	M	Y
N	W	R	O	H	A		M	E	R	O	R
O	P	R	E	M	O		T	H	A	R	M
P	T	H	E	R	A		Y	R	A	L	L
Q	Z	O	O	N	O		H	E	R	E	X
R	D	R	A	S	S		S	T	E	M	I
S	C	A	L	E	N		A	R	E	G	G
T	F	O	R	I	G		N	A	L	T	A
U	M	I	P	L	A		U	E	C	A	B
V	O	T	I	S	I		T	E	R	O	N
W	E	S	P	A	R		L	E	N	S	H
X	B	L	O	C	E		N	T	U	S	K
Y	M	E	R	C	A		O	E	B	O	D
Z	S	H	U	F	I		T	E	E	N	Y

Answers on page 356

Anagrams

The letters of each word in this list can be rearranged in multiple ways to form other words. We provide the word and the number of anagrams that are possible to make. (*Remember, you must use ALL the letters in the given word.*) You should give your brain a rest if you can solve all of these anagrams in two minutes.

1. Lake (2) _____ _____

2. Tars (4) _____ _____ _____ _____

3. Flow (2) _____ _____

4. Wider (2) _____ _____

5. Torso (2) _____ _____

6. Thing (1) _____

7. Claps (2) _____ _____

8. Takers (2) _____ _____

Answers on page 356

RIDDLE ME THIS

Riddles often require some unconventional thinking and are a great brain exercise. Think outside the box as you try to solve this classic riddle.

What has many holes but can still hold water?

Answer on page 356

good going

All of the answers in this quiz contain the word GOOD.

1. Purveyor of ice cream novelties, sold from trucks and in stores.

2. Candy-coated licorice pieces.

3. This women's magazine published its first issue in 1885.

4. This is one way to get your prison sentence reduced.

5. A nonprofit organization that provides job training and other services largely through a large network of retail thrift stores.

6. This film, starring Robin Williams, is set in Saigon in 1965.

7. This 1990 film, directed by Martin Scorsese, follows the rise and fall of the Lucchese family.

8. According to poet Robert Frost, "good fences make . . ." these.

9. Charlie Brown's favorite exclamation.

10. This might be said when you're happy to see someone go away.

11. The first African American Supreme Court justice.

12. He "looked out on the feast of Stephen, when the snow lay round about, deep and crisp and even."

13. This researcher is acknowledged as the foremost expert on chimpanzees.

Answers on page 356

Easy as Pie

Similes are comparative expressions that use the words *like* or *as*. In this game, we provide the first half of a familiar simile and you must give the rest. To make this a more vigorous brain exercise, try to answer all the questions in one minute.

1. Cute as _____

2. Flat as _____

3. Neat as _____

4. Nutty as _____

5. Pale as _____

6. Pleased as _____

7. Shiny as _____

8. Smart as _____

9. Sober as _____

10. Sturdy as _____

11. Thin as _____

Answers on page 356

CHARACTER STUDY

long-term memory

These movie characters are often named in lists of the "greatest movie characters of all time." Can you name the movie they're featured in *and* the actor who played them?

1. Rhett Butler

2. Fanny Brice

3. Princess Leia Organa

4. Norma Rae

5. Clyde Barrow

6. Marty McFly

7. Mrs. Robinson

8. Maria von Trapp

9. Bob Woodward

10. George Bailey

11. Butch Cassidy

12. Indiana Jones

13. Atticus Finch

14. Charles Foster Kane

15. Michael Corleone

Answers on page 356

Common Bonds

long-term memory
executive functioning
attention to detail

The pictures in this puzzle may seem like they have nothing in common. But if you look carefully, you'll see a theme emerge. What is the common bond among these three images?

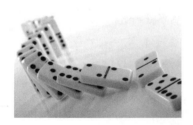  

Answer on page 356

State of the Word

Each word in the list below contains the postal abbreviation for a US state (with apologies to Texas, Vermont, and West Virginia, for which we could find no words). Given the first letter and a blank line for each missing letter, can you figure out a word for each US state?

long-term memory
executive functioning
attention to detail

1. C ___ ___ **AL**

2. A ___ **AK** ___

3. G ___ **AZ** ___

4. D ___ **AR** ___

5. V ___ **CA** ___

6. A**CO** ___ ___

7. C ___ **CT** ___ ___

8. M ___ **DE** ___

9. R ___ **FL** ___

10. C ___ **GA** ___

11. S**HI** ___ ___

12. G ___ **ID** ___

13. U ___ ___ **IL**

14. T ___ **IN** ___

15. P___ ___ ___ **IA**

16. B ___ ___ ___ **KS**

17. S ___ ___ ___ **KY**

18. P**LA** ___ ___ ___

19. C ___ **ME** ___ ___

20. G ___ **MD** ___ ___ ___

21. F ___ ___ **MA**_

22. D ___ **MI** ___ ___

23. C ___ ___ **MN** ___ ___

24. F ___ ___ **MS** _

25. K ___ **MO** ___ ___

26. W ___ ___ **MT** ___

27. S**NE** ___ ___ ___

28. C ___ **NV** ___ ___

29. U**NH** ___ ___ ___ ___

30. B ___ **NJ** ___

31. I**NM** ___ ___ ___

32. B ___ ___ ___ ___ **NY**

33. P ___ **NC** ___

34. A ___ ___ **ND** ___ ___

35. A ___ ___ **OH** ___ ___

36. P ___ ___ ___ **OK** ___

37. C ___ ___ ___ ___ **OR** ___

38. P ___ **PA** ___ ___

39. F ___ ___ **RI** ___

40. E**SC** ___ ___ ___

41. W ___ **SD** ___ ___

42. C ___ **TN** ___ ___

43. S ___ **UT** ___ ___ ___

44. C ___ ___ **VA** ___

45. F ___ ___ **WA** ___ ___

46. D ___ ___ **WI** ___ ___

47. L ___ **WY** ___ ___

Answers on page 356

Semordnilap

A *semordnilap* is a word that spells a different word forward and backward, such as *faced* and *decaf*. (*Give yourself a pat on the back if you noticed something special about the word* semordnilap*!*)

long-term mem
executive functior

1. Forward, it's a prevaricator; backward, it's what a train moves on.

2. Forward, it's an insect; backward, it's the astronauts' beverage.

3. Forward, they're a part of the mouth; backward, it means self-satisfied or conceited.

4. Forward, it's a group of Apple computers; backward, it's fraud or a dishonest scheme.

5. Forward, it was a Russian space station; backward, it's the edge of a basketball hoop.

6. Forward, they're sharpeners for straight razors; backward, they include baseball, luge, and diving.

7. Forward, they're the noises little dogs make; backward, it's the process of removing the ovaries of a dog or cat.

8. Forward, it's an archaic term for a poet; backward, it means dull, colorless, or uninteresting.

9. Forward, it's a wanderer or desert traveler; backward, it's the last name of the actor who played the title role in *Good Will Hunting*.

10. Forward, it's exemplified by Betelgeuse or the Sun; backward, they're rodents.

11. Forward, it's a one-mast sailboat; backward, they're places to swim.

Answers on page 357

---

 trivia

KITCHEN SCIENCE

long-term memory
executive functioning

There's a lot of science in the foods we make and eat.

❶ The first person to receive a degree in veterinary medicine in the United States also gave his last name to this genus of bacteria that causes severe food poisoning.

❷ Oddly enough, if you eat bagels topped with these, you could test positive for heroin.

❸ What kind of food additive is aspartame?

❹ MSG is a common flavor-enhancing food additive. What is MSG short for?

Answers on page 357

How Much Is . . .?

This game involves simple addition . . . but you have to figure out which numbers to add up. For example: *How much is . . . the number of dalmatians in the Disney movie + the number of items in a half dozen?* The answer: *107 (101 + 6).*

1. How much is . . . the temperature at which water freezes (in Fahrenheit) plus the temperature at which water boils (in Celsius)?

2. How much is . . . the year that Pearl Harbor was attacked plus the year that Richard Nixon resigned the presidency?

3. How much is . . . the number of letters in the English alphabet plus the highest possible score in a string of tenpin bowling?

4. How much is . . . two score plus two dozen?

5. How much is . . . the number of strings on a typical banjo plus your height, in inches, if you are 6'3"?

6. How much is . . . the number of degrees in a circle plus the number of angles in a rectangle?

7. How much is . . . the Downing Street address of the British prime minister's residence plus the Manhattan street where the "Christmas miracle" occurred in the 1947 film starring nine-year-old Natalie Wood?

8. How much is . . . the number of Abraham Lincoln's presidency plus the number of Ronald Reagan's presidency?

9. How much is . . . the number of John F. Kennedy's PT boat during WWII plus the number of ounces in a pound weight?

10. How much is . . . the number of "Heinz varieties" plus the number that corresponds to the letters PQRS on a standard telephone?

long-term memory
executive functioning
multitasking

Answers on page 357

ALPHABET TRIVIA

The only thing these trivia questions have in common is that all of the answers begin with the letter K.

long-term memory
executive functioning

1. You'll be doing great if you can identify three of the six world countries whose names begin with the letter K.

2. What are the two US states that begin with the letter K?

3. Name two marsupials that begin with the letter K.

4. Name two martial arts that begin with the letter K.

5. What is the name of a traditional Japanese garment?

6. Name the Oscar-winning film starring Dustin Hoffman and Meryl Streep as a divorcing couple.

7. Which Muppet had a hit song with "It's Not Easy Being Green"?

8. What is the form of entertainment in which people sing lyrics over prerecorded music tracks?

9. This company's donuts are sold around the world.

10. A one-person boat.

11. A week-long African American holiday.

12. A mountain located in Tanzania.

13. What is the full name of the actor who starred in *The Big Chill* and *A Fish Called Wanda*?

14. He became famous as O.J. Simpson's "house guest."

Answers on page 357

Vivienne's Vowels

executive functioning
long-term memory
attention to detail
processing speed

Vivienne is an odd one. She has an aversion to the letters A, E, I, O, and U. Can you fix her list of geographical locations by putting back the missing vowels? *Note: Any geographical location, from bodies of water and landmarks to cities, states, and countries, is acceptable.* You can make this a more strenuous brain exercise by adding some time pressure: Try to solve this puzzle in two minutes.

1. R D JNR _____
2. HVN _____
3. STRL _____
4. JMC _____
5. NTR, CND _____

6. RSS _____
7. STTL _____
8. STH FRC _____
9. NRB _____
10. SL _____

11. PRG _____
12. RGY _____
13. RB _____

Answers on page 357

endings & beginnings

In this game, we provide the first half of a two-word phrase or compound word and the second half of another. For example, given *Credit _____ trick*, the one word that completes both clues is *Card*, i.e., *Credit card* and *Card trick*. (If you get stuck, the first letter of the answer is provided in a hint below.)

1. Throw _____ fight
2. Times _____ dance
3. Watch _____ paddle
4. Criminal _____ player
5. Air _____ gum

6. Forbidden _____ cocktail
7. Puppy _____ sick
8. Crawl _____ shuttle
9. River _____ robber
10. Net _____ force

Hints: 1 p; 2 s; 3 d; 4 r; 5 b; 6 f; 7 l; 8 s; 9 b; 10 w

Answers on page 357

WORD TOWER

Every word in a word tower begins with the same two letters. You build the tower by increasing the length of each word by one letter. For example, a five-word tower built on the letters FA could include: FAN, FAST, FABLE, FACTOR, FAILURE.

How far can you go before you get stumped? Using the letters HI, we made a tower twelve words high. (*Note: Proper nouns are not allowed, and you cannot just add an s to make a longer word. For example, if your four-letter word is* hire, *your five-letter word cannot be* hires.) For an extra brain boost, see how tall your tower of words can get in two minutes.

1. HI

2. HI___

3. HI___ ___

4. HI___ ___ ___

5. HI___ ___ ___ ___

6. HI___ ___ ___ ___ ___

7. HI___ ___ ___ ___ ___ ___

8. HI___ ___ ___ ___ ___ ___ ___

9. HI___ ___ ___ ___ ___ ___ ___ ___

10. HI___ ___ ___ ___ ___ ___ ___ ___ ___

11. HI___ ___ ___ ___ ___ ___ ___ ___ ___ ___

12. HI___ ___ ___ ___ ___ ___ ___ ___ ___ ___ ___

Answers on page 357

MAKING CONNECTIONS

Given nine words or phrases randomly placed in a grid, can you find the three groups of three connected items AND explain why they are connected? Here's a sample grid:

RED	HONEY	BLUE
VIEIRA	HARVEST	PURPLE
FULL	LAUER	COURIC

GROUP 1 WORDS:
Red, Blue, Purple

THEME:
Colors

GROUP 2 WORDS:
Vieira, Lauer, Couric

THEME:
Today show hosts

GROUP 3 WORDS:
Full, Honey, Harvest

THEME:
_____moon

BLUE	YORK	FORD
WHITE	SWISS	MEXICO
GOAT	JERSEY	CROCKER

GROUP 1 WORDS

_____ _____ _____

THEME:

_____

GROUP 2 WORDS

_____ _____ _____

THEME:

_____

GROUP 3 WORDS

_____ _____ _____

THEME:

_____

Answers on page 358

Group Therapy

Group Therapy is the game that proves there is more than one correct answer to a question . . . and we tell you the minimum number of answers you need to come up with. For an extra brain boost, put a one-minute limit on each question.

1. Name seven words that end in the letters IC.

2. Name six things that many people buy or pay for that commonly cost more than $1,000.

3. Name four famous people (living or dead) whose last name begins with Van or Von.

4. Name five types or brands of snack chips.

5. Name ten US rivers.

6. Name four careers that begin with the letter A.

7. Name four brands of over-the-counter (i.e., nonprescription) pain pills.

8. Name five countries in which Spanish is the official or primary language.

Answers on page 358

IMPROBABLE PAIRS

long-term memory

executive functioning

Be careful whom you marry or you might end up with an outlandish name!

❶ If John Lennon's second wife married Cher's first husband she'd be . . .

❷ If the well-endowed country singer and star of *9 to 5* married the Spanish surrealist painter with the flamboyant moustache she'd be . . .

❸ If the sexy blond star of the movie *10* married the late Hawaiian traditional and pop singer she'd be . . .

❹ If the female co-star of *Grease* married the Las Vegas–based entertainer and singer of "Danke Schoen," divorced him, and then married the British singer/songwriter known for his showy eyeglasses, she'd be . . .

Answers on page 358

long-term memory

working memory

processing speed

Blank Book

How many single words can you come up with in two minutes that complete the compound word or two-word phrase _____ *book*?

_____ _____ _____

_____ _____ _____

_____ _____ _____

_____ _____ _____

_____ _____ _____

_____ _____ _____

_____ _____ _____

_____ _____ _____

_____ _____ _____

_____ _____ _____

_____ _____ _____

Answers on page 358

fill in the letters

long-term memory
executive functioning
attention to detail

Fill in the blank spaces with letters to make common English words (no proper nouns allowed). For example, __ **a t** yields twelve answers: *bat, cat, eat, fat, hat, mat, oat, pat, rat, sat, tat, vat. (Note: The number in parentheses indicates how many common English words can be made.)*

1. __ **u** __ **e**   (32)

2. __ __ **n g**   (26)

3. __ **e a d**   (6)

4. **t** __ **i** __   (11)

5. __ **l a** __   (25)

6. **m i** __ __   (20)

7. **s w i** __ __   (7)

8. **s h** __ __ **e**   (12)

Answers on page 359

WHAT'S THE SPORT?

We provide the name of the movie. Can you name the key sport that was featured in it?

1. *Jerry Maguire* (1996)

2. *Chariots of Fire* (1981)

3. *Days of Thunder* (1990)

4. *Bull Durham* (1988)

5. *The Big Lebowski* (1998)

6. *Raging Bull* (1980)

7. *The Hustler* (1961)

8. *Breaking Away* (1979)

9. *Bend It Like Beckham* (2002)

10. *The Legend of Bagger Vance* (2000)

11. *National Velvet* (1944)

12. *The Mighty Ducks* (1992)

13. *Kansas City Bomber* (1972)

14. *Invictus* (2009)

15. *The Other Side of the Mountain* (1975)

16. *The Endless Summer* (1966)

Answers on page 359

Name That Musical

Can you identify the Broadway musical from two of its well known songs?

1. "It's the Hard-Knock Life" and "Tomorrow"

2. "Kids" and "One Last Kiss"

3. "Memory" and "Mr. Mistoffeles"

4. "I Whistle a Happy Tune" and "Shall We Dance?"

5. "Sunrise, Sunset" and "Matchmaker, Matchmaker"

6. "I'd Be Surprisingly Good for You" and "Don't Cry for Me Argentina"

7. "Easy to Be Hard" and "Good Morning Starshine"

8. "Dulcinea" and "The Impossible Dream"

9. "Tonight" and "I Feel Pretty"

10. "Do You Hear the People Sing?" and "I Dreamed a Dream"

11. "The Rain in Spain" and "Get Me to the Church on Time"

12. "Judas' Death" and "I Don't Know How to Love Him"

13. "Sixteen Going on Seventeen" and "So Long, Farewell"

14. "People Will Say We're in Love" and "Oh, What a Beautiful Mornin'"

15. "Summer Nights" and "Hopelessly Devoted to You"

Answers on page 359

prime-time❖rhyme❖

Each question in this quiz has three different answers . . . and they all rhyme.

For example:

Clues: One plus one; not false; azure color.

Answers: Two; true; blue.

long-term memory
working memory

1. Modest or unpretentious; almost fall; speak indistinctly

2. To throw pieces around randomly; to lavish praise, usually insincerely; to break suddenly into many small pieces

3. A short, simple song; metropolis; a young cat

4. The system in an automobile that is activated by a key; a basic arithmetic operation; to try out for a play

5. A canine, for example; frequent choice in restaurant seating; veracity

6. A device that strengthens or supports; the product of tatting; a sprint or marathon

7. A hobo; a rustic vacation place; postage

8. A mismatch of colors; garbage; the sound of something hitting water

9. A typical feature on an iron; a homeless dog; a horse sound

10. An energetic style; first hit in a tennis game; to turn abruptly or change direction

11. To put a prisoner in chains; a feature of American football; wall repair material

12. An aromatic mix of dried flowers and spices; a basketball or soccer official; the Volunteer State

13. House shoe; a TV dolphin; a clothing fastener

Answers on page 359

What a Pair

Harvard and Yale, Thunder and Lightning, Coke and Pepsi are all common pairs . . . but what about *Wonder and Perrier*? If you redefine *Wonder and Perrier* correctly, you'll come up with the more familiar pairing *Bread and Water*. How many familiar pairs can you make from the clues below?

1. The distance from one street to the next . . . and to wrestle an opposing football player to the ground.

_____

2. Bowling targets . . . and knitting implements.

_____

3. Swiss Army tool . . . and a split in the road.

_____

4. A use for worms . . . and the device that activates a lamp.

_____

5. A formal dance . . . and a group of restaurants owned by the same company.

_____

6. Automobile . . . and a golf club with a wooden head.

_____

7. Diarist Anne and family . . . and legumes.

_____

8. Urban green area . . . and travel on a horse, bicycle, or bus.

_____

9. Sergeant or Captain . . . and fingernail shaper.

_____

10. Small hat with a brim . . . and a formal dress.

_____

11. Car or plane accident . . . and overcook the toast.

_____

Answers on page 359

it's quitting time

long-term memory
executive functioning
attention to detail
processing speed

For each clue below, can you put the missing letters Q-U-I-T back in the correct order to reveal a common English word? To make this a more vigorous brain exercise, try to solve this quiz in three minutes.

1. __ __ __ L __

2. E __ __ __ __ Y

3. __ __ A __ N __

4. S __ __ __ N __

5. S __ __ __ R __

6. AN __ __ __ __ E

7. __ RAN __ __ __ L

8. __ E __ __ __ LA

9. L __ __ __ IDA __ E

10. MOS __ __ __ __ O

11. __ __ __ N __ ET

12. __ __ __ E __ ER

13. __ __ AN __ __ TY

14. E __ __ AL __ __ Y

15. __ __ __ CKES __

16. CRI __ __ __ __ E

17. __ ECHN __ __ __ E

18. E __ __ ES __ R __ AN

Answers on page 360

SOUP'S ON

long-term
memory

executive
functioning

**Get all these right
and you'll earn a
PhD in Soup-ology.**

❶ The main difference between a typical American vegetable soup and this Italian specialty lies in the vegetables used.

❷ The word for this clear broth comes from the French phrase "to have made complete."

❸ This rich soup is made thick by pureed seafood. Sometimes even lobster shells are ground to a fine paste and added in.

❹ This soup gave its name to a summer resort area of the Catskill Mountains that was popular among Jewish vacationers from the 1920s to the 1970s.

Answers on page 360

ALPHABET TRIVIA

The only thing these trivia questions have in common is that all of the answers begin with the letter L.

1. How many of the nine countries that begin with the letter L can you name?

2. What is the only US state that begins with the letter L?

3. Name the only US president whose last name begins with the letter L.

4. Which one of the seven deadly sins begins with the letter L?

5. Name the three US state capitals that begin with the letter L.

6. Which two signs of the zodiac start with the letter L?

7. What is the largest European city that begins with the letter L?

8. What is the largest US city that begins with the letter L?

9. In the Bible (King James Version) one book in the Old Testament and one in the New Testament begin with the letter L. Can you name them?

10. How many different animals that begin with the letter L can you name?

11. Which US holiday begins with the letter L?

12. Name the brother-and-sister characters in the Peanuts comic strip whose first names begin with the letter L.

13. What is the numeric value of the Roman numeral L?

14. Name three of the dozens of *Superman* characters whose initials are LL.

15. Name the "Coal Miner's Daughter" who became a country music star.

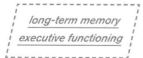

long-term memory
executive functioning

Answers on page 360

alphabetically speaking

Everyone knows that January is the first month of the year. But "alphabetically speaking," April is the first month because it begins with the letters AP. In this game, can you figure out what comes first, last, or next . . . alphabetically speaking?

1. Alphabetically speaking, this is the first of Canada's thirteen provinces and territories.

2. Alphabetically speaking, this human body part is first in most dictionaries.

3. Alphabetically speaking, this is the last color in the color spectrum.

4. Alphabetically speaking, this is the first borough of New York City.

5. Alphabetically speaking, this US national park is last.

6. Alphabetically speaking, this is the first number (between 1 and 10) when spelled out.

7. Alphabetically speaking, this is the first railroad property on a Monopoly board.

8. Alphabetically speaking, this is the last Ivy League college.

9. Alphabetically speaking, he is the first US president by first name.

10. Alphabetically speaking, this is the next book of the Bible after Proverbs.

11. Alphabetically speaking, this is the first Roman numeral.

12. Alphabetically speaking, this is the last chess piece.

Answers on page 360

INITIAL QUIZ

long-term memory
working memory

All of the two-word answers in this quiz begin with the initials AA.

1. Don Draper's milieu in the television series *Mad Men*.

2. The policy of favoring members of a disadvantaged group who have suffered discrimination within their culture.

3. Organization founded in 1935 by Bill Wilson and Dr. Bob Smith.

4. The name of this capital city of Ethiopia means either "new flower" or "natural springs," depending on which dialect is spoken.

5. Famous painters in this genre include Piet Mondrian and Wassily Kandinsky.

6. The sixth-largest city in Michigan and the location of the main campus for the University of Michigan.

7. Former #1-ranked professional tennis player.

8. This common name for the laryngeal prominence is derived from the fact that it is more prominent in men than in women.

9. A popular movie genre.

10. From 1997 to 2004, this was the name of a West Coast Major League Baseball team.

11. Photographer famous for his photos of natural landscapes.

Answers on page 360

Common Bonds

The pictures in this puzzle may seem like they have nothing in common. But if you look carefully, you'll see a theme emerge. What is the common bond among these three images?

long-term memory
executive functioning
attention to detail

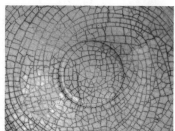

Answer on page 360

ODD MAN OUT

All of the items in each list have something in common—with one exception. Your job is to find which item doesn't fit and to explain why it is the "odd man out."

1. Idiotic, Expenses, Tweezers, Needles, Reserved

2. St. Louis, Aspirin, Human feet, McDonald's

3. Bridges, Radley, Diddley, Tie

4. Lieberman, Kennedy, Edwards, Bentsen

5. Chocolate, Potato, Blue, Telephone

6. Your tongue, Your legs, Your t's, Your heart

7. Racer, Madam, Level, Civic

8. Morse, Bar, Sergeant, Area

Answers on page 360

"I" exam

All of the answers in this quiz begin with the letter I.

1. Inactive or lazy.

2. Anti-inflammatory drug used for pain relief.

3. Time or space without end.

4. Sloped typeface often used for titles.

5. A time or place that is extremely happy, peaceful, or picturesque.

6. Remote, cut off from others.

7. A travel plan document.

8. Most suitable, perfect.

9. Apparatus for hatching eggs.

10. Smitten, besotted, crazy about someone.

11. Unachievable, unworkable, impractical.

12. Behavior, often unconventional, that is peculiar to an individual.

Answers on page 361

Memorable TV Lines

Can you identify the television show from these memorable lines? And for an extra brain workout, try to remember the character (in fiction TV) or the real-life person (in nonfiction TV) who said each line.

1. "Yabba dabba doo!"

_____

2. "De plane, de plane!"

_____

3. "Nanu-nanu."

_____

4. "Let's be careful out there."

_____

5. "Hello caller, I'm listening."

_____

6. "Holy crap!"

_____

7. "Bam!"

_____

8. "Is that your final answer?"

_____

9. "You're fired!"

_____

10. "I know nothing!"

_____

11. "I'm Larry, this is my brother Darryl, and this is my other brother Darryl."

_____

12. "Norm!"

_____

Answers on page 361

RIDDLE ME THIS

Riddles often require some unconventional thinking and are a great brain exercise. Think outside the box as you try to solve this classic riddle.

**Feed me and I'll grow quickly.
Give me water and I will die. What am I?**

Answer on page 361

Vowel States

How many of the twelve US states that begin with a vowel can you name in one minute?

_____   _____   _____

_____   _____   _____

_____   _____   _____

_____   _____

Answers on page 361

Alma's Shopping List

Alma is a great shopper but a bad speller. Every word on her shopping list is misspelled by one letter. Can you fix Alma's list? Remember, you should not move any letters; just change one to reveal the correct word. (*Note: All of the items are common brand names or generic names for food and other products that are usually sold in a grocery store.*) For an extra brain boost, see how many correct answers you can get in two minutes.

1. Ace Creak

2. Apply

3. Bold Guts

4. Cheat Break

5. Broad Crumps

6. Union Kings

7. Cave Six

8. Child Peepers

9. Per Soul

10. Rakish

11. Fax Pager

12. Fight Bulls

Answers on page 361

THE NAME GAME

This is a two-part game. First answer the clues. Then put the answers in the correct order to reveal the name of a famous person (living or dead, real or fictional). Example question: *The sound of a growl + men's neckwear + the forest.* Answer: *Grrr + tie + woods* (*Tiger Woods*).

1. To leave or depart + the opposite of yes + fifteenth letter of the alphabet + the yellow of an egg

2. A toy that flies in the wind + structure that separates two rooms + a person from Istanbul + President Reagan, informally

3. Light black color + four of this makes a bushel + word to describe a violent and bloody movie

4. Doll boyfriend of Barbie + a Christmas song + Mr. Fisher, the singer + a long queue of people

5. Not out + hot dogs + cheer sound you might hear at a football game + painting or sculpture

6. Armed conflict + a conjunction + a corridor in a house or building + the fifth letter of the alphabet

7. Unwell + invoice + vegetable that looks like an oversized scallion + joint between the hand and arm

8. To tremble or vibrate + document that bequeaths money or property + a stem of asparagus + a sweet potato

9. The sixth letter of the alphabet + cubicle where a horse sleeps + Mr. Namath and Mr. Montana + not out

Answers on page 361

Finish the Proverb

Given the first couple of words of a familiar proverb or saying, can you complete it? To make this a more vigorous brain exercise, try to answer all the questions in one minute.

1. What goes _____.

2. Look before _____.

3. A journey of _____.

4. An ounce of _____.

5. The road to _____.

6. Youth is _____.

7. Those who do not learn _____.

8. Absolute power _____.

9. It's better to have _____.

10. If you can't stand _____.

11. Laugh and the _____.

Answers on page 361

By the Letter

long-term memory
executive functioning

In this game, players need to guess a word—one letter at a time. Place the letter called for in each question in the line below (the first answer above the number 1, the second above the number 2, and so on).

1.
The first letter of the capital city of Denmark.

2.
The first letter of the species that experts believe is, along with the brown rat, the most numerous mammal on Earth.

3.
The first letter of the name of the biological system that protects humans from disease.

4.
The first letter of the name of this insect that can tell the temperature.
(*Just add 40 to the number of chirps it emits in 15 seconds.*)

5.
The first letter of the name of the basketball team that was formed in 1946 and whose home arena is Madison Square Garden.

6.
The first letter of the name of a French pastry that is a typically oblong-shaped light dough, filled with cream or custard, and topped with icing.

7.
The last letter of the name for a deep gorge, usually cut into the earth by a flowing river.

____ ____ ____ ____ ____ ____ ____
  1   2   3   4   5   6   7

Answers on page 362

Vivienne's Vowels

executive functioning
long-term memory
attention to detail
processing speed

Vivienne is an odd one. She has an aversion to the letters A, E, I, O, and U. Can you fix her list of foods by putting back the missing vowels? *Note: Anything that is edible, i.e., brand names, generic names, restaurant dishes, etc., is acceptable.* You can make this a more strenuous brain exercise by adding some time pressure: Try to solve this puzzle in two minutes.

1. SFD SLD _____

2. SLM _____

3. BNNS _____

4. PPY _____

5. MCRN _____

6. PPLSC _____

7. P SP _____

8. QCH _____

9. CHRS _____

10. RNGS _____

11. SPRGS _____

12. NNS _____

Answers on page 362

Number Please

In this game, the "numbers" have been removed from the words. Can you put them back in the blank space? For example, the answer to *WRIT____* is *WRIT 10*, i.e., *written.* (*Note: Numbers may be repeated.*)

1. BARS _____ L

2. U _____ SIL

3. BE _____

4. PHY _____

5. BAR _____ DER

6. PRIM _____

7. CA _____

8. _____ EST

9. CAR _____ N

10. FR _____

11. CLAS _____

12. EF _____ T

Answers on page 362

HETERONYMS

Heteronyms are words that are spelled the same, but have different meanings and are sometimes pronounced differently. For example, the word *number* can be a numeral and it can also mean "more numb." *Entrance* can be a doorway and, with the stress on the second syllable, can mean "to charm or delight." Given two definitions, can you identify the heteronym?

1. To rip . . . and eye lubricant.

2. Very small . . . and a unit of time.

3. A soft and malleable metal . . . and to head up a group of people or to be first in a parade.

4. Not legitimate, worthless . . . and a disabled or sick person.

5. A flaw or imperfection in something . . . and to leave your country for another, usually because of politics or ideology.

6. A collection of published material . . . and to absorb nutrients from food.

7. Subject matter or information . . . and satisfied, at peace.

8. To argue a point . . . and a competitive event.

9. To anger or enrage . . . and an aromatic gum that produces a sweet odor when burned.

10. A physician in training . . . and to confine someone for political or military reasons.

11. Average in amount, intensity, or degree . . . and to preside over a debate.

12. To show a movie on a screen . . . and a low-income housing complex.

13. More precipitation than before . . . and a snowcapped mountain in Washington state.

Answers on page 362

complete the words

Complete the words in the grid below using the three-letter words from the list to its left. Each three-letter word will be used once.

ACT	P	A	P				I	T	E	R
BAG	O	V	A				I	O	N	E
BAN	T	S	A				R	S	E	X
CAT	S	P	R				I	C	E	L
ERA	F	O	R				F	U	L	Y
FEE	C	A	S				G	L	E	R
GET	S	U	N				L	I	N	G
HER	H	A	V				G	E	R	Y
INN	H	U	S				D	E	R	S
LIE	B	I	S				N	I	O	N
MUG	A	B	E				V	E	N	D
WHO	A	R	C				Y	E	A	K
WOO	G	A	R				E	L	L	Y
PET	A	S	K				Y	O	L	K

Answers on page 362

WORD PARTS

The word *bather* is defined as "a person that takes a bath or goes swimming." In this game, however, we supply the definition not of a word, but of its parts. For example, given the first clue *Louisville Slugger*, plus the second clue *the opposite of him*, the answer is *bather* (*bat* + *her*).

1. Coca-Cola's first diet drink + to allow

2. For each + verdict deciders

3. Stylish, fashionable + Barbie's beau

4. To sharpen + a pig's hangout

5. To spray tiny droplets of water + formation of iron oxide on steel

6. Commercial, for short + clergyman

7. Cleopatra's snake + first letter of the alphabet + an old piece of cloth + you and me

8. A baseball hat + sick, unwell + March/April's zodiac sign

9. Mr. Rather + place for cold cuts, cheeses, salads, etc. + not off

10. Person who uses scuba gear + the opposite of stand + the penultimate letter of the alphabet

11. Performer who overacts + to mimic someone scornfully

12. Hawaiian singer, Don _____ + to expectorate + Mr. Gore

13. Opposite of out + a devotee of a celebrity + to attempt

14. Note that follows do, re, . . . + black bird + hand gesture used for hello or goodbye

Answers on page 362

ALPHABET TRIVIA

long-term memory
executive functioning

The only thing these trivia questions have in common is that all of the answers begin with the letter M.

1. What are the eight US states that begin with the letter M?

2. Name four mammals that begin with the letter M.

3. What is the only country in the Western Hemisphere that begins with the letter M?

4. Which two planets in our solar system begin with the letter M?

5. What is the only Canadian province that begins with the letter M?

6. What is the value of the Roman numeral *M*?

7. Name the two New York Yankee players who competed in a 1961 race to beat Babe Ruth's single-season home run record.

8. What is Romeo's last name?

9. This country was once known as Burma.

10. This city was once known as Bombay.

11. Who wrote *Gone with the Wind*?

12. What was John Wayne's real name?

13. In the Bible, who was the first person to witness the resurrection of Jesus?

14. When she married Arthur Miller, her initials became MMM.

15. What do these acronyms stand for?
MADD
MGM
MIA
MIT
MoMA
MPG
MRI

Answers on page 362

what's their job?

Given the names of three well-known people, what careers do they all share?
Note: While some of the individuals mentioned may hold other jobs, we're looking for the one job that the three people in the clue all have in common.

1. Edvard Munch, Gustav Klimt, Roy Lichtenstein

_____

2. Berkeley Breathed, Jim Davis, Hank Ketcham

_____

3. Viktor Petrenko, Johnny Weir, Sonja Henie

_____

4. Alton Brown, Ina Garten, Michael Symon

_____

5. Hank Stram, Chuck Noll, Bill Parcells

_____

6. Calvin Borel, Victor Espinoza, Angel Cordero

_____

7. Ernie Banks, Bob Gibson, Steve Carlton

_____

8. Nellie Melba, Jessye Norman, Renée Fleming

_____

9. Bertolt Brecht, August Strindberg, David Mamet

_____

10. Chuck Lorre, Sherwood Schwartz, Steven Bochco

_____

11. Chesley Sullenberger, Steve Fossett, Chuck Yeager

_____

12. Drew Peterson, Daryl Gates, William Bratton

_____

Answers on page 363

---

 trivia

"LADIES" THINGS

long-term memory
executive functioning

All of the answers in this quiz include a woman's first name.

❶ Vodka and tomato juice—maybe with a little Tabasco sauce or horseradish.

❷ A rotating, usually circular, tray for serving or storage.

❸ Nickname for the Ford Model T.

❹ An eighteenth-century wool-making machine.

❺ A tournament or competition in which each participant plays in turn against every other.

Answers on page 363

TED'S TERRIBLE TITLES

long-term memory
executive functioning

Poor Ted. He is a connoisseur of culture but he can never remember the titles of some of his favorite books, plays, songs, magazines, television shows, etc. Can you fix Ted's titles by correcting his mistakes?

1. A Row of Synchronized Dancers and Singers

2. An Oak Becomes Larger in a Borough of New York City

3. The Covert Existence of Drones and Queens

4. Small Dwelling on the Grassland

5. The Star Closest to Earth Ascends Too

6. The Small-Fruit-That-Grows-in-Clusters-on-Vines of Anger

7. Smallest Coins from Paradise

8. Lots of Hubbub Concerning Zilch

9. Misplaced Saturday and Sunday

10. Joyful Twenty-Four-Hour Spans Are in This Location Once More

11. Hard Gems Exist Eternally

12. Illegal Behavior and Disciplinary Measures

Answers on page 363

 **RIDDLE ME THIS**

executive functioning
attention to detail

Riddles often require some unconventional thinking and are a great brain exercise. Think outside the box as you try to solve this classic riddle.

Besides breathing, what is everyone doing at the same time?

Answer on page 363

MAKING CONNECTIONS

Given nine words or phrases randomly placed in a grid, can you find the three groups of three connected items AND explain why they are connected? Here's a sample grid:

RED	HONEY	BLUE
VIEIRA	HARVEST	PURPLE
FULL	LAUER	COURIC

GROUP 1 WORDS:
Red, Blue, Purple

THEME:
Colors

GROUP 2 WORDS:
Vieira, Lauer, Couric

THEME:
Today show hosts

GROUP 3 WORDS:
Full, Honey, Harvest

THEME:
_____moon

TEDDY	ROCKY	RIGHT
GRAY	BLUE	BLACK
SMOKEY	GREEN	SMOKY

GROUP 1 WORDS

_____ _____ _____

THEME:

_____

GROUP 2 WORDS

_____ _____ _____

THEME:

_____

GROUP 3 WORDS

_____ _____ _____

THEME:

_____

Answers on page 363

bird watching

long-term memory
executive functioning
attention to detail

Get out your binoculars and see how many of these birds you can identify. We're just looking for their common names.

A _____

B _____

C _____

D _____

E _____

F _____

G _____

H _____

I _____

J _____

K _____

L _____

M _____

N _____

Answers on page 363

Group Therapy

Group Therapy is the game that proves there is more than one correct answer to a question . . . and we tell you the minimum number of answers you need to come up with. For an extra brain boost, put a one-minute limit on each question.

1. Name eight geographical locations with two-word names.

2. Name six famous men (past or present, real or fictional) who are well known for having facial hair (i.e., moustache, beard, or both).

3. Name six stand-up comedians, past or present.

4. Name five people (past or present, real or fictional) named Charles or Charlie.

5. Name eight words with four syllables.

6. Name seven Irish surnames.

7. Name five fruits and/or vegetables that begin with the letter C.

8. Name five insects that fly.

Answers on page 363

---

trivia

A RIVER RUNS THROUGH IT

long-term memory
executive functioning

From the source to the mouth, can you name these world rivers?

❶ This river runs 2,530 miles from Lake Itasca, Minnesota, south to the Gulf of Mexico.

❷ This river runs 1,896 miles from Canby Mountain in Colorado south to Matamoros in Mexico, where it empties into the Gulf of Mexico.

❸ This river runs 215 miles east from Gloucestershire to the North Sea.

❹ This river begins at the Côte d'Or, in Burgundy, and runs 482 miles northwest to the English Channel.

❺ This Asian river, which starts in Qinghai, China, shares its name with the Delta where it ends in Vietnam.

Answers on page 364

OSCAR MOMENTS

Given a list of memorable quotes from Academy Award shows, can you identify the name of the speaker? And for extra kudos, can you name the film, where appropriate?

1. "You like me. Right now, you really like me."

_____

2. "I'm king of the world!"

_____

3. "   _(Actor's name)_   very regretfully cannot accept this very generous award. And the reason for this being is the treatment of American Indians today by the film industry."

_____

4. "Hello, Gorgeous!"

_____

5. "I just said to Matt, 'Losing would suck, and winning would be really scary'—and it's really, really scary!"

_____

6. "Oh my God. Oh my God. I'm sorry. This moment is so much bigger than me. This moment is for Dorothy Dandridge, Lena Horne, Diahann Carroll. . . . And it's for every nameless, faceless woman of color that now has a chance because this door tonight has been opened."

_____

7. "Whoever Keyser Soze is, I can tell you he is going to get gloriously drunk tonight."

_____

8. "I'm in shock. And I'm so in love with my brother right now. He just held me and said he loved me."

_____

9. "Mom and dad, yeah, look! Whoo! Thank you, Mom and Dad, for turning me on to such a groovy profession."

_____

10. "Thank you very much indeed."

_____

11. "The only laugh that man will ever get in his life is by stripping and showing off his shortcomings."

_____

12. "Did I really earn this? Or did I just wear y'all down?"

_____

Answers on page 364

executive functioning

attention to detail

wacky wordies

Quite	I have _dea
❶ ______	❷ ______
goodalltime	cut cut cut cut
❸ ______	❹ ______

To solve these fun puzzles, look carefully at each frame, because the arrangement of the letters is a key clue to the familiar phrase contained within. For example, if the word *school* were placed high up in the frame, the answer would be *high school*. Or, if the words *easy pieces* occurred five times in the frame, the answer would be *five easy pieces*.

Answers on page 365

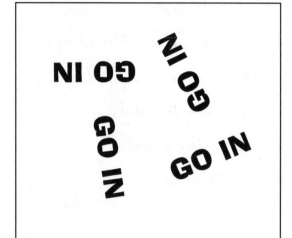

MEN
MEN
MEN

5 _____

6 _____

the bag

7 _____

8 _____

Rivals

We provide one half of a famous feuding pair (it could be a decades-long rivalry or a one-time face-off). Can you provide the name of the opposition?

1. Billie Jean King and _____

2. Robin Hood and _____

3. The Capulets and _____

4. Abraham Lincoln and _____

5. Dorothy and _____

6. Alexander Hamilton and _____

7. Captain Ahab and _____

8. Wolfgang Amadeus Mozart and ___

9. Magic Johnson and _____

10. Luke Skywalker and _____

11. Wile E. Coyote and _____

12. The Bloods and _____

Answers on page 365

busy as a bee

Similes are comparative expressions that use the words *like* or *as*. In this game, we provide the second half of a familiar simile (that includes a type of animal) and you must come up with the first half. To make this a more vigorous brain exercise, try to answer all the questions in one minute.

1. _____ as a beaver.

2. _____ as a lamb.

3. _____ as a goose.

4. _____ as a jaybird.

5. _____ as a loon.

6. _____ as a peacock.

7. _____ as a fox.

8. _____ as a clam.

9. _____ as an eel.

10. _____ as a bull.

11. _____ as a cat.

12. _____ as a dog.

13. _____ as a bird.

14. _____ as a bat.

Answers on page 365

TRIMBLE

Trimble is a trivia game and a word jumble combined. First, answer the trivia questions (all related to music) and cross out the letters of each answer in the letter grid. Then rearrange the remaining letters (those that have not been crossed out) to reveal another word or phrase related to the same theme.

A	A	A	A	B	C	D	E	E	E	F	G	H
H	H	I	J	J	K	L	L	M	M	N	N	N
N	N	N	O	O	O	O	P	R	R	R	S	T
T	U	U	V	Y	Y							

1. Debuting in 1953 and featuring cowboy Curly McLain and farmhand Jud Fry, this was the first musical written by the team of Rodgers & Hammerstein.

_____

2. This musical instrument was featured in a memorable "duel" in the 1972 film *Deliverance*.

_____

3. This musical, which premiered on Broadway in 1964, was based on the life of actress/singer Fanny Brice.

_____

4. He was born Henry John Deutschendorf Jr. in New Mexico, but he adopted this last name because Colorado was his favorite state.

_____

5. It's the name of an elephant's call . . . and Dizzy Gillespie's instrument.

_____

Word Jumble hint:
Country, rock, and gospel singer.

Answers on page 365

it's madness!

long-term memory
working memory

All of the answers in this quiz begin with the letters MAD.

1. A young unmarried woman in France.

2. An appellation for the Virgin Mary.

3. The large island off the southeast coast of Africa.

4. This Manhattan street is synonymous with the US advertising industry.

5. Former football player and color commentator for NFL telecasts.

6. The capital of Spain.

7. A type of lightweight Indian cotton fabric, usually in a plaid design.

8. Meaning crazy, wacky, or nutty, this term is often applied to comedy films.

9. A region of Portugal, or the name of a wine that comes from there.

10. This very small French cake evoked memories of his youth for author Marcel Proust.

11. A Renaissance and early Baroque song, usually involving three to six voices.

12. This 1979 dystopian film features a world in which law and order has broken down following a major energy crisis.

Answers on page 365

Vivienne's Vowels

executive functioning
long-term memory
attention to detail
processing speed

Vivienne is an odd one. She has an aversion to the letters A, E, I, O, and U. Can you fix her list of famous people by putting back the missing vowels?
Note: All well-known people, male or female, living or dead, and those who are known by one name, two names, or more are all acceptable. You can make this a more strenuous brain exercise by adding some time pressure: Try to solve this puzzle in two minutes.

1. THMS DSN_____

2. RSTTL _____

3. RDY GLN _____

4. NN KLY _____

5. MR NTNTT_____

6. MLY BRNT_____

7. L PCN _____

8. J MNTN _____

9. SN PNN _____

10. DS RNZ _____

11. BBBY RR _____

Answers on page 365

"QUOTATION STATION"

Move the letters in each vertical column of the top grid to the spaces in the column just below it in the bottom grid. The letters will not necessarily be moved in the order in which they appear. If you move the letters to the correct positions, they will spell out a quotation (reading from left to right) from American editorial cartoonist Frank Tyger. (*Note: A black square indicates the end of a word. Words may continue from one horizontal line to the next.*)

Before attempting the big puzzle, try this example first—without looking at the answer to the right:

T	H	I	R	A	M	O	R
E		T	H	I	F	K	
I		E		E	N		

Example Answer:

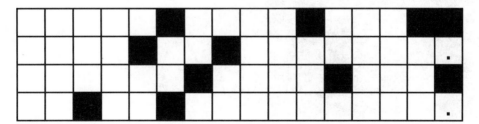

D	I	K	E	S	G	H	H	F	P	T	N	O	O	S	
D	I	I	I	N	I	S	W	H	A	I	Y	D	O	U	
L	O	K	I	G		W	A	A	R	E	E	E	U	M	
L	O		N				P	T			Y	S			

Answer on page 365

WORD PICTURES

Put one picture together with one word part (in any order) to come up with the names of eight cities or countries.

SON	UGAL	WAR	ENIA
EA	AMA	TI	LAND

Answers on page 365

ALPHABET TRIVIA

The only thing these trivia questions have in common is that all of the answers begin with the letter N.

1. How many of the ten sovereign countries that begin with the letter N can you name?

2. Name the eight US states that begin with the letter N.

3. Name the five Canadian provinces and territories that begin with the letter N.

4. What is the only US state capital that begins with the letter N?

5. Can you name the three actors (whose last name begins with the letter N) who have won the Academy Award for Best Actor?

6. What is the noble gas that produces uniquely bright reddish-orange light, especially useful for advertising signs?

7. Name two national department stores that begin with the letter N.

8. How many men's names that begin with N can you come up with?

9. Which spice begins with the letter N?

10. Which planet begins with the letter N?

11. Name the only US president whose last name begins with N.

12. Identify the following acronyms/abbreviations:
NAACP
NASA
NATO
NBC
NIMBY
NOW
NPR
NRA

Answers on page 366

FAMOUS CARS

Here are a few questions about some well-known wheels.

❶ In this 1980s TV series, the bright-orange 1969 Dodge Charger with the confederate flag painted on the roof was named "The General Lee."

❷ In the 1963 film *The Love Bug*, what model car was Herbie, the self-driving automobile that was capable of human emotions?

❸ The title characters in this 1991 film drove a classic 1966 Ford Thunderbird over a cliff and into the Grand Canyon.

❹ What kind of car was A. C. Cowlings driving in the infamous "slow car chase" in which O.J. Simpson sat in the back seat with a gun to his own head?

Answers on page 366

Fictional Occupations

You might remember these classic television characters, but do you know what their occupation was? And, for an extra memory exercise, can you name the television series that featured each character?

long-term memory
executive functioning

1. Ralph Kramden

2. Rhoda Morgenstern

3. Howard Cunningham

4. Dorothy Zbornak

5. Michael Brady

6. Gomer Pyle

7. Jack Tripper

8. Sally Rogers

9. Tony Banta

10. Murray Slaughter

11. Newman

12. Floyd Lawson

Answers on page 366

Order, Please!

long-term memory
working memory
executive functioning
multitasking

Put the following list of countries in order of the size of their landmass, starting with the largest.

___ Iran

___ Brazil

___ Japan

___ France

___ Canada

___ Germany

___ Australia

___ Argentina

___ Saudi Arabia

___ United States

Answers on page 366

Finish the Poetry

Given the first part of a line of poetry, can you supply the end?

1. "Somewhere men are laughing, and somewhere children shout.
But there is no joy in Mudville, mighty . . ." _____

2. "For of all sad words of tongue or pen,
the saddest are . . ." _____

3. "I am the master of my fate. I am . . ." _____

4. "The time has come, the Walrus said,
to talk of many things:
of shoes and ships and sealing-wax,
of . . ." _____

5. "If music be the . . ." _____

6. "They also serve who . . ." _____

7. "Do not go gentle . . ." _____

8. "A little learning is . . ." _____

9. "Because I could not stop for . . ." _____

10. "This is the way the world ends.
Not with a bang . . ." _____

11. "We few, we happy few, . . ." _____

12. "In the room the women come and go . . ."

_____

Answers on page 366

long-term memory
executive functioning
multitasking
attention to detail

complete the words

Place a letter in each blank space below to make a word of five letters or more. All twenty-six letters are used only once. And each correct answer uses at least one space on the right and one space on the left of the inserted letter. No hyphenated words, plurals, or proper nouns are allowed.

A	E	T	R	A	M		O	L	I	N	E
B	C	U	R	R	C		O	W	D	E	R
C	N	A	G	A	R		I	C	O	T	Z
D	B	A	I	R	P		R	T	E	L	L
E	E	A	S	T	H		A	G	A	N	G
F	P	I	L	L	O		C	A	S	E	W
G	T	U	B	A	N		O	Y	F	E	E
H	M	A	L	W	A		S	T	A	N	N
I	V	B	E	H	A		I	O	R	Y	H
J	O	P	T	M	I		T	U	R	E	Q
K	P	U	B	I	O		R	A	P	H	Y
L	Q	U	A	C	O		R	A	G	G	I
M	I	F	R	I	S		Y	E	A	R	T
N	D	E	O	D	O		A	N	T	H	E
O	D	O	G	L	A		C	O	M	A	N
P	S	K	N	I	T		I	N	G	R	O
Q	P	A	N	T	I		U	E	S	H	R
R	C	L	U	M	E		I	U	M	M	Y
S	S	I	R	I	F		G	H	T	E	R
T	G	L	O	B	I		A	R	R	E	W
U	C	H	A	N	D		O	M	E	T	I
V	P	L	K	N	U		K	L	E	D	Y
W	B	L	U	M	B		R	G	A	T	T
X	M	O	O	T	A		T	R	U	M	O
Y	B	L	I	N	D		O	L	D	E	D
Z	M	O	T	H	T		N	G	O	T	H

Answers on page 367

Beginnings & Endings

From *Aroma* to *Yearly*, can you come up with words for each letter of the alphabet that begin and end with the same letter? And for an extra brain boost, see how many words you can get in three minutes.

long-term memory
working memory
executive functioning
processing speed

A _____

B _____

C _____

D _____

E _____

F _____

G _____

H _____

I (Obscure) _____

J (None)

K _____

L _____

M _____

N _____

O _____

P _____

Q (None)

R _____

S _____

T _____

U (Obscure) _____

V (Obscure) _____

W _____

X _____

Y _____

Z (None)

Answers on page 367

FIND THE WORDS

Find the 83 words in the picture that start with the letter B.

Answers on page 368

ODD MAN OUT

All of the items in each list have something in common—with one exception. Your job is to find which item doesn't fit and to explain why it is the "odd man out."

1. Trousers, A banana, A pool table, A marsupial

2. Beaker, Skiff, Snifter, Flute

3. Dozen, Dancing, High school, Harry

4. Scarlet, Spring, Bacon, Saturday night

5. Denver, Wayne, Miami, Candy

6. A fish, A Weight Watchers meeting, A driving instructor, A music student

7. Knee, Kidney, Shower, Thinking

8. Kennedy, Roosevelt, Fear, May

Answers on page 367

---

honorific titles

In English, words such as *Mr., Mrs., Ms., Dr., Uncle, Captain*, etc., are called "honorific titles." Can you identify the honorific title for each character in this quiz?

1. "In the meadow we can build a snowman, and pretend that he is . . ." who?

2. She's also called "Hot Lips."

3. Richard Chamberlain played this hospital intern on 1960s TV.

4. Joe DiMaggio was the spokesman for this small appliance.

5. In the 1950s, he was known as Mr. Television and by this nickname.

6. "You've got to accentuate the positive, eliminate the negative, latch on to the affirmative, and don't mess with . . ." who?

7. He couldn't refrain from "squeezing the Charmin."

8. Jackie Coogan played this member of the Addams Family on TV.

9. A brand of cookies, especially chocolate chip.

Answers on page 367

Blue Blank

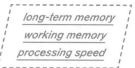

long-term memory
working memory
processing speed

How many single words can you come up with in two minutes that complete the compound word or two-word phrase *Blue _____* ?

_____ _____ _____

_____ _____ _____

_____ _____ _____

_____ _____ _____

_____ _____ _____

_____ _____ _____

_____ _____ _____

_____ _____ _____

_____ _____ _____

_____ _____ _____

Answers on page 370

DOUBLE TROUBLE

Can you find the one word that follows each list of words to make a common two-word phrase or compound word? For example, the one word that completes *honey*, *polar*, and *teddy* is *bear* (*honey bear*, *polar bear*, *teddy bear*). If you get stuck, we've provided the first letter of the correct answer as a hint at the bottom of the page.

1. Car, hog, mouth

2. Sand, thunder, snow

3. Cross, ox, rain

4. Electric, arm, high

5. Poker, baby, type

6. Slot, time, sewing

7. Hair, king, clothes

8. Pep, pillow, small

9. Black, table, tree

10. Butter, chocolate, whole

Hints: 1 w; 2 s; 3 b; 4 c; 5 f; 6 m; 7 p; 8 t; 9 t; 10 m

Answers on page 370

MAKING CONNECTIONS

Given nine words or phrases randomly placed in a grid, can you find the three groups of three connected items AND explain why they are connected? Here's a sample grid:

executive functioning
attention to detail

RED	HONEY	BLUE
VIEIRA	HARVEST	PURPLE
FULL	LAUER	COURIC

GROUP 1 WORDS:
Red, Blue, Purple

THEME:
Colors

GROUP 2 WORDS:
Vieira, Lauer, Couric

THEME:
Today show hosts

GROUP 3 WORDS:
Full, Honey, Harvest

THEME:
_____moon

CUTTER	ROBINSON	HOUDINI
TRUMAN	SCOW	DORY
DAVIS	HAMLIN	ROOSEVELT

GROUP 1 WORDS   THEME:

_____ _____ _____   _____

GROUP 2 WORDS   THEME:

_____ _____ _____   _____

GROUP 3 WORDS   THEME:

_____ _____ _____   _____

Answers on page 370

ALPHABET TRIVIA

The only thing these trivia questions have in common is that all of the answers begin with the letter O.

1. Which US president's last name begins with the letter O?

2. What are the three world capital cities that begin with the letter O? (*Note: One of them is obscure.*)

3. Which three US states begin with the letter O?

4. How many musical instruments that begin with the letter O can you name? (We found three.)

5. How many edible fruits and vegetables that begin with the letter O can you name? (We found four.)

6. Which Shakespeare character smothered his wife in a jealous rage?

7. Which Greek epic poem, attributed to Homer, begins with an O?

8. How many "O" animals can you name? (We found thirteen.)

9. Name three gemstones that begin with the letter O.

10. Identify these famous folks whose last names begin with O:
   a. He played Archie Bunker.
   b. Although she played John Wayne's wife in five movies, she's probably best remembered as Natalie Wood's mother in *Miracle on 34th Street*.
   c. He led the US program to build an atomic bomb during WWII.
   d. He wore number 4 for the Boston Bruins.
   e. He wrote *1984* and *Animal Farm*.

11. Identify the following acronyms:
OB-GYN
OCD
OD
OED
OJ
OMG
OPEC
OR

Answers on page 370

President in Name Only

Although this is not a quiz about US presidents, every answer includes the last name of a US president.

1. What is the name of the theater where President Lincoln was assassinated?

2. Johnny Cash married this blue-eyed daughter of a traditional American folk music family.

3. This former football player was instrumental in capturing the man who shot Robert F. Kennedy.

4. Who is the twentieth-century abstract artist famous for his "drip paintings"?

5. Before the 1994 Winter Olympics, she conspired to injure her skating rival.

6. He is the author of *Breakfast at Tiffany's*.

7. This movie's theme song includes the lyrics: "If you get caught between the moon and New York City, the best that you can do . . . is fall in love."

8. Also called Denali, this is the highest mountain peak in North America.

9. This "First Lady of the American Theatre" made her stage debut in 1905, when she was five years old.

10. She wrote *Dinner at the Homesick Restaurant* and *The Accidental Tourist*.

Answers on page 370

> long-term memory
> executive functioning

RIDDLE ME THIS

> executive functioning
> attention to detail

Riddles often require some unconventional thinking and are a great brain exercise. Think outside the box as you try to solve this classic riddle.

When Jack and Leah went to the seashore, they saw a boat filled with people. Yet there wasn't a single person on the boat. How is that possible?

Answer on page 371

Word Rebus

long-term memory
executive functioning
attention to detail

In this game, each rebus represents one word. If you get the right word or sound for each image, you should be able to sound out the answer. Here's an example of a one-word rebus—and be sure to pay attention to the plus sign (+) or minus sign (-) to know whether to add or subtract a sound:

The answer is LOVEBIRD (glove – G = love + bird)

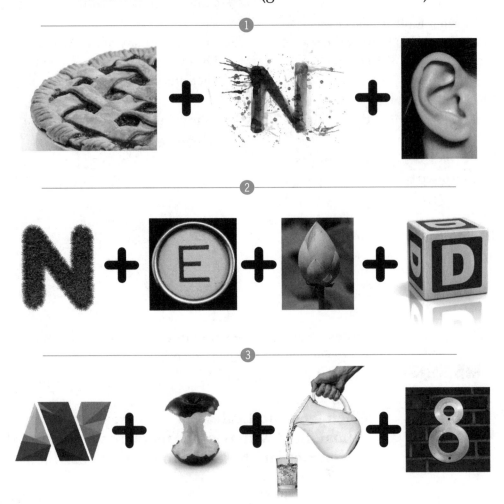

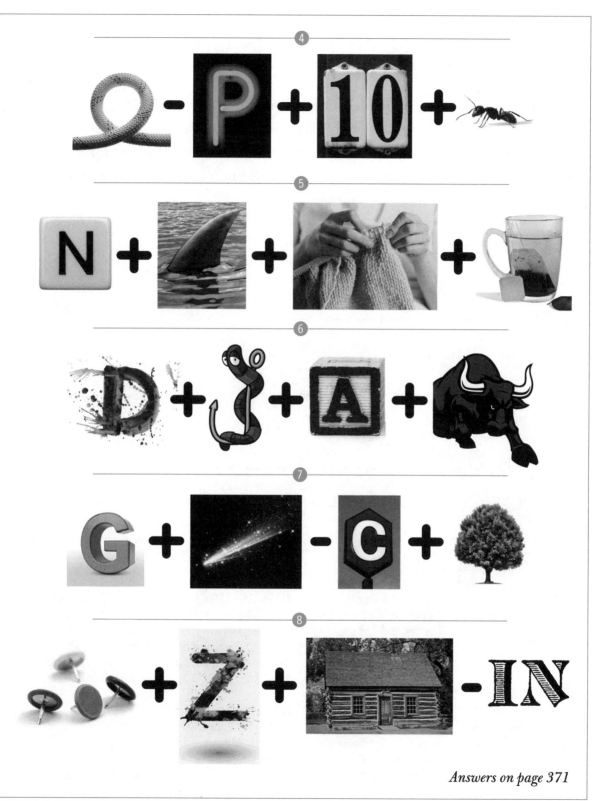

Answers on page 371

Anagrams

The letters of each word in this list can be rearranged in multiple ways to form other words. We provide the word and the number of anagrams that are possible to make. (*Remember, you must use ALL the letters in the given word.*) You should give your brain a rest if you can solve all of these anagrams in three minutes.

1. Dome (2) _____ _____

2. Buts (3) _____ _____ _____

3. Meta (4) _____ _____ _____ _____

4. Scion (3) _____ _____ _____

5. Slime (3) _____ _____ _____

6. Voles (2) _____ _____

7. Palest (5) _____ _____ _____ _____ _____

8. Caller (2) _____ _____

Answers on page 371

---

 trivia

A BRIDGE TOO FAR

long-term memory
executive functioning

How well do you know these North American bridges?

❶ The Edmund Pettus Bridge in this US state is the infamous site of "Bloody Sunday," when armed police attacked peaceful civil rights marchers in 1965.

❷ The Bourne Bridge connects this peninsula with the rest of Massachusetts.

❸ The Seven Mile Bridge, also called the Overseas Highway, carries US Highway 1 to its southernmost point in this state.

❹ The George Washington Bridge, which connects New Jersey and Manhattan, spans what river?

❺ The Rainbow Bridge, which spans this river, connects the United States and Canada. It replaced the Honeymoon Bridge, which collapsed in 1938.

Answers on page 371

water, water everywhere

All of the answers in this quiz contain the word WATER.

1. Where Napoleon met his final defeat.

2. Idiom that means "in spite of all obstacles." For example, "I will climb Mt. Everest, come _____."

3. A flush toilet . . . or a room containing a flush toilet.

4. Until 1972, this was simply the name of a large office/apartment complex in Washington, DC.

5. Ducks, geese, and swans, for example.

6. Idiom that means that family is the most important thing.

7. Fast-moving shallow stretches of a river favored by adventurous rafters.

8. Idiom that means you're in deep trouble.

9. This white vegetable, which grows in marshes, usually provides the crunch in Chinese stir-fry.

10. This saying means that the quietest people can be the wisest.

11. This now classic 1972 novel by Richard Adams is about a group of rabbits, including a young runt named Fiver.

12. When you're not feeling comfortable where you are, you are feeling like this.

13. These aquatic flowering plants are the subject of a very famous series of paintings by Claude Monet.

Answers on page 371

Letter Play

long-term memory
executive functioning
multitasking
attention to detail

Complete each word below by filling in the missing letter. Then, unscramble those letters to form the eight-letter word indicated by the given clue. *Note: This game can be quite challenging. Many of the words below can be completed with more than one letter, but only one will work to form the correct eight-letter word.*

1

___RAFT   NA___ED   P ___ ACH

FE___ON   PL___NT   CA___DY

BRAV___   BA___ON

___ ___ ___ ___ ___ ___ ___ ___

(A standstill or stalemate)

2

C___ONE   G___AND   ___OUND

P___ACH   S___ORE   LE___ST

MAN___R   ___ROWN

___ ___ ___ ___ ___ ___ ___ ___

(Many people are down with this sport.)

3

___LIGHT   SLE___T   S___ARK

RE___TER   BRAW___   S___NGS

S___AMP   ST___AP

___ ___ ___ ___ ___ ___ ___ ___

(What Androcles took from the lion)

Answers on page 371

Signature Songs

Sometimes a song is associated with a particular performer no matter how many others record it. In this quiz, we give the song title. Can you name the singer or group most closely identified with it?

1. "Georgia on My Mind" _____

2. "Moon River" _____

3. "Mack the Knife" _____

4. "Fever" _____

5. "My Heart Will Go On" _____

6. "Thank Heaven for Little Girls" _____

7. "Day-O" (The Banana Boat Song) _____

8. "There's No Business Like Show Business" _____

9. "Mona Lisa" _____

10. "I Am Woman" _____

11. "Downtown" _____

12. "I've Gotta Be Me" _____

13. "Hey There" _____

14. "Buttons and Bows" _____

15. "A-Tisket, A-Tasket" _____

Answers on page 371

exonyms

long-term memory
executive functioning

An exonym is a name in one language for a place that has a different name in its own country or language. For example, did you know that the word *Misr* is the Egyptian word for Egypt? Or that *Osterreich* is the Austrian (German) word for Austria? In this game, we provide the name of the location in its native language. What do we call it in English?

1. Venezia

2. München

3. Firenze

4. Kobenhavn

5. Hellas

6. Genova

7. Wien

8. Cote d'Azur

9. Nippon

10. Eire

11. Den Haag

12. Norge

13. Moskva

Answers on page 371

Secret Word

executive functioning
long-term memory
attention to detail
processing speed

How many four- and five-letter common English words can you find in the word below? The more words you find, the more likely you are to also get the secret word—a word that is generally a little harder to spot. (We found thirty-eight 4-letter words and twenty-five 5-letter words.) To make this game even more challenging—and a better brain exercise—try to find at least twenty 4- and 5-letter words in one minute.

PSYCHOLOGY

Answers (including the secret word) on page 372

WORD PICTURES

The object of this game is to put one preposition with one picture to come up with the ten compound words. For example:

ABOVE

The preposition *above* plus the picture of the wooden *board* makes the word *aboveboard*. It is important to note that:

1) prepositions will always begin the word,

2) although a preposition might work with more than one picture, each preposition and each picture will be used only once, and

3) in some circumstances, the spelling of the resulting compound word may not be exact, but the pronunciation will always be correct.

PREPOSITIONS:	
BACK	OFF
OUT	IN
OVER	AFTER
UNDER	WITH
DOWN	BEFORE

Answers on page 372

last name please

Do you ever have trouble remembering names? Try these names, which are also titles of books and movies, on for size.

1. *Annie* _____

2. *Being John* _____

3. *Lorna* _____

4. *Myra* _____

5. *Pippi* _____

6. *Pudd'nhead* _____

7. *Stuart* _____

8. *The Brothers* _____

9. *The Magnificent* _____

10. *The Talented Mr.* _____

Answers on page 372

endings & beginnings

In this game, we provide the first half of a two-word phrase or compound word and the second half of another. For example, given *Credit* _____ *trick*, the one word that completes both clues is *Card*, i.e., *Credit card* and *Card trick*. (If you get stuck, the first letter of the answer is provided in a hint below.)

1. Drift _____ shed

2. Court _____ stick

3. Sweet _____ beat

4. Social _____ guard

5. About _____ lift

6. Blue _____ burger

7. Space _____ case

8. Second _____ split

9. Sheet _____ candy

10. Gift _____ lift

Hints: 1 w; 2 a; 3 h; 4 s; 5 f; 6 c; 7 s; 8 b; 9 r; 10 s

Answers on page 372

Follow the Rules

If you follow each instruction precisely, you will discover the second half of the phrase "Never put an age . . ." We've provided the first line, and the rest is up to you. A gold star to the solver who gets it right on the first try. (*This game is harder than you might think.*)

1. Without spaces between the letters, write down the phrase: N E V E R P U T A N A G E

1 <u>N E V E R P U T A N A G E</u>

2. Remove the third letter and replace it with an M.

2 _____

3. Replace the first two E's with I's.

3 _____

4. Remove all A's, then put an A in the last position.

4 _____

5. Put the initials of the actress who starred in *Kramer vs. Kramer* and *Out of Africa* at the end.

5 _____

6. Remove the fifth letter, double it, and place both before the letter G.

6 _____

7. Remove the sixth letter and place it before the first R.

7 _____

8. Place an O before and after the second N.

8 _____

9. Place an L before the first N and a Y after the second N.

9 _____

10. Place the fourth letter of the alphabet in the fourteenth position.

10 _____

11. Remove the second, sixth, and sixteenth letters.

11 _____

Did you get the right answer?

Answers on page 373

What a Pair

Harvard and Yale, Thunder and Lightning, Coke and Pepsi are all common pairs . . . but what about *Wonder and Perrier*? If you redefine *Wonder and Perrier* correctly, you'll come up with the more familiar pairing *Bread and Water*. How many familiar pairs can you make from the clues below?

1. Carillons . . . and informers blow these.

_____

2. Don Knotts's Barney . . . and a percussion instrument.

_____

3. Difficult . . . and speedy.

_____

4. Secretariat . . . and infested with insects.

_____

5. Pursue an animal for food . . . and one quarter of a bushel.

_____

6. Green pod vegetables . . . and waiting lines, especially in Britain.

_____

7. A negative term for very rural areas . . . and British units of weight that equal fourteen pounds.

_____

8. Hammer or wrench . . . and expire

_____

9. One of the five senses . . . and what a green light signals.

_____

10. Newman's wife . . . and legendary conductor and composer.

_____

Answers on page 372

what's the title?

Given the first few words of a long book or movie title, can you supply the ending?

1. Been Down So Long . . . _____

2. Dr. Strangelove or: How I Learned . . . _____

3. Fried Green Tomatoes . . . _____

4. Midnight in the Garden . . . _____

5. Divine Secrets of . . . _____

6. The Englishman Who . . . _____

7. The Assassination of Jesse James by . . . _____

8. The Best Little . . . _____

9. Come Back to the . . . _____

10. To Wong Foo, . . . _____

Answers on page 373

fill in the letters

long-term memory
executive functioning
attention to detail

Fill in the blank spaces with letters to make common English words (no proper nouns allowed). For example, __ **a t** yields twelve answers: *bat, cat, eat, fat, hat, mat, oat, pat, rat, sat, tat, vat.* (*Note: The number in parentheses indicates how many common English words can be made.*)

1. **f __ n __**   (12)

2. **g __ __ e**   (13)

3. **w __ s __**   (6)

4. **__ __ t h**   (11)

5. **__ a t e r**   (10)

6. **b l __ __ d**   (7)

7. **p r __ __ e**   (11)

8. **__ __ e e __ e**   (8)

Answers on page 373

ALPHABET TRIVIA

The only thing these trivia questions have in common is that all of the answers begin with the letter P.

1. How many of the ten nations that start with the letter P can you name?

2. Which two nineteenth-century US presidents had last names that began with the letter P?

3. Name the two birthstones that begin with the letter P.

4. What are the three US state capitals that begin with the letter P?

5. Can you name all three NFL teams that begin with the letter P? (Team names, not city names.)

6. Can you name four brands of automobiles that start with the letter P? (Brands or manufacturer names, not models.)

7. How many species of animals that start with the letter P can you name? (We found 21, many of which are birds.)

8. He was the most rotund of The Three Tenors.

9. Identify Santa's only reindeer whose name begins with the letter P.

10. The name of which US state begins with the letter P?

11. What was Johannes Gutenberg's fifteenth-century invention?

12. Identify the following acronyms:
PBS
PETA
PG
PIN
PLO
POW
PTA
PTSD

Answers on page 373

long-term memory
executive functioning
attention to detail

Sentence Sleuth

A true sentence sleuth can find the one word that is hidden somewhere in a sentence. In this case, can you find the name of a country or international city? The correct answer could be spread over one, two, or several words, and you should ignore all punctuation, capital letters, etc., when looking for the hidden geographical location.

1. "Chop suey," said Susanne, "is really an American adaptation of a Chinese dish."

2. "That hamster damaged the couch and the rug!" Mom shouted, after Nibbles escaped from her cage.

3. The governor argued fiercely, saying, "It's logical! Cut taxes and you spur public sector spending."

4. When young John Lynch was arrested for drunk driving, his dad and mum bailed him out of jail.

5. To help him get over his paralyzing stage fright, Anne pushed the actor onto the stage.

6. Sophia has odd eating habits; she likes sugar on tomatoes and basil on donuts.

7. Rosa was mortified when her youngest brother put down his saxophone in the middle of a performance, waved, and yelled "Hi Ros, hi Ma!"

8. Tristan bullied his next-door neighbor for years until the boy grew taller than he.

Answers on page 374

INITIAL QUIZ

All of the two-word answers in this quiz begin with the initials CD.

1. Presidential getaway.

2. Author of *Oliver Twist*.

3. "Seize the day."

4. Venue for the Kentucky Derby.

5. British scientist who developed the scientific theory of evolution.

6. Famous American lawyer who is best remembered for defending John T. Scopes in the 1925 Scopes "Monkey" trial against opposing attorney William Jennings Bryan.

7. Product made by the Smith Brothers since 1852. (*You'll have to decide whether it's a candy or a medicine.*)

8. This sparkling wine was invented in Detroit and is made up of a mix of one part California red wine and two parts of New York sparkling wine.

9. This French phrase, which is used all over the world, means the sudden, illegal removal of a government, which is then often replaced by another governing body, usually military.

10. General term for ailments of the heart and/or blood vessels.

11. This compound, emitted as a result of burning fossil fuels, is a greenhouse gas that plays a major role in global climate change.

Answers on page 374

INFAMOUS NICKNAMES

long-term memory
executive functioning

We provide the name of the criminal, you tell us his nickname.

❶ What nickname did the press give an unknown serial murderer in the 1960s, who later turned out to be Albert DeSalvo?

❷ What nickname did Al Capone acquire from injuries sustained in a fight in Brooklyn, NY?

❸ What nickname did the FBI give to Theodore Kaczynski in the 1980s, long before they learned who he was and arrested him in 1996?

❹ What nickname did David Berkowitz give himself during his 1976–1977 killing spree in New York City?

❺ What epithet did the Los Angeles media give to Angelo Buono and Kenneth Bianchi, who tortured and killed 10 women in the 1970s?

Answers on page 374

WORD TOWER

Every word in a word tower begins with the same two letters. You build the tower by increasing the length of each word by one letter. For example, a five-word tower built on the letters FA could include: FAN, FAST, FABLE, FACTOR, FAILURE.

How far can you go before you get stumped? Using the letters OR, we made a tower thirteen words high. (*Note: Proper nouns are not allowed, and you cannot just add an* s *to make a longer word. For example, if your five-letter word is* organ, *your six-letter word cannot be* organs.) For an extra brain boost, see how tall your tower of words can get in two minutes.

1. OR
2. OR___
3. OR___ ___
4. OR___ ___ ___
5. OR___ ___ ___ ___
6. OR___ ___ ___ ___ ___
7. OR___ ___ ___ ___ ___ ___
8. OR___ ___ ___ ___ ___ ___ ___
9. OR___ ___ ___ ___ ___ ___ ___ ___
10. OR___ ___ ___ ___ ___ ___ ___ ___ ___
11. OR___ ___ ___ ___ ___ ___ ___ ___ ___ ___
12. OR___ ___ ___ ___ ___ ___ ___ ___ ___ ___ ___
13. OR___ ___ ___ ___ ___ ___ ___ ___ ___ ___ ___ ___

Answers on page 374

Group Therapy

Group Therapy is the game that proves there is more than one correct answer to a question . . . and we tell you the minimum number of answers you need to come up with. For an extra brain boost, put a one-minute limit on each question.

1. Name five root vegetables.

2. Name five famous people, dead or alive, who are bald or mostly bald.

3. Name seven countries that share either one or zero land borders with another country.

4. List four things that you might find in a typical first aid kit.

5. Name six hotel chains.

6. Name six automobile makes or models that begin with the letter C.

7. Name eight words that end with the letter X.

8. Name seven large cities in Europe.

Answers on page 374

sibling rivalry

We give you the first names of some famous siblings; can you provide their last names?

1. John, Robert, and Edward

   _____

2. Tom and Ray _____

3. Dick and Jerry _____

4. Dennis and Randy _____

5. Eric and Julia _____

6. James and Peter _____

7. Caroline and John _____

8. Ben and Casey _____

9. Richard and Karen _____

10. Jane and Peter _____

Answers on page 375

Vivienne's Vowels

Vivienne is an odd one. She has an aversion to the letters A, E, I, O, and U. Can you fix her list of geographical locations by putting back the missing vowels? *Note: Any geographical location, from bodies of water and landmarks to cities, states, and countries, is acceptable.* You can make this a more strenuous brain exercise by adding some time pressure: Try to solve this puzzle in two minutes.

1. BNS RS   _____

2. THT   _____

3. THRN, RN   _____

4. JN, LSK   _____

5. VNN, STR   _____

6. PRT RC   _____

7. BS, DH   _____

8. MN   _____

9. GN, RGN   _____

10. CLND   _____

Answers on page 375

change a letter

Change the first letter of the three words in each list to create three new words that all start with the same letter. For example, given the words *whine, plant,* and *reason,* what one letter can replace the first letter of each word to make three new words? The answer is S—*shine, slant,* and *season.*

1. Wide, Scorn, Olive

2. Baked, Eight, Yearly

3. Wart, Chick, Great

4. Grid, Hiding, Suction

5. Dough, Mover, Grown

6. Warm, Reading, Worse

7. Unit, Snow, Help

8. Gel, Plastic, Jarring

9. Danish, Ease, Sanity

10. Math, Basis, Doze

Answers on page 375

pour le "ban"

All of the answers in this quiz contain the consecutive letters BAN.

1. An elaborate, formal meal.
2. Circular, nonflexible bracelet.
3. Tropical fruit that is very high in potassium.
4. Early forms of this musical instrument were fashioned by Africans in nineteenth-century America.
5. Headdress worn by male members of the Sikh religion.
6. Mexican-born actor who played Mr. Roarke in the television series *Fantasy Island*.
7. An insolvent debtor.
8. Of, or relating to, areas just outside of a city.
9. Capital, and most populous, city in Thailand.
10. Fundamentalist Islamic political group that ruled Afghanistan from 1996 to 2001.
11. To cast out a person as a form of punishment.
12. The class in boxing that applies to fighters who weigh between 115 and 118 pounds.

Answers on page 375

ODD MAN OUT

All of the items in each question have something in common—with one exception. Your job is to find which item doesn't fit and to explain why it is the "odd man out."

1. De La Renta, Armani, Von Furstenberg, Dior
2. Merit, Write, Remit, Timer
3. Glenn Miller, Jimmy Hoffa, Amelia Earhart, Greta Garbo
4. Chipper, Vinyl, Wood, Iron
5. Prison gangs, Bicycles, Baseball gloves, Mountains
6. Chaplin, Alda, Gretzky, Redford, Mantle
7. Veteran's Day, Thanksgiving, Election Day, Halloween

Answers on page 375

long-term memory
executive functioning
attention to detail

Sentence Sleuth

A true sentence sleuth can find the one word that is hidden somewhere in a sentence. In this case, can you find the name of an animal? The correct answer could be spread over one, two, or several words, and you should ignore all punctuation, capital letters, etc., when looking for the hidden animal.

1. Frustrated by all the wedding arrangements, Constance and Grant eloped instead.

2. Last autumn, Petey watched his Grandpa rake Etta's yard after she hurt her back.

3. Seymour didn't notice that his naked toddler had run out onto the sidewalk.

4. "Sometimes, it's okay to be average," said Kate to her stressed-out teenage daughter.

5. After he made the withdrawal, Rusty bought his new car with the cash he got from his dad.

6. "Brooke cannot terminate her cell phone contract until next year," said her sister Cecelia.

7. When she saw the wreckage on television, Salvatore's sister shouted, "Sal, a man derailed the train to Chicago!"

8. "I like Rikki's new boyfriend Jack a lot," said Rachel slyly.

Answers on page 376

One-Syllable Anatomy

How many one-syllable names of body parts can you come up with in one minute?

long-term memory
working memory
processing speed

Answers on page 376

By the Letter

In this game, players need to guess a word—one letter at a time. Place the letter called for in each question in the line below (the first answer above the number 1, the second above the number 2, and so on).

1. First letter of the name of the mineral that was removed from the desert in Death Valley by "20-mule teams" and made into a laundry detergent.

2. First letter of an alternative word for *hors d'oeuvre*.

3. First letter of the third-largest city in Italy. It's the city nearest to the volcanic ruins of Pompeii and it's where pizza originated.

4. First letter of the first name of Mr. Carnegie, Mr. Wyeth, or Mr. Lloyd Webber.

5. First letter of the name of the Roman god of freshwater and the sea.

6. First letter of the name of the northeastern mountain range that spans from Georgia in the south to Newfoundland and Labrador in the north.

___ ___ ___ ___ ___ ___
 1   2   3   4   5   6

Answers on page 376

RIDDLE ME THIS

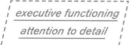

Riddles often require some unconventional thinking and are a great brain exercise. Think outside the box as you try to solve this classic riddle.

Which word in the dictionary is always spelled incorrectly?

Answer on page 376

complete the words

long-term memory
executive functioning
multitasking
attention to detail

Place a letter in each blank space below to make a word of five letters or more. All twenty-six letters are used only once. And each correct answer uses at least one space on the right and one space on the left of the inserted letter. No hyphenated words, plurals, or proper nouns are allowed.

A	C	O	R	S	Y		D	R	O	M	E
B	A	M	O	T	H		R	M	O	X	I
C	M	I	C	R	O		H	O	N	E	K
D	E	T	T	J	O		N	T	H	O	D
E	D	I	G	I	N		U	R	Y	E	W
F	Q	A	T	L	L		M	A	P	P	Y
G	K	C	E	L	E		R	A	T	E	H
H	H	O	T	J	I		S	A	W	X	O
I	S	C	R	E	A		U	R	E	L	L
J	P	S	E	I	Z		R	E	M	U	M
K	F	R	U	M	O		F	I	C	E	
L	T	T	O	T	U		U	A	L	L	Y
M	D	E	S	K	A		A	T	E	V	Y
N	W	Q	S	W	O		P	G	H	A	C
O	F	F	L	A	W		E	R	X	Y	Z
P	H	U	R	R	I		A	N	E	L	L
Q	D	I	V	I	C		I	N	I	C	H
R	B	A	P	T	I		E	D	E	A	D
S	C	A	R	N	I		A	L	I	U	A
T	Z	I	P	A	R		I	N	G	G	Y
U	Y	E	L	H	A		M	E	R	I	N
V	U	P	I	F	T		I	N	G	E	V
W	V	A	B	I	S		O	P	C	E	D
X	F	O	G	R	A		J	U	S	T	L
Y	K	M	Y	S	E		U	I	N	S	S
Z	C	O	N	T	E		T	Y	S	E	D

Answers on page 376

ALPHABET TRIVIA

The only thing these trivia questions have in common is that all of the answers begin with the letter Q.

1. What is the only nation that begins with the letter Q?

2. What is the only world capital city that begins with the letter Q?

3. What Canadian province begins with the letter Q?

4. What Australian state begins with the letter Q?

5. Name the US vice president whose last name begins with a Q.

6. What two commonly used punctuation marks begin with a Q?

7. What is the name of Australia's largest airline?

8. What is a popular brand name of motor oil?

9. What is the name of a fast-food sub shop?

10. What is the name of a mid-cost hotel chain?

11. Name the foods that begin with the letter Q:
    a. French egg-and-cheese dish
    b. Mexican cheese-and-tortilla dish
    c. Hard-shelled clams usually used in clam chowder
    d. Very small game bird
    e. The main flavoring in tonic water, it's also used to treat malaria

12. Name the former leader of Libya who was killed by rebel forces in 2011.

13. This president of Norway assisted Nazi Germany as it conquered his own country so that he could continue to rule.

14. He'll always be remembered as *Zorba the Greek*.

Answers on page 376

A Spoonful of Medicine

These days, there are many commercials on television for prescription drugs, but sometimes it's hard to know what disease they are for. In this quiz, we provide the name of the medicine; can you name the disease or condition it treats?

long-term memory
executive functioning

1. Insulin

2. Nitroglycerin

3. L-dopa (or Levodopa)

4. Ritalin

5. Albuterol

6. Vicodin

7. Crestor

8. Nexium

9. Cymbalta

Answers on page 377

walk a *mile*

In each clue below, can you put the missing letters M-I-L-E back in the correct order to reveal a common English word? To make this a more vigorous brain exercise, try to solve this quiz in three minutes.

1. S __ __ __ __

2. D __ __ P __ __

3. H __ __ __ U __

4. __ __ __ B __ R

5. __ __ __ P __ D

6. __ __ D D __ __

7. __ __ __ D __ W

8. __ __ N G __ __

9. P __ __ P __ __

10. B __ __ __ __ S H

11. C __ __ __ A T __

12. D __ C __ __ A __

13. D __ __ __ __ M A

14. H __ __ S __ __ F

15. __ __ __ T __ N G

16. __ __ N __ R A __

17. D __ __ O __ __ S H

18. H __ __ R __ O O __

19. __ A S C U __ __ N __

20. __ __ __ O U S I N __

Answers on page 377

long-term memory
executive functioning
attention to detail
processing speed

TED'S TERRIBLE TITLES

Poor Ted. He is a connoisseur of culture but he can never remember the titles of some of his favorite books, plays, songs, magazines, television shows, etc. Can you fix Ted's titles by correcting his mistakes?

1. Inquisitive Mr. Clooney

2. Your Unfaithful Organ that Pumps Blood Throughout the Human Body

3. Words of Affection

4. Unfamiliar Person in a Peculiar Terrain

5. Being Seated on the Pier of the Inlet of the Sea

6. A Century of Aloneness

7. Penitentiary Boulder

8. In Frigid Plasma

9. The Way to Triumph in Commerce Minus the Effort

10. Ascend All Peaks

11. So Long, So Long, Blue Jay

12. Everything Concerning the First Woman

Answers on page 377

Sleep Deprived

You can't go to sleep until you answer these questions.

1. The story of Sleeping Beauty was first told in 1697 by Charles Perrault, and by these German brothers more than 100 years later.

2. In his 1973 comedy film *Sleeper*, the main character is cryogenically frozen (without his consent) and thawed out 200 years later.

3. He wrote *The Legend of Sleepy Hollow*, featuring the schoolmaster Ichabod Crane and the famous Headless Horseman.

4. He wrote *The Big Sleep*, *Farewell, My Lovely*, and *The Long Goodbye*, all featuring the hardboiled Los Angeles detective Philip Marlowe.

Answers on page 377

WORD PICTURES

Each picture represents one part of a word or common two-word phrase. For example, if you combined a picture of a *hole* and a picture of a *key*, you would get the word *keyhole*. How many of the eight words or two-word phrases can you find? Each picture will only be used once.

Answers on page 377

pot head

All of the answers in this quiz contain the word POT.

1. According to Irish lore, this is what a leprechaun hides at the end of the rainbow.

2. A group meal in which each participant contributes a dish.

3. Damage to a roadway that often appears after a tough winter.

4. A popular brand of slow cooker.

5. In olden days, this was a portable toilet that was kept in the bedroom.

6. This idiom indicates that a person is guilty of the very thing of which he accuses another.

7. To put in additional money to the total sum of bets made in poker.

8. Chinese dumpling.

9. Phrase used to describe a multicultural society, such as the United States.

10. Brutal communist dictator and leader of Cambodia's Khmer Rouge from 1963 to 1997.

11. A low-quality novel or play, usually written by the author just for the income.

12. Mr. _____, the mean banker in *It's a Wonderful Life*.

13. This proverb, ascribed to Benjamin Franklin, means that time seems to slow down when you're waiting for something to happen.

Answers on page 377

Where's the Suburb?

Given the names of three suburbs, can you identify their closest major US city?

1. Redmond, Kirkland, Bellevue

2. Alpharetta, Smyrna, Decatur

3. Eden Prairie, Edina, St. Cloud

4. Frisco, Mesquite, Arlington

5. Windsor, Sterling Heights, Ypsilanti

6. Mesa, Glendale, Chandler

7. Carmel, Zionsville, Danville

8. Ellicott City, Columbia, Towson

9. McKeesport, Monroeville, Carnegie

10. Lakewood, Maple Heights, Euclid

Answers on page 377

MAKING CONNECTIONS

Given nine words or phrases randomly placed in a grid, can you find the three groups of three connected items AND explain why they are connected? Here's a sample grid:

RED	HONEY	BLUE
VIEIRA	HARVEST	PURPLE
FULL	LAUER	COURIC

GROUP 1 WORDS:
Red, Blue, Purple

THEME:
Colors

GROUP 2 WORDS:
Vieira, Lauer, Couric

THEME:
Today show hosts

GROUP 3 WORDS:
Full, Honey, Harvest

THEME:
_____moon

LAND ARMY	LIME	OLD FAIR
FOREST	COAL ODOR	BAN
SURE	MINT	SECRET

GROUP 1 WORDS

_____ _____ _____

THEME:

_____

GROUP 2 WORDS

_____ _____ _____

THEME:

_____

GROUP 3 WORDS

_____ _____ _____

THEME:

_____

Answers on page 377

prime-time ❖ rhyme ❖

Each question in this quiz has three different answers . . . and they all rhyme.
For example:

Clues: One plus one; not false; azure color.

Answers: Two; true; blue.

1. Swore or pledged; a large gathering of people; moved soil

2. Trash or debris; five o'clock shadow; a sphere formed by soap

3. Soft candy that is often made with chocolate; a blurred mark or smear; a courtroom boss

4. A feeling; noisy; a reduction in rank or status

5. To meditate or be curious about something; a mistake or gaffe; effect that results from the rapid expansion of air caused by lightning

6. Music of W. C. Handy, Bessie Smith, and Muddy Waters; a short, light nap; a discoloring of the skin due to injury

7. Eerie; to transform or convert; canine skin disease

8. A tempest; a large, dense group of insects; college housing

9. A computer accessory; a sliver of wood; season caused when Earth's axis is farthest from the sun

10. To pull through a very dangerous circumstance; to reach your destination; breathing and active

11. Rubber ring that seals a juncture between two pipes or parts; a woven container; a coffin

12. An untidy collection of things; a speech disorder; churned cream

Answers on page 378

What's the Nationality?

long-term memory
executive functioning
attention to detail

There are, of course, French and Dutch people. But things are often connected to nationalities too—such as a *French twist* or a *Dutch uncle*. In this game, we provide the "thing" and you need to come up with its nationality (language group, region, etc.).

1. _____ Glass

2. _____ Taffy

3. _____ Meatballs

4. _____ Broth

5. _____ Man o'war

6. _____ Treat

7. _____ Cotton

8. _____ Hat

9. _____ Falcon

10. _____ Beetle

11. _____ Ink

12. _____ Urn

13. _____ Geese

14. _____ Nut

15. _____ Nights

Answers on page 378

THE PLAY'S THE THING

long-term memory

executive functioning

It's playtime for theatergoers.

Answers on page 378

❶ This three-act play by Thornton Wilder is set in a graveyard in Grover's Corners, New Hampshire.

❷ In this 1965 Neil Simon play, the Pigeon sisters live upstairs.

❸ This is believed to be Tennessee Williams's most autobiographical play. It focuses on his difficult mother and sickly sister.

❹ When this Arthur Miller play debuted in 1949, it starred Lee J. Cobb as Willy.

❺ In this "absurdist" play by Samuel Beckett, two characters, Vladimir and Estragon, wait endlessly and in vain for the arrival of a person with this name.

❻ The musical *My Fair Lady* was an adaptation of this 1913 play by George Bernard Shaw.

❼ What 1957 musical, set in a blue-collar New York City neighborhood, was inspired by Shakespeare's *Romeo and Juliet*?

❽ In 2013, this musical, book by Harvey Fierstein and music and lyrics by Cyndi Lauper, won the Tony Award for Best Musical.

TWO > MINUTE > MADNESS

Chicken Blank

How many single words can you come up with in two minutes that complete the compound word or two-word phrase *Chicken* _____ ?

Answers on page 378

Common Bonds

long-term memory
executive functioning
attention to detail

The pictures in this puzzle may seem like they have nothing in common. But if you look carefully, you'll see a theme emerge. What is the common bond among these three images?

Answer on page 378

Group Therapy

Group Therapy is the game that proves there is more than one correct answer to a question . . . and we tell you the minimum number of answers you need to come up with. For an extra brain boost, put a one-minute limit on each question.

1. Name five genres or styles of music.

2. Name six words that complete the compound word or two-word phrase _____court.

3. Name six famous dogs (real or fictional).

4. Name six common Spanish/Hispanic surnames.

5. Name six types of oil.

6. Name six animals with three-letter names.

7. Name five "red" foods.

8. Name seven official US holidays.

Answers on page 378

Word Rebus

long-term memory
executive functioning
attention to detail

In this game, each rebus represents one word. If you get the right word or sound for each image, you should be able to sound out the answer. Here's an example of a one-word rebus—and be sure to pay attention to the plus sign (+) or minus sign (-) to know whether to add or subtract a sound:

The answer is LOVEBIRD (glove – G = love + bird)

①

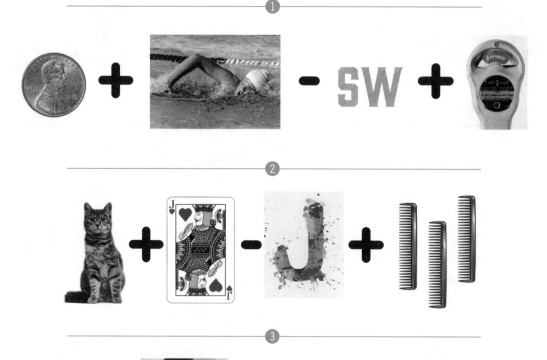

②

③

④

— ARD + 🚬

⑤

—KE+ 🚪 + ◯ + 💵 —DO

⑥

—M+ 👣 + 🏈 —HEL+

⑦

—B+ 🥓 —BA+ 🧙 +Ɛ

⑧

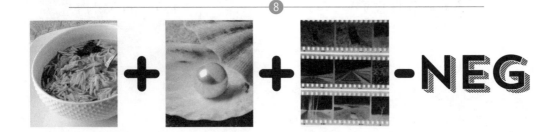

+ 🦪 + —NEG

Answers on page 379

Eights & Fours

In each square below, there are eight scrambled letters. Arrange the letters to make one eight-letter word and two four-letter words. For example, given the letters RSPDTAAE, you could make the eight-letter word ADAPTERS and the four-letter words DARE and PAST. Note: The four-letter words must not form a part of the eight-letter words. For example, the words HARD and WARE cannot be used if the eight-letter word is HARDWARE.

1.

AEIRSSTW

_ _ _ _ _ _ _ _

_ _ _ _

_ _ _ _

2.

AEEOHRSS

_ _ _ _ _ _ _ _

_ _ _ _

_ _ _ _

3.

AUFHKLNT

_ _ _ _ _ _ _ _

_ _ _ _

_ _ _ _

4.

EEIOCLNT

_ _ _ _ _ _ _ _

_ _ _ _

_ _ _ _

5.

AEEDBRT.W

_ _ _ _ _ _ _ _

_ _ _ _

_ _ _ _

6.

AIOCHMNP

_ _ _ _ _ _ _ _

_ _ _ _

_ _ _ _

Answers on page 379

Find the Quotation

Cross out words in the grid below according to the instructions, then rearrange the remaining words to reveal a quotation.

AGUA	SUE	AREN'T	AVOCADO	BARB
BED	BEST	BLUE	BROOKLYN	CINCO
CYAN	DOE	FLO	HILLSIDE	IDAHO
IN	IOWA	LIFE	MAP	DUCK
OBESITY	OHIO	PANDA	PESO	PIN
PINK	SCRATCH	SHEETS	SLOTH	STRETCH
TEAL	THE	THINGS	THINGS	TWELFTH

INSTRUCTIONS:

1. Cross out all Spanish words.

2. Cross out all US states.

3. Cross out all four syllable words.

4. Cross out all three-letter words (except "the").

5. Cross out all female names.

6. Cross out all names of animals.

7. Cross out all words with double letters.

8. Cross out all names of colors.

9. Cross out all words that are seven-letters long and contain only one vowel.

Answers on page 379

Finish the Poetry

Given the first part of a line of poetry, can you supply the end?

1. "The woods are lovely, dark and deep
   But I have promises to keep
   and . . ."_____

2. "Grow old along with me!
   The best . . ."_____

3. "All the world's a stage
   And all the men and women . . ."

   _____

4. "Beauty is truth, truth beauty
   that is all ye know on earth/and
   . . ."_____

5. "Hush, little baby, don't say a word,
   Papa's gonna buy you a mockingbird.
   And if that mockingbird don't sing,
   Papa's gonna . . ."

   _____

6. "I think that I shall never see
   A poem . . ."

   _____

7. "What happens to a dream deferred?
   Does it dry up
   Like . . ."_____

8. "How do I love thee? Let me count the ways
   I love thee to the depth and breadth and height . . ."

   _____

9. "She walks in beauty, like the night
   Of cloudless climes and starry skies
   And all that's best of dark and bright
   Meet in her aspect . . ."

   _____

10. "Shall I compare thee to a summer's day?
    Thou art more lovely and . . ."

    _____

Answers on page 379

Stinky Pinky

We have humorist George S. Kaufman to thank for this game (and for its unusual title). Each Stinky Pinky answer contains two words that rhyme—but you have to figure out what that answer is from an offbeat definition. For example, the answer to the clue *Mrs. Onassis' tan pants* is *Jackie's Khakis*.

1. A communication device made of rock.

2. Where you learn about diamonds.

3. Plates for a flounder.

4. The first year ballplayer's Mint Milanos.

5. The pastor's instructor.

6. Epidermis at the bottom on your leg.

7. A golf club made of a dairy spread.

8. A carrying container for Old Glory.

9. One way to ask Mary and Joseph's son if he wants Gouda and Edam.

10. Mrs. George H. W. Bush's candleholders.

Answers on page 380

alphabetically speaking

long-term memory
executive functioning
attention to detail

Everyone knows that January is the first month of the year. But "alphabetically speaking," April is the first month because it begins with the letters AP. In this game, can you figure out what comes first, last, or next . . . alphabetically speaking?

1. Alphabetically speaking, this is the last official US holiday.

2. Alphabetically speaking, this small dog is the last breed recognized by the American Kennel Club.

3. Alphabetically speaking, this is the last of the original weapons in the board game Clue.

4. Alphabetically speaking, this is the first sport of the Summer Olympics.

5. Alphabetically speaking, this is the last of Jane Austen's six novels.

6. Alphabetically speaking, what flower follows "dahlia" in the dictionary?

7. Alphabetically speaking, this state capital comes after Helena and before Indianapolis.

8. Alphabetically speaking, this is the first country in the world.

9. Alphabetically speaking, this is the first US state capital.

10. Alphabetically speaking, he is the first Beatle.

11. Alphabetically speaking, this is the first of Santa's "eight tiny reindeer."

Answers on page 380

What's Their Job?

Given the names of three well-known people, what careers do they all share?
Note: While some of the individuals mentioned may hold other jobs, we're looking for the one job that the three people in the clue all have in common.

1. Chuck Woolery, Bill Cullen, Wink Martindale

2. Anne Tyler, Dan Brown, Anne Rice

3. Oliver Sacks, Ron Paul, Paul Farmer

4. Kate Moss, Kathy Ireland, Paulina Porizkova

5. Cale Yarborough, Kyle Busch, A. J. Foyt

6. Ted Olson, Gloria Allred, Nelson Mandela

7. Deke Slayton, Gordon Cooper, Mark Kelly

8. Cristobal Balenciaga, Mary Quant, Stella McCartney

9. Art Blakey, Ringo Starr, Buddy Rich

10. Tom Carvel, Burt Baskin, Ben Cohen

11. Pablo Neruda, Wallace Stevens, Shel Silverstein

12. Hakeem Olajuwon, David Robinson, Karl Malone

Answers on page 380

long-term memory
attention to detail

ALPHABET TRIVIA

The only thing these trivia questions have in common is that all of the answers begin with the letter R.

1. What is the name of the two European and one African countries that begin with the letter R?

2. The last name of which three US presidents begins with the letter R?

3. Which two US state capitals begin with the letter R?

4. Name at least three world capitals that begin with the letter R.

5. Identify at least three Major League Baseball teams whose team names begin with the letter R.

6. Can you name all three Shakespeare dramas that begin with the letter R?

7. How many species of animals that start with the letter R can you name? (We found ten.)

8. How many types of fruits and vegetables can you name that begin with the letter R? (We found five.)

9. Can you name the three rivers (more than 500 miles long) that begin with the letter R?

10. What is the only US state that begins with the letter R?

11. Identify the meaning of these acronyms:
R&B
RBI
RCMP
RFD
RIP
ROTC
RPM
R&R
RSVP
RV

Answers on page 380

Sentence Sleuth

A true sentence sleuth can find the one word that is hidden somewhere in a sentence. In this case, can you find the name of a color? The correct answer could be spread over one, two, or several words, and you should ignore all punctuation, capital letters, etc., when looking for the hidden color.

long-term memory
executive functioning
attention to detail

1. "Isaiah," said his mother, "the sign says that you are not supposed to feed, frighten, or anger the caged animals at most zoos."

2. The new knitting craze will spur plenty of young people to make hats and mittens for charity.

3. The custom agent allowed Grandma Bielski to bring her homemade pickles into the country.

4. When it comes to acting, Ray Romano got better with experience.

5. The O'Boyle family decided just to spin Kenny's globe and visit whatever country the arrow landed on.

6. What made Mateo's car lethal were the bald tires and worn brakes.

7. When the hawk flew onto the porch, I dove under the stairs.

8. When the kids started fighting in the boat, Josh laid down the law. "Bob, row now. And Catalina will row after lunch."

Answers on page 380

flower power

Exercise your brain and your green thumb by identifying these flowers—by their common names only.

A _____

B _____

C _____

D _____

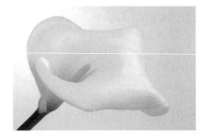

E _____

F _____

G _____

H _____

I _____

J _____

K _____

L _____

M _____

N _____

Answers on page 380

ODD MAN OUT

All of the items in each list have something in common—with one exception. Your job is to find which item doesn't fit and to explain why it is the "odd man out."

1. Jefferson, Madison, Monroe, Buchanan, Carter

2. China, Cabbage, Bottle, Herring

3. Vietnam, China, Laos, Japan

4. Hay, Jackpot, Star, Brakes

5. Inner, Middle, Toothpaste, Vacuum

6. Drain, North, Stone, Twist

7. *Oklahoma!, South Pacific, The Sound of Music, West Side Story*

8. Fife, Saxophone, Rubble, Google

Answers on page 381

RIDDLE
ME THIS

Riddles often require some unconventional thinking and are a great brain exercise. Think outside the box as you try to solve this classic riddle.

A policeman in New York City watched a taxi driver go down a one-way street the wrong way, pass a stop sign without stopping, and take a left in front of a no left turn sign, but he just let him go? Why?

Answer on page 381

THE NAME GAME

This is a two-part game. First answer the clues. Then put the answers in the correct order to reveal the name of a famous person (living or dead, real or fictional). Example question: *The sound of a growl + men's neckwear + the forest.* Answer: *Grrr + tie + woods* (*Tiger Woods*).

long-term memory
executive functioning
multitasking

1. Pen fluid + place of eternal suffering + objective form of she + twelfth letter

2. Fourth letter of the alphabet + twelfth letter of the alphabet + to give money to someone temporarily + giving, big-hearted

3. Device on city streets to limit parking time + place for indoor exercise, for short + to put money in the pot in poker

4. The first letter of the alphabet + middle leg joint + to send a rocket on its way

5. Obese + the opposite of no + a mistake or inaccuracy + title given to a knight

6. Actress, Ms. Bancroft + ice cream holder + fifteenth letter of the alphabet + fourteenth letter of the alphabet + to force open

7. Indelible marker fluid + lions' lairs + two thousand pounds + twelfth letter of the alphabet + to clean with soap and water

8. To knock someone into a dazed or semiconscious state + a place of worship + opposite of lose + sick

9. Fourth letter of the alphabet + fifth letter of the alphabet + twenty-second letter of the alphabet + Vice President Quayle + foot digit

Answers on page 381

Vivienne's Vowels

executive functioning
long-term memory
attention to detail
processing speed

Vivienne is an odd one. She has an aversion to the letters A, E, I, O, and U. Can you fix her list of animals by putting back the missing vowels? *Note: "Animals" includes creatures of any type, from the ant to the whale.* You can make this a more strenuous brain exercise by adding some time pressure: Try to solve this puzzle in three minutes.

1. KL _____

2. CTPS _____

3. GS _____

4. LN _____

5. NTTR _____

6. GN _____

7. PND _____

8. TTR _____

9. TRTS _____

10. FL _____

11. M _____

12. P _____

Answers on page 381

Order, Please!

Put the following list of historical events in order of when they occurred, starting with the earliest. For a better brain boost, try to complete this quiz in two minutes.

___ US Women Get the Vote

___ Nelson Mandela Freed

___ O.J. Simpson Not Guilty

___ *Hindenburg* Explodes

___ Nixon Resigns

___ Hurricane Katrina

___ Insulin Discovered

___ First Polio Vaccine

___ Martin Luther King Jr. Shot

___ *Titanic* Sinks

___ Berlin Wall Falls

___ Man Walks on Moon

Answers on page 381

What Month Is It?

All of the answers in this quiz contain the name of a month of the year. (*Note: Not all months are used, and a month may occur more than once.*)

1. Charity founded by President Franklin Roosevelt to combat polio.

2. This Rochester, Minnesota, medical research center is one of America's top hospitals.

3. The first mention of this day of pranks was in Geoffrey Chaucer's *The Canterbury Tales* in 1392.

4. Title of war veteran Ron Kovic's memoir of being paralyzed during the Vietnam War, recovering, and becoming a political and peace activist.

5. The capital of Alaska.

6. Top elected city or town official.

7. Tom Clancy's first novel. It was made into a film starring Alec Baldwin as former Marine–turned–CIA analyst Jack Ryan.

8. This 1956 comedy, starring Marlon Brando and Glenn Ford, satirizes the US occupation and Americanization of the island of Okinawa following the end of World War II.

Answers on page 381

---

 trivia

IT'S OFFAL FOOD

long-term memory
executive functioning

Offal refers to the internal organs and entrails of a butchered animal. Have fun!

❶ Pâté de foie gras is a delicacy made from this organ of a duck or goose that has been specially fattened.

❷ Although this organ is a delicacy in some cultures, it also carries increased risk of transmitting fatal neurological ailments, such as Mad cow disease.

❸ This may sound like dessert, but it's actually the thymus gland or pancreas of a calf.

❹ This white, net-like food, which is used in soups and sausages, is actually the stomach lining of a cow.

❺ This traditional Scottish dish contains sheep's heart, liver, and lungs wrapped in a sheep's stomach.

Answers on page 381

INITIAL QUIZ

All of the two-word answers in this quiz begin with the initials ID.

1. This ceremonial event occurs every four years in January.

2. A mixture of oil, vinegar, and a variety of herbs and spices.

3. This sport has been included in the Winter Olympics since 1976.

4. Italian nickname for Mussolini that means "The Leader."

5. Examples of this are the flu, the common cold, and cholera.

6. The man who shot President Ronald Reagan escaped the death penalty by using this plea successfully.

7. Crack cocaine or LSD.

8. The Fourth of July.

9. Professional who makes the space inside your house more beautiful and functional.

10. What Popeye might develop if he doesn't eat his spinach.

11. This modern dance pioneer died in France in 1927 when the scarf wrapped around her neck became entangled in the open-spoke wheels of the car she was riding in.

Answers on page 381

RIDDLE ME THIS

Riddles often require some unconventional thinking and are a great brain exercise. Think outside the box as you try to solve this classic riddle.

What gets wetter the more it dries?

Answer on page 382

TRIMBLE

Trimble is a trivia game and a word jumble combined. First, answer the trivia questions (all related to world geography) and cross out the letters of each answer in the letter grid. Then rearrange the remaining letters (those that have not been crossed out) to reveal another word or phrase related to the same theme.

A	A	A	A	A	A	A	A	A	A	A	A	A	A
A	A	A	A	A	B	C	C	C	D	D	D	E	E
G	G	H	I	I	I	I	I	I	I	J	L	L	L
M	M	N	N	N	N	N	N	P	P	R	R	R	R
R	S	S	S	S	S	T	T	T	U	W	Z	Z	

1. The most populous country in South America.

2. A large island nation off the east coast of Africa.

3. The only one-syllable name of a country that begins with the letter S. (*If you need a hint, it's in Europe.*)

4. Russia may be the largest country (by area), but this nation is in second place.

5. Surprisingly, this is the second most common language in South America.

6. Andrew Lloyd Weber's famous musical *Evita* is about the wife of this country's President Juan Perón.

7. Only one genus of tree kangaroo lives in Papua New Guinea; all the rest live in this country.

8. This country is divided into twenty-six states called cantons. Its two most populous cantons are Zurich and Bern.

Word Jumble hint: The Big Island of Hawaii is about the same size as this island that is about 5,000 miles away.

Answers on page 382

"QUOTATION STATION"

Move the letters in each vertical column of the top grid to the spaces in the column just below it in the bottom grid. The letters will not necessarily be moved in the order in which they appear. If you move the letters to the correct positions, they will spell out a quotation (reading from left to right) from the Irish playwright George Bernard Shaw. (*Note: A black square indicates the end of a word. Words may continue from one horizontal line to the next.*)

Before attempting the big puzzle, try this example first—without looking at the answer to the right:

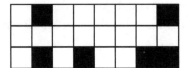

Example Answer:

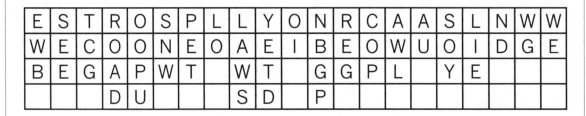

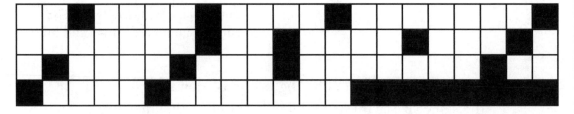

Answer on page 382

no trix!

long-term memory
working memory

All of the answers in this quiz end in the letter X.

1. The voice box.

2. A fraud or deception.

3. Precursor to shingles.

4. A subsidiary or addition to a building.

5. An ending added to a word.

6. To veto or refuse to agree to something.

7. A conclusion that is far less powerful than expected.

8. Supplementary material at the end of a book.

9. Disease that was eradicated in 1980.

10. To persuade or cajole someone to do something.

11. The bottom point of the human spinal column.

12. The moment when winter turns to spring and summer turns to autumn.

Answers on page 382

Common Bonds

long-term memory
executive functioning
attention to detail

The pictures in this puzzle may seem like they have nothing in common. But if you look carefully, you'll see a theme emerge. What is the common bond among these three images?

Answer on page 382

ALPHABET TRIVIA

The only thing these trivia questions have in common is that all of the answers begin with the letter S.

long-term memory
executive functioning

1. If you can name four of the seven European countries that begin with the letter S, you're doing very well.

2. Which six US state capitals begin with the letter S?

3. The names of which two of Disney's seven dwarfs begin with the letter S?

4. Which two of the five traditional human senses begin with the letter S?

5. Which one of the seven deadly sins begins with the letter S?

6. Which two signs of the zodiac begin with the letter S?

7. Name these Oscar-winning movies that begin with the letter S:
a. The singing Von Trapp family escapes the Nazis.
b. Newman and Redford play grifters who con a mob boss.
c. A German businessman saves more than a thousand Jews during WWII.

8. How many "S" animals (not including insects) can you name? (We found seventeen.)

9. Identify the following people with the initials SS:
a. She played Gloria Stivic in TV's *All in the Family*.
b. Composer and lyricist who wrote *West Side Story*, *Gypsy*, and *Sweeney Todd*.
c. She played Chrissy in TV's *Three's Company*.
d. She was Louise in *Thelma and Louise*.

10. Identify the following acronyms that begin with the letter S:
SALT
SAT
SCOTUS
SNAFU
SNL
SOS
SSN
SWAK

Answers on page 382

MAKING CONNECTIONS

Given nine words or phrases randomly placed in a grid, can you find the three groups of three connected items AND explain why they are connected? Here's a sample grid:

RED	HONEY	BLUE
VIEIRA	HARVEST	PURPLE
FULL	LAUER	COURIC

GROUP 1 WORDS:
Red, Blue, Purple

THEME:
Colors

GROUP 2 WORDS:
Vieira, Lauer, Couric

THEME:
Today show hosts

GROUP 3 WORDS:
Full, Honey, Harvest

THEME:
_____moon

NICKEL	CABBAGE	DOUGH
BREAD	SILVER	CLAMS
SNAILS	IRON	CRABS

GROUP 1 WORDS

_____   _____   _____

THEME:

_____

GROUP 2 WORDS

_____   _____   _____

THEME:

_____

GROUP 3 WORDS

_____   _____   _____

THEME:

_____

Answers on page 382

Alma's Shopping List

Alma is a great shopper but a bad speller. Every word on her shopping list is misspelled by one letter. Can you fix Alma's list? Remember, you should not move any letters; just change one to reveal the correct word. (*Note: All of the items are common brand names or generic names for food and other products that are usually sold in a grocery store.*) For an extra brain boost, see how many correct answers you can get in two minutes.

1. Belts

2. Card Caddy

3. Coin Ships

4. Fat Foot

5. Naked Bears

6. Pin Crest

7. Swim Mile

8. Wish Stocks

9. Brag Flames

10. Brash Bats

11. Omen Cleaver

12. Car Sitter

Answers on page 382

fill in the letters

long-term memory
executive functioning
attention to detail

Fill in the blank spaces with letters to make common English words (no proper nouns allowed). For example, __ **a t** yields twelve answers: *bat, cat, eat, fat, hat, mat, oat, pat, rat, sat, tat, vat.* (*Note: The number in parentheses indicates how many common English words can be made.*)

1. **e __ __ t**   (4)

2. **__ h a __**   (15)

3. **l __ __ __ l**   (7)

4. **b l a __ __**   (9)

5. **b __ i __ e**   (4)

6. **q u i __ __**   (9)

7. **t h __ __ __**   (24)

8. **__ __ i s t __ __**   (13)

Answers on page 383

Blank Stick

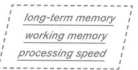

long-term memory

working memory

processing speed

How many single words can you come up with in two minutes that complete the compound word or two-word phrase _____ *stick*?

Answers on page 383

Group Therapy

Group Therapy is the game that proves there is more than one correct answer to a question . . . and we tell you the minimum number of answers you need to come up with. For an extra brain boost, put a one-minute limit on each question.

1. Name six famous scientists (past or present).

2. Name five Westerns or cowboy movies.

3. Name ten words that begin with the letters CAT.

4. Name seven countries that begin with the letter C.

5. Name six famous female authors.

6. Name five ballroom/dancehall dances.

7. Name seven internal organs of the human body.

8. Name twelve famous artists.

Answers on page 383

Common Bonds

The pictures in this puzzle may seem like they have nothing in common. But if you look carefully, you'll see a theme emerge. What is the common bond among these three images?

Answer on page 384

TED'S TERRIBLE TITLES

long-term memory
executive functioning

Poor Ted. He is a connoisseur of culture but he can never remember the titles of some of his favorite books, plays, songs, magazines, television shows, etc. Can you fix Ted's titles by correcting his mistakes?

1. The Flawless Tempest

2. The Unclothed and the Non-breathing

3. The Lengthy and Curving Thoroughfare

4. Insurgent Devoid of a Reason

5. Egotism and Bigotry

6. I Am Cognitive of the Reason the Imprisoned Flying Vertebrate Warbles

7. Pleasant Daybreak, Communist Asian Country

8. Moves Rhythmically with Members of the *Canis lupis* Species

9. Azure Brushed-Leather Footwear

10. More Improved Domiciles and Cultivated Areas

11. A Collection of Maps Moved Its Shoulders Up and Down

12. The Day Before Today

Answers on page 384

MIND YOUR BUSINESS

long-term memory
executive functioning

Here are a few questions from the business world.

❶ John Patchett opened the first commercial winery in this California valley in 1859. By 1900 there were 140 wineries there.

❷ S. Duncan Black and this business partner filed a patent for a new kind of hand drill in 1916.

❸ At its peak, this home movie and video game rental company owned more than 9,000 stores. It went bust in 2013.

❹ After 77 years as the world's top automaker, this company took second place to Toyota in 2008.

❺ If you're a frankfurter fan, you might know the first name of Mr. Handwerker, who opened a hot dog stand on Coney Island in 1916.

Answers on page 384

in the middle

Can you identify this list of famous people by their middle name?

1. Conan
2. Luther
3. Wilkes

4. Lloyd
5. Tyler
6. Sebastian
7. May

8. Makepeace
9. Allan
10. Jefferson
11. Washington

12. Jean
13. Wadsworth

Answers on page 384

CHARACTER STUDY

These movie characters are often named in lists of the "greatest movie characters of all time." Can you name the movie they're featured in *and* the actor who made them famous?

1. Dr. Hannibal Lecter
2. Rick Blaine
3. Norma Desmond
4. Lou Gehrig
5. Travis Bickle
6. Rose Sayer
7. Crash Davis
8. Ratso Rizzo

9. Norman Bates
10. Holly Golightly
11. King Mongkut
12. Father Flanagan
13. Professor Henry Higgins
14. Oda Mae Brown
15. Aurora Greenway
16. Miranda Priestly

Answers on page 384

Semordnilap

A *semordnilap* is a word that spells a different word forward and backward, such as *faced* and *decaf*. (*Give yourself a pat on the back if you noticed something special about the word* semordnilap!)

1. Forward, it's an initial bet in poker; backward, it's a mountain in Italy.

_____

2. Forward, it's an uncultivated tract of land, a heath; backward, it's a division of a house enclosed by walls.

_____

3. Forward, it's a sturdy fabric; backward, it means searched for and/or obtained coal, copper, etc.

_____

4. Forward, it's one of the six simple machines identified by Renaissance scientists; backward, it means to enjoy yourself in a lively and noisy way, especially with drinking and dancing.

_____

5. Forward, it's a sheet of dried seaweed often used to wrap sushi; backward, it removes wrinkles.

_____

6. Forward, it's fit for a monarch; backward, it's a type of beer that is often lighter in color and body.

_____

7. Forward, it's an emotional state; backward, it's death, destruction, or some other terrible fate.

_____

8. Forward, it means to discharge or give forth; backward, it's often referred to as the fourth dimension and it includes the past, present, and future.

_____

9. Forward, it means twofold or double; backward, it's high praise.

_____

10. Forward, it's a famous Middle East canal; backward, he's the Greek king of the gods.

_____

Answers on page 385

camp out

All of the answers in this quiz contain the word CAMP.

1. A college hot shot.

2. The official title of this Stephen Foster song is "Gwine to Run All Night."

3. Military training center for recruits where strict discipline is enforced.

4. Finish the lyric from this 1963 novelty song by Allan Sherman: "Hello Muddah, Hello Faddah. Here I am . . ."

5. To work in an organized way to achieve elected office.

6. Since 1869, this company's product has been "Mmm mmm good."

7. Shrimp cooked in garlic butter and wine and served over noodles.

8. This chemical is mainly used as a moth repellent, but it's also an ingredient in Vicks VapoRub.

9. Island in northern Maine, on the Canadian border, made famous as the summer retreat for the Roosevelt family.

10. Italian aperitif with a distinctive red color and bittersweet, fruity flavor.

11. This section of the brain is thought to be the center of emotion and memory.

Answers on page 385

ODD MAN OUT

All of the items in each list have something in common—with one exception. Your job is to find which item doesn't fit and to explain why it is the "odd man out."

1. Florentine, Fortune, Lisbon, Girl Scout

2. War, Barry, Junk, Saxophone

3. Squirrel, Fork, Buttress, Saucer

4. Coffee, Pool, Picnic, Eclipse

5. Capuchin, Pelican, Howler, Mandrill

6. Elizabeth, Zachary, Phoebe, James

7. Oliver Twist, Martin Chuzzlewit, Dorian Gray, Edwin Drood

8. Alexander, Expectations, Lakes, Tim

Answers on page 385

long-term memory
executive functioning
attention to detail

Sentence Sleuth

A true sentence sleuth can find the one word that is hidden somewhere in a sentence. In this case, can you find the name of car makes or models? The correct answer could be spread over one, two, or several words, and you should ignore all punctuation, capital letters, etc., when looking for the hidden automobile.

1. Elise did not want to dish on David because she was secretly in love with him.

2. Even though Susanne was a Democrat, she voted for Dwight Eisenhower in 1952.

3. When their oldest daughter moved out, Jeannie and Steve gave her a bureau, divan, and hutch for her new apartment.

4. Mr. Brink told the chef, "If I ate your cooking every day, I would put on a hundred pounds."

5. Stephanie laughed when she was asked her opinion of a TV commercial for running shoes. "Just watching that energetic ad, I'll ache for days," she said.

6. Mr. Ostrow was distressed when his daughter decided to join the military. "Go into the army if you must, Angie, but please wait until you're twenty-one."

7. "The Mexican restaurant in the mall near Sears sells a taco roll and an apple-and-guacamole salad to die for," said Leo.

8. As soon as Zoë finished her tuna sub, a rush of nausea came over her.

Answers on page 385

WORD PICTURES

Put one picture together with one word part (in any order) to come up with eight names of animals.

CO	ER	FIN	MANA
GUIN	CHIM	ELOPE	THON

Answers on page 385

Group Therapy

Group Therapy is the game that proves there is more than one correct answer to a question . . . and we tell you the minimum number of answers you need to come up with. For an extra brain boost, put a one-minute limit on each question.

1. Name five famous lawyers (real or fictional, past or present).

2. Name five elements on the Table of Elements that are classified as gases.

3. Name seven words that begin with the letters TH.

4. Name six Shakespeare plays.

5. Name five types of hats, or words for hat.

6. Name four things that people typically buy a half-dozen times or fewer in their lives.

7. Name four television series, drama or comedy, that are or were set primarily in New York City (any of the five boroughs).

8. Name six sports that begin with the letter S.

Answers on page 385

---

trivia

HARVARD DROPOUTS

long-term memory
executive functioning

Judging by these folks, even *dropping out of Harvard* is a key to success.

❶ He dropped out of Harvard in 1974 to start a computer software company. Today, he ranks among the richest men in the world.

❷ This legendary folk musician dropped out of Harvard in 1938 when his political activism led to poor grades and the loss of his scholarship money.

❸ This poet, who was 86 years old when he recited a poem at the inauguration of John F. Kennedy, dropped out of both Dartmouth College and Harvard.

❹ He left Harvard and his hometown of Cambridge, MA, in 1992 to pursue his acting career. Four years later he co-won an Academy Award for Best Original Screenplay.

❺ He left Harvard in his sophomore year to expand his social networking company, called Facebook.

Answers on page 386

ALPHABET TRIVIA

The only thing these trivia questions have in common is that all of the answers begin with the letter T.

1. Which two US states begin with the letter T?

2. Name two of the five largest world cities (population greater than two million) that begin with the letter T.

3. Which three US state capitals begin with the letter T?

4. The last names of which four US presidents begin with the letter T?

5. Who is the only twentieth-century British prime minister whose last name begins with the letter T?

6. Name four musical instruments that begin with the letter T.

7. Name three fruits and/or vegetables that begin with the letter T.

8. Name five animals of any type that begin with the letter T.

9. Name the two senses that begin with the letter T.

10. Name the one sign of the zodiac that begins with the letter T.

11. Name a one-word movie title that begins with the letter T.

Answers on page 386

 RIDDLE
ME THIS

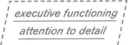

Riddles often require some unconventional thinking and are a great brain exercise. Think outside the box as you try to solve this classic riddle.

What has four fingers and a thumb but is not alive?

Answer on page 387

DON'T BUG ME

long-term memory

executive functioning

Test your insect IQ with these questions.

❶ Despite its name, this family of bugs can have a varying number of legs, from 15 to more than 300.

❷ This type of bug transmits Lyme disease and Rocky Mountain spotted fever.

❸ The name of this bug, which spreads malaria and yellow fever, is Spanish for "little fly."

❹ After a month, the May beetle is known by this name.

Answers on page 387

Anagrams

working memory

executive functioning

processing speed

The letters of each word in this list can be rearranged in multiple ways to form other words. We provide the word and the number of anagrams that are possible to make. (*Remember, you must use ALL the letters in the given word.*) You should give your brain a rest if you can solve all of these anagrams in three minutes.

1. Tush (3) _____ _____ _____

2. Agree (1) _____

3. Steno (4) _____ _____ _____ _____

4. Being (2) _____ _____

5. Marines (2) _____ _____

6. Ranged (3) _____ _____ _____

7. Ethics (1) _____

8. Aspired (3) _____ _____ _____

Answers on page 387

Vivienne's Vowels

Vivienne is an odd one. She has an aversion to the letters A, E, I, O, and U. Can you fix her list of book, movie, and television show titles by putting back the missing vowels? You can make this a more strenuous brain exercise by adding some time pressure: Try to solve this puzzle in three minutes.

1. XDS _____

2. LLT _____

3. MGN _____

4. CBRT _____

5. KLHM _____

6. MMM M _____

7. GRS _____

8. NV _____

9. L LW _____

10. LSS _____

11. JN YR _____

12. RTS _____

13. TH SPRNS _____

Answers on page 387

Letter Play

Complete each word below by filling in the missing letter. Then, unscramble those letters to form the eight-letter word indicated by the given clue. *Note: This game can be quite challenging. Many of the words below can be completed with more than one letter, but only one will work to form the correct eight-letter word.*

__EAD   __ELLOW   ST__RE

PA__TS   __ROOM   __HICK

F__LL   ME__AL

____ ____ ____ ____ ____ ____ ____ ____

(Annual event)

Answers on page 387

Finish the Proverb

Given the first couple of words of a familiar proverb or saying, can you complete it? To make this a more vigorous brain exercise, try to answer all the questions in one minute.

1. That which does not _____.

2. Revenge is _____

3. Spare the _____.

4. It's better to light _____.

5. A rising tide _____.

6. Time and _____.

7. A chain is _____.

8. There's no such _____.

Answers on page 387

---

honorific titles

In English, words such as *Mr., Mrs., Ms., Dr., Uncle, Captain*, etc., are called "honorific titles." Can you identify the honorific title for each character in this quiz?

1. Robin Williams's only movie role in female dress.

2. In *A Tale of Two Cities*, she stitched into her knitting the names of those who should die after the French Revolution.

3. Samantha's "magical" physician on *Bewitched*.

4. A brand of children's sleeping garment with attached feet.

5. He was a gambler, gunfighter, dentist, and pal of Wyatt Earp.

6. TV character played by Eve Arden (1948 to 1957).

7. This knight's affair with the queen ultimately brought about the end of King Arthur's reign.

8. Dorothy Gale's guardian and mother figure.

9. Jim Backus was the voice of this nearsighted cartoon character.

10. Bess Myerson, Phyllis George, or Vanessa Williams.

Answers on page 387

THE NAME GAME

This is a two-part game. First answer the clues. Then put the answers in the correct order to reveal the name of a famous person (living or dead, real or fictional). Example question: *The sound of a growl + men's neckwear + the forest.* Answer: *Grrr + tie + woods* (*Tiger Woods*).

1. To mix liquids with a spoon + British slang for bathroom + opposite of present + the fifth letter of the alphabet

2. Large leg joint + plus or in addition to + the fifth letter of the alphabet + a mixture of flour and butter used as a basis for sauces

3. Use a bathroom scale + to "do this" is human + in the act of shortening a skirt or dress + a bird's home

4. Appendage on a fish + to leave or depart + boxlike vehicle, larger than a car and smaller than a bus + one penny

5. Tree fluid + to manually propel a boat + boats like Noah's

6. A scrap of cloth used to cover a hole + the fifth letter of the alphabet + a high mountain in Europe, such as Mont Blanc or the Matterhorn + the opposite of yes

7. JFK Jr. to Jackie Onassis + L. Frank Baum's "Emerald City" + the last letter + sound made by a bell, especially at a funeral

8. Your male child + the lowest face card + locks don't work without this + great happiness or joy

9. A unit of speech which, with others, forms a sentence + interrogative word meaning "in what way" + many female sheep

Answers on page 387

endings & beginnings

In this game, we provide the first half of a two-word phrase or compound word and the second half of another. For example, given *Credit _____ trick*, the one word that completes both clues is *Card*, i.e., *Credit card* and *Card trick*. (If you get stuck, the first letter of the answer is provided in a hint below.)

1. Full _____ river

2. Irish _____ grinder

3. Table _____ water

4. Work _____ line

5. Toilet _____ bag

6. Shirt _____ wind

7. First _____ bug

8. Hand _____ road

9. Dead _____ zone

10. Brown _____ cube

Hints: 1 m; 2 c; 3 s; 4 c; 5 p; 6 t; 7 l; 8 r; 9 e; 10 s

Answers on page 387

long-term memory
working memory
executive functioning

Group Therapy

Group Therapy is the game that proves there is more than one correct answer to a question . . . and we tell you the minimum number of answers you need to come up with. For an extra brain boost, put a one-minute limit on each question.

long-term memory
executive functioning
multitasking
processing speed

1. Name six cities (anywhere, any size) that begin with the letter P.

2. Name six brands or varieties of tea.

3. Name four inventions or innovations we have today that did not exist before World War II.

4. Name six countries in which English is the official or the *de facto* language.

5. Name five famous people who use initials as part of their names.

6. Name four species of rodent.

7. Name ten wearable items (of any kind) that begin with the letter S.

Answers on page 387

executive functioning

attention to detail

wacky wordies

MputY cents
cents

E A K C

❶ ______

❷ ______

look

look

P
R
I
C
E

❸ ______

❹ ______

To solve these fun puzzles, look carefully at each frame, because the arrangement of the letters is a key clue to the familiar phrase contained within. For example, if the word *school* were placed high up in the frame, the answer would be *high school*. Or, if the words *easy pieces* occurred five times in the frame, the answer would be *five easy pieces*.

Answers on page 388

5 _____

6 _____

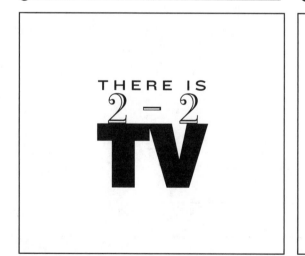

7 _____

8 _____

WORD TOWER

Every word in a word tower begins with the same two letters. You build the tower by increasing the length of each word by one letter. For example, a five-word tower built on the letters FA could include: FAN, FAST, FABLE, FACTOR, FAILURE.

How far can you go before you get stumped? Using the letters GO, we made a tower twelve words high. (*Note: Proper nouns are not allowed, and you cannot just add an* s *to make a longer word. For example, if your four-letter word is* good, *your five-letter word cannot be* goods.) For an extra brain boost, see how tall your tower of words can get in two minutes.

1. GO
2. GO___
3. GO___ ___
4. GO___ ___ ___
5. GO___ ___ ___ ___
6. GO___ ___ ___ ___ ___
7. GO___ ___ ___ ___ ___ ___
8. GO___ ___ ___ ___ ___ ___ ___
9. GO___ ___ ___ ___ ___ ___ ___ ___
10. GO___ ___ ___ ___ ___ ___ ___ ___ ___
11. GO___ ___ ___ ___ ___ ___ ___ ___ ___ ___
12. GO___ ___ ___ ___ ___ ___ ___ ___ ___ ___ ___

Answers on page 388

Add Some Letters

long-term memory
executive functioning
attention to detail

The first word in each clue below has one letter missing. Without moving the letters around, how many words can you make by placing a letter in the blank spot? For example: RE ___ TED would yield the answers RENTED and RESTED. The second word in each question has the same letters in the same order. These words also follow the same rules, but this time there are two letters missing. The number in parentheses indicates the number of words we found. *Note: No proper nouns are allowed.*

1. MI ___ ED (5) _____

   MI ___ ___ ED (9) _____

2. ___ ATTER (8) _____

   ___ ___ ATTER (9) _____

3. B ___ ING (4) _____

   B ___ ___ ING (18) _____

4. ___ IPPED (8) _____

   ___ ___ IPPED (13) _____

5. LA ___ ER (7) _____

   LA ___ ___ ER (14) _____

Answers on page 389

RIDDLE ME THIS

Riddles often require some unconventional thinking and are a great brain exercise. Think outside the box as you try to solve this classic riddle.

**If you have me, you'll want to share me.
But if you share me, I will no longer exist. What am I?**

Answer on page 389

FIND THE WORDS

Find the 71 words in the picture that start with the letter M.

working memory
executive functioning
attention to detail
multitasking

Answers on page 390

Memorable TV Lines

Can you identify the television show from these memorable lines? And for an extra brain workout, try to remember the character (in fiction TV) or the real-life person (in nonfiction TV) who said each line.

1. "This tape will self-destruct in five seconds."

_____

2. "Just one more thing . . ."

_____

3. "You hear that, Elizabeth? I'm coming to join you, honey."

_____

4. "You rang?"

_____

5. "The thrill of victory and the agony of defeat."

_____

6. "God will get you for that."

_____

7. "Jane, you ignorant slut."

_____

8. "Who loves ya, baby?"

_____

9. "Kiss my grits!"

_____

10. "Dy-no-mite!"

_____

11. "Up your nose with a rubber hose."

_____

12. "What'choo talkin' 'bout, Willis?"

_____

Answers on page 389

Letter Play

Complete each word below by filling in the missing letter. Then, unscramble those letters to form the eight-letter word indicated by the given clue. *Note: This game can be quite challenging. Many of the words below can be completed with more than one letter, but only one will work to form the correct eight-letter word.*

long-term memory
executive functioning
multitasking
attention to detail

__AGER   WIN__   STUN__   SCA__E

S__ACK   N__TION   D__MP   MANI__

___ ___ ___ ___ ___ ___ ___ ___

(The spoken word)

Answers on page 389

MAKING CONNECTIONS

Given nine words or phrases randomly placed in a grid, can you find the three groups of three connected items AND explain why they are connected? Here's a sample grid:

RED	HONEY	BLUE
VIEIRA	HARVEST	PURPLE
FULL	LAUER	COURIC

GROUP 1 WORDS:
Red, Blue, Purple

THEME:
Colors

GROUP 2 WORDS:
Vieira, Lauer, Couric

THEME:
Today show hosts

GROUP 3 WORDS:
Full, Honey, Harvest

THEME:
_____moon

PEPPER	DANE	LAKES
GO	YORK	SORRY
LIFE	BRITAIN	SHRIVER

GROUP 1 WORDS
_____ _____ _____

THEME:
_____

GROUP 2 WORDS
_____ _____ _____

THEME:
_____

GROUP 3 WORDS
_____ _____ _____

THEME:
_____

Answers on page 389

ALPHABET TRIVIA

The only thing these trivia questions have in common is that all of the answers begin with the letter U.

long-term memory
executive functioning

1. Can you name the seven countries that begin with the letter U?

2. What mythical animal begins with the letter U?

3. Name two of the four most common three-letter English words that begin with the letter U.

4. The name of this US state is derived from the name of the Native American tribe that lived there. It means "people of the mountains."

5. When William Herschel discovered this planet in 1781, he named it *Georgium Sidus* (George's Star) in honor of King George III. Not popular outside of Britain, the name was soon changed.

6. Which "U" element is necessary to build a nuclear weapon?

7. What Eurasian socialist state collapsed in 1991?

8. This type of submachine gun was designed by an officer in the Israeli Defense Forces in the late 1940s.

9. Which "U" football player, nicknamed "The Golden Arm," played college football at Louisville and spent most of his pro career with the Baltimore Colts?

10. Name the only human bone that begins with the letter U.

11. The name of which of the original *Star Trek* crew members begins with the letter U?

12. Identify the following acronyms that start with the letter U:
UCLA
UFO
UHF
UN
UNCF
UPI
UPS
USAF

Answers on page 389

Letter Play

long-term memory
executive functioning
multitasking
attention to detail

Complete each word below by filling in the missing letter. Then, unscramble those letters to form the eight-letter word indicated by the given clue.

Note: This game can be quite challenging. Many of the words below can be completed with more than one letter, but only one will work to form the correct eight-letter word.

D__WN   __ONKEY   DO__LY

__OFFEE   R__CK   PAST__

MEA__ER   SLEE__

____ ____ ____ ____ ____ ____ ____ ____

(Increasing the family)

Answers on page 389

Chapter Eight

RUN THE ALPHABET

Cars

long-term memory
working memory
executive functioning
processing speed

From *Audi* to *Zephyr*, can you come up with the names of automobile makes or models that start with each letter of the alphabet? And for an extra brain boost, see how many you can get in three minutes. *Note: Both current cars and former models are acceptable.*

A _____   N _____

B _____   O _____

C _____   P _____

D _____   Q (None)

E _____   R _____

F _____   S _____

G _____   T _____

H _____   U _____

I _____   V _____

J _____   W _____

K _____   X (None)

L _____   Y _____

M _____   Z _____

Answers on page 392

TRIMBLE

Trimble is a trivia game and a word jumble combined. First, answer the trivia questions (all related to TV characters) and cross out the letters of each answer in the letter grid. Then rearrange the remaining letters (those that have not been crossed out) to reveal another word or phrase related to the same theme.

A	A	A	B	B	B	B	C	D	D	D	D
E	E	E	E	E	E	E	E	F	H	H	H	I
I	K	L	L	L	M	M	N	N	N	O	O
O	O	O	O	O	P	P	R	R	R	R
R	R	S	S	S	S	T	U	U	Y	Y

1. She was Laverne's best friend from 1976 to 1983.

_____

2. Rachel, Monica, and this character were the female friends on *Friends*.

_____

3. This TV character lived in a high-rise apartment in Seattle.

_____

4. What was the name of Fred and Wilma Flintstone's daughter?

_____

5. Dick Van Dyke's sitcom character Rob worked with Sally and this character, played by Morey Amsterdam.

_____

6. This character lived upstairs from Mary Richards and worked as a window dresser in a department store.

_____

7. What was the full name of Ralph Kramden's friend and neighbor—the one who worked in the New York City sewers?

_____

8. *Car 54, Where Are You?* followed the adventures of two New York police officers named Gunther Toody and Francis . . . what was his last name?

_____

Word Jumble hint: He knew how to make an entrance.

Answers on page 392

WORD PICTURES

Put one picture of an animal together with one word part to come up with eight common words. (*Note: The spelling of the answer might not always be correct, but the pronunciation will be.*)

MENT	SEL	KA	TERY
GENT	TROT	EGORY	ARD

Answers on page 392

INITIAL QUIZ

All of the two-word answers in this quiz begin with either the initials AM or PM.

1. Collective term for commas, question marks, and semicolons.

2. The computer made this technology basically obsolete.

3. US Postal Service flat rate package delivery service.

4. Security officers who ride on planes.

5. Breed of dog that is popular at the Iditarod.

6. The only member of the Beatles who fits this game's criteria.

7. Latin phrase for the school that one attended.

8. Precursor technology to voicemail.

9. Dr. Silmer's Swamp Root and Lydia Pinkham's Vegetable Compound are two examples of this type of product that was largely out of use by the mid-twentieth century.

10. Plant that is often used by farmers and gardeners to condition dry, sandy soil.

11. This arcade fixture was pretty much replaced in the 1980s by video games.

12. Organic gardeners welcome this long and thin insect because it eats copious amounts of crop-destroying insects.

Answers on page 392

---

 trivia

BODY OF EVIDENCE

long-term memory
executive functioning

Test your knowledge of human anatomy with this quiz.

❶ What is the name of the rope-like connection between a fetus and the placenta?

❷ This transparent membrane that covers the iris is one of the few areas of the body with no blood vessels.

❸ Every human hair grows out of these pouchlike openings.

❹ What is the name for the large veins in the neck that drain blood from the head?

Answers on page 392

prime-time ❖ rhyme ❖

Each question in this quiz has three different answers . . .
and they all rhyme. For example:
Clues: One plus one; not false; azure color.
Answers: Two; true; blue.

1. A barrel maker; a state police officer; a funny error caught on film

2. A small rodent raised for fur; a member of the nonhuman primate family; the capital of the Philippines

3. To argue or raise objections about a trivial matter; to write something quickly and carelessly; small pellets of dry dog food

4. A woodwind instrument commonly used in classical music and jazz; a string puppet; a woman who fought for the right to vote

5. To ask a question; cheerful and lively; a small pitted fruit

6. The eggs of a fish or frog; reflex associated with boredom; chess piece

7. A visible mass of condensed water vapor; a great deal of volume; a large number of people gathered together

8. An indeterminate number of things; a feeling or guess based on intuition; a jab

9. Popular style of boots in the 1960s; an animal best known for being extinct; a children's toy

10. Full of moxie; a drug addict; a playful primate

11. Feeling nauseated; squalid or sordid; achieved without great difficulty

12. Scared; double-crossed someone; a celebratory procession

13. To set free; to asphyxiate; to embellish a cake

Answers on page 392

alphabetically speaking

long-term memory
executive functioning
attention to detail

Everyone knows that January is the first month of the year. But "alphabetically speaking," April is the first month because it begins with the letters AP. In this game, can you figure out what comes first, last, or next . . . alphabetically speaking?

1. Alphabetically speaking, this is the first Ivy League College.

2. Alphabetically speaking, she is the first of the Andrews sisters

3. Alphabetically speaking, this is the first real estate property on a Monopoly board.

4. Alphabetically speaking, this is the first Shakespeare comedy.

5. Alphabetically speaking, this is the first gas in the Periodic Table of Elements. (*Hint: If it helps, it's also a noble gas.*)

6. Alphabetically speaking, this is the last country in Africa.

7. Alphabetically speaking, this is the last US state capital.

8. Alphabetically speaking, he is the last US president by first name.

9. Alphabetically speaking, this is the last country in Europe. (*Note: For the purposes of this quiz, we're not including Vatican City.*)

10. Alphabetically speaking, this is the first US National Park.

Answers on page 392

nicknames

Can you identify the person, place, or thing by its nickname?

1. The Great One _____

2. The Greatest _____

3. The Hostess with the Mostes' _____

4. The Lady with the Lamp _____

5. Charlie Hustle _____

6. Seward's Folly _____

7. The Land of Enchantment _____

8. The Swedish Nightingale _____

9. Lady Lindy _____

10. The Granite State _____

11. Foggy Bottom _____

12. The Fourth Estate _____

Answers on page 392

Common Bonds

The pictures in this puzzle may seem like they have nothing in common. But if you look carefully, you'll see a theme emerge. What is the common bond among these three images?

long-term memory
executive functioning
attention to detail

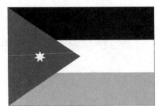

Answer on page 393

TWO>MINUTE>MADNESS

Blank Number

How many single words can you come up with in two minutes that complete the compound word or two-word phrase _____ number? *Note: Only one-word answers are allowed. For example,* social security number *would not be a correct answer because it has two words in front of the word* number.

Answers on page 393

DOUBLE TROUBLE

Can you find the one word that precedes each list of words to make a common two-word phrase or compound word? For example, the one word that completes *weed, coast,* and *sick* is *sea* (*seaweed, seacoast, seasick*). If you get stuck, we've provided the first letter of the correct answer as a hint at the bottom of the page.

1. Birth, noon, shave

_____

2. Basket, winner, pudding

_____

3. Balance, clockwise, point

_____

4. Beat, line, lock

_____

5. Bird, sick, seat

_____

6. Key, piece, mind

_____

7. Fight, talk, case

_____

8. Oil, pit, bite

_____

9. Beat, stairs, date

_____

10. Button, flop, laugh

_____

Hints: 1 a; 2 b; 3 c; 4 d; 5 l; 6 m; 7 p; 8 s; 9 u; 10 b

Answers on page 393

What's Their Job?

Given the names of three well-known people, what careers do they all share?
Note: While some of the individuals mentioned may hold other jobs, we're looking for the one job that the three people in the clue all have in common.

1. William McGuffey, Christa McAuliffe, Jaime Escalante

2. Clement Attlee, Stanley Baldwin, John Major

3. David Blaine, Doug Henning, David Copperfield

4. Margaret Mead, Louis Leakey, Franz Boaz

5. Lisa Murkowski, Mary Landrieu, Olympia Snowe

6. John Maynard Keynes, Ben Bernanke, John Kenneth Galbraith

7. Howard Zinn, C. Vann Woodward, Doris Kearns Goodwin

8. Blaise Pascal, Jacob Bernoulli, George Boole

9. Gustav Fabergé, Louis Comfort Tiffany, Harry Winston

10. Amory Lovins, John Muir, Rachel Carson

11. Rosemary Woods, Evelyn Lincoln, Marguerite "Missy" LeHand

12. B. F. Skinner, Jean Piaget, Ivan Pavlov

Answers on page 393

long-term memory
attention to detail

ALPHABET TRIVIA

The only thing these trivia questions have in common is that all of the answers begin with the letter V.

1. Which South American country begins with the letter V?

2. Which Asian country begins with the letter V?

3. Name the only US president whose last name begins with V.

4. Which two US states begin with the letter V?

5. This English part of speech begins with the letter V.

6. Name Santa's only reindeer whose name begins with the letter V.

7. What are the two "V" instruments commonly used in an orchestra?

8. Which sign of the zodiac begins with the letter V?

9. Which two brands of foreign cars currently sold in the United States begin with the letter V?

10. Which planet begins with the letter V?

11. Name the two most common types of alcoholic beverages that begin with the letter V.

12. What is the "V" name for a chamber of the heart?

13. What is the "V" name for the bones that form the human backbone?

14. What is the "V" name for the circulatory tubes?

Answers on page 393

TITLE TRANSLATIONS

long-term memory
executive functioning

You can't judge a book by its cover, but maybe by its title.

❶ In Sweden, the title of this pre–Civil War American novel is *Onkel Tomms Stuga*.

❷ In France, the title of this macabre short story is "La Chute de la Maison Usher."

❸ In Mexico, the title of this novel set during the US Civil War is *El Rojo Emblema del Valor*.

❹ In Italy, the title of this novel about a wounded war veteran and a promiscuous divorcée is *Il Sole Anche Sorge*.

Answers on page 393

By the Letter

In this game, players need to guess a word—one letter at a time. Place the letter called for in each question in the line below (the first answer above the number 1, the second above the number 2, and so on).

1. First letter of the last name of the TV actor who played Little Joe Cartwright in the 1960s, Charles Ingalls in the 1970s, and Jonathan Smith, an angel on "probation," in the 1980s.

2. First letter of the name of the second-largest country in South America. It was the setting for the long-running Broadway musical *Evita*.

3. First letter of the anatomical system that includes the stomach and intestines.

4. First letter of the name of the first US National Park, established in 1872 by President Theodore Roosevelt.

5. First letter of the last name of this television comedy legend who appeared on the cover of *TV Guide* more than any other star in the history of the magazine.

6. Last letter of the word for a traditional form of Japanese poetry that consists of three lines—the first with five syllables, the second with seven syllables, and the last with five syllables.

7. First letter of the name of the branch of science or medicine that deals with aging and the problems of older persons.

<u>   </u> <u>   </u> <u>   </u> <u>   </u> <u>   </u> <u>   </u> <u>   </u>
 1   2   3   4   5   6   7

Answers on page 393

Follow the Rules

If you follow each instruction precisely, you will discover the second half of the phrase "Science is true even if..." We've provided the first line, and the rest is up to you. A gold star to the solver who gets it right on the first try. (*This game is harder than you might think.*)

1. Without spaces between the letters, write down the phrase:
   S C I E N C E   I S   T R U E   E V E N   I F

   1. <u>S C I E N C E I S T R U E E V E N I F</u>

2. If Columbus is the capital of Ohio, replace all C's with O's. If Cincinnati is the capital of Ohio, replace all C's with H's.

   2. _____

3. Replace the first S with a Y and the second S with a D.

   3. _____

4. Remove the first two E's.

   4. _____

5. If Detroit is the capital of Michigan, place a D in the twelfth position. If Lansing is the capital of Michigan, place an L in the twelfth position.

   5. _____

6. Remove the sixth letter and place it after the L.

   6. _____

7. Remove the fourth and fifth letters, switch their position, and place them after the D.

   7. _____

8. Replace the last letter with a T.

   8. _____

9. Remove the ninth letter and place it in the fourth position.

   9. _____

10. Replace the R with the first letter of the capital of the state of Idaho.

    10. _____

11. Remove the letters that are third from the front and third from the end.

    11. _____

Did you get the right answer?

Answers on page 394

out of this world

All of the answers in this quiz contain the word WORLD.

1. First part of the poetry line that ends ". . . weep and you weep alone."

2. The first edition of this compendium of knowledge, published in 1917, had 8 volumes. By 1988, there were 22 volumes.

3. Popular title given to Dvořák's *Symphony No. 9 in E minor*, which he wrote while he was the director of the National Conservatory of Music of America in the late 1800s.

4. Title of the Louis Armstrong song that begins with the lyrics: "I see trees of green, red roses too."

5. We may do this figuratively, but Atlas (of Greek mythology) did it literally.

6. In the 1997 movie, this is what Jack Dawson shouted as he leaned over the prow of the doomed *Titanic*.

7. What the "www" stands for in every online address.

8. According to the old adage, "The hand that rocks the cradle . . ." does what?

9. These include the Hanging Gardens of Babylon, the Temple of Artemis at Ephesus, and five other sites.

10. This 1985 song, written by Michael Jackson and Lionel Richie, was recorded by a star-studded group of musicians and it raised more than $63 million for humanitarian aid in Africa.

Answers on page 393

 **RIDDLE ME THIS**

Riddles often require some unconventional thinking and are a great brain exercise. Think outside the box as you try to solve this classic riddle.

I am nothing. Yet the more you take from me, the bigger I get. What am I?

Answer on page 394

WORD PICTURES

In this game, you just need to combine one image with one letter to make a word. It is important to note that the "name" of the letter, not its sound, is used here. For example, if there were a picture of a *can* and the letter *E*, the answer would **not** be *cane*; rather, it would be *canny* (*can* + *E*). The letter can also precede the picture, i.e., the picture of a *witch* with the letter *B* would yield the word *bewitch* (*B* + *witch*). (*Note: Each picture and each letter will be used once.*)

ABDFMOSV

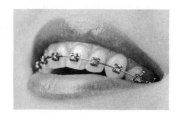

Answers on page 394

Vivienne's Vowels

executive functioning
long-term memory
attention to detail
processing speed

Vivienne is an odd one. She has an aversion to the letters A, E, I, O, and U. Can you fix her list of companies by putting back the missing vowels? You can make this a more strenuous brain exercise by adding some time pressure: Try to solve this puzzle in three minutes.

1. MTRL _____

2. MRCN RLNS _____

3. FCBK _____

4. RD SHCK _____

5. VLV _____

6. CC-CL _____

7. BNG _____

8. GGL _____

9. SRS _____

10. NK _____

11. VS _____

12. YH _____

Answers on page 394

bravO!

long-term memory
working memory

All of the answers in this quiz end with the letter O.

1. A loose-fitting robe worn as a formal garment in Japan.

2. A printed cotton fabric . . . or a multicolored cat.

3. He was both the son of Zeus and the god of music.

4. This bird gets its pink coloring because its key food is shrimp.

5. A machine or gadget—especially one whose name you don't know or can't recall.

6. An artificially high-pitched singing voice.

7. A disaster, debacle, or flop.

8. A raging fire.

9. The largest land animal in North America.

10. 1970s subculture featured in the movie *Saturday Night Fever*.

11. Phenomenon caused by the reflection of sound waves off of a surface.

12. Soup made from tomatoes and other vegetables and served cold.

Answers on page 394

TED'S TERRIBLE TITLES

Poor Ted. He is a connoisseur of culture but he can never remember the titles of some of his favorite books, plays, songs, magazines, television shows, etc. Can you fix Ted's titles by correcting his mistakes?

1. Small Adult Females

2. A Fellow for Every Part of the Year

3. Creature Cultivation Fields

4. All People Are Enamored with the Man Who Played Perry Mason

5. Kin Fight

6. Leave and Utter It upon the Elevated Land Feature

7. Allow the Splendid Moments to Rotate

8. Existence Is Only a Container of Small Red Pitted Fruits

9. Turbulent Atmospheric Conditions

10. Athletic Competitions Pictorialized

11. Cover with Dirt My Central Human Organ at Injured Leg Joint

12. Courageous Unused Planet

Answers on page 394

fill in the letters

Fill in the blank spaces with letters to make common English words (no proper nouns allowed). For example, __ **a t** yields twelve answers: *bat, cat, eat, fat, hat, mat, oat, pat, rat, sat, tat, vat.* (*Note: The number in parentheses indicates how many common English words can be made.*)

1. __ n __ w   (5)

2. __ e __ n   (20)

3. __ __ i v e   (6)

4. t r __ __ t   (6)

5. __ i __ i t   (4)

6. s __ a __ e   (25)

7. __ o __ s t   (12)

8. __ n __ i __ e   (11)

Answers on page 394

long-term memory
executive functioning
attention to detail

292   417 MORE GAMES, PUZZLES & TRIVIA CHALLENGES

MAKiNG CoNNECTioNS

Given nine words or phrases randomly placed in a grid, can you find the three groups of three connected items AND explain why they are connected? Here's a sample grid:

RED	HONEY	BLUE
VIEIRA	HARVEST	PURPLE
FULL	LAUER	COURIC

GROUP 1 WORDS:
Red, Blue, Purple

THEME:
Colors

GROUP 2 WORDS:
Vieira, Lauer, Couric

THEME:
Today show hosts

GROUP 3 WORDS:
Full, Honey, Harvest

THEME:
_____moon

BOXCARS	STATES	EARL
S.	XII	NATIONS
AIRLINES	HUSSEIN	2²X3

GROUP 1 WORDS

_____ _____ _____

THEME:

_____

GROUP 2 WORDS

_____ _____ _____

THEME:

_____

GROUP 3 WORDS

_____ _____ _____

THEME:

_____

Answers on page 395

How Much Is . . . ?

This game involves simple addition . . . but you have to figure out which numbers to add up. For example: *How much is . . . the number of Dalmatians in the Disney movie + the number of items in a half-dozen?* The answer: *107 (101 + 6)*.

1. How much is . . . the number of visible stars in the Big Dipper + the number of minutes in a day?

2. How much is . . . the Roman numeral XX + the Roman numeral CC?

3. How much is . . . the number of teaspoons in a tablespoon + the number of tablespoons in a stick of butter?

4. How much is . . . the number of wives Henry VIII had + the number of husbands Elizabeth Taylor had?

5. How much is . . . the number of days (or nights) according to the Bible that it rained before the earth was covered with water + the number of days before Jesus was resurrected after he was crucified?

6. How much is . . . the year that Neil Armstrong walked on the moon + the number of the Apollo spaceflight that brought Armstrong and crew to the moon?

7. How much is . . . the number of zeros in one billion + the number of Canadian provinces and territories?

8. How much is . . . the number of stars in the Big Dipper (or, in the Little Dipper) + the number of hydrogen atoms in a molecule of water?

9. How much is . . . the year that William Shakespeare died + the number of sovereign countries in continental South America?

10. How much is . . . the national speed limit set in 1974 (and later repealed) + the number of senators in the US senate?

Answers on page 395

complete the words

long-term memory
executive functioning
multitasking
attention to detail

Place a letter in each blank space below to make a word of five letters or more. All twenty-six letters are used only once. And each correct answer uses at least one space on the right and one space on the left of the inserted letter.

No hyphenated words, plurals, or proper nouns are allowed.

A	G	O	B	U	B		L	E	A	R	Y
B	M	A	B	U	R		L	A	R	Y	G
C	R	E	C	O	G		I	Z	E	N	T
D	S	W	E	E	P		T	A	K	E	S
E	S	C	R	I	S		Y	N	E	F	F
F	R	I	B	L	A		E	S	O	D	A
G	A	Y	A	Y	E		L	O	W	E	R
H	E	G	L	A	D		A	C	E	N	T
I	U	F	R	I	S		U	A	L	L	E
J	E	X	A	L	O		D	F	A	L	L
K	W	M	O	U	T		W	A	S	H	Y
L	T	W	O	N	D		R	G	R	Y	S
M	E	C	A	P	R		N	B	A	R	S
N	W	O	O	L	S		A	M	P	U	N
O	C	A	N	O	N		M	O	U	S	E
P	A	C	C	O	M		O	D	A	T	E
Q	T	S	C	R	A		I	E	S	T	Y
R	J	A	N	D	E		I	L	O	N	G
S	E	D	U	C	A		E	A	P	O	R
T	O	O	P	I	C		L	E	A	R	N
U	V	I	L	L	A		N	T	H	E	E
V	A	B	P	A	J		M	A	S	R	T
W	O	R	C	H	I		P	E	S	S	O
X	S	C	H	A	R		O	A	L	E	W
Y	Q	U	A	V	I		E	N	I	N	G
Z	K	A	D	A	F		O	D	I	L	K

Answers on page 395

THE NAME GAME

This is a two-part game. First answer the clues. Then put the answers in the correct order to reveal the name of a famous person (living or dead, real or fictional). Example question: *The sound of a growl + men's neckwear + the forest.* Answer: *Grrr + tie + woods (Tiger Woods)*

1. To be in debt + to steal + cause pain or injury + a loud, prolonged noise + hearing organ

_____

2. Word your doctor often wants you to say + use needle and thread + traditional stories or teachings + charge or cost + not out

_____

3. A shaft of sunlight + monthly invoice + an excessively theatrical actor + the L in sports' MLB

_____

4. Mr. Rickles + the part of the earth not covered in water + first person possessive pronoun + to phone someone

_____

5. The fifteenth letter in the alphabet + "Say ___," said the doctor holding a tongue depressor + outer covering of a mollusk + pronoun used when referring to oneself + explosive device

_____

6. The opposite of low + famous collie dog + rental contract + to vend or peddle goods

_____

7. What one does to inflate a balloon + two-letter word for Dad + appreciative sounds, oohs and _____ + the fifteenth letter of the alphabet + tool to break ice blocks

_____

8. Where you live + ninth letter of the alphabet + payment to use a highway + slangy way to say yes + good fortune + joint that enables you to bend your leg + the first letter of the alphabet

_____

9. Your brother's daughter, to you + foot digit + Ms. Winfrey + negative response

_____

Answers on page 395

HETERONYMS

Heteronyms are words that are spelled the same, but have different meanings and are sometimes pronounced differently. For example, the word *number* can be a numeral and it can also mean "more numb." *Entrance* can be a doorway and, with the stress on the second syllable, can mean "to charm or delight." Given two definitions, can you identify the heteronym?

1. A type of fish . . . and, a musical instrument, typically with four strings.

2. A queue or line . . . and, a fight or argument.

3. To rent again . . . and, to liberate or set free.

4. A main goal or purpose . . . and, to express disagreement or disapproval.

5. Thoughtful, methodical, purposeful . . . and, to consider issues and decisions very carefully.

6. A cabinet for a television or radio . . . and, to comfort someone at a time of grief or disappointment.

7. A reason or explanation to justify a fault or offense . . . and, to release someone from an obligation.

8. Most recent . . . and, final.

9. Fun pastime, leisure activity . . . and, simulation of an event from the past, often for dramatic purposes.

10. To have doubts or uncertainty about doing something . . . and, secured accommodations at a restaurant or hotel.

11. Drainage pipes . . . and, a needlecrafter.

12. To be knocked about, especially by wind or rough seas . . . and, a meal that you serve yourself.

Answers on page 395

ALPHABET TRIVIA

The only thing these trivia questions have in common is that all of the answers begin with the letter W.

1. Can you name the four world capitals that begin with the letter W? (*Note: One of them is very difficult.*)

2. Which four US states begin with the letter W?

3. Name the two US presidents whose last names begin with the letter W.

4. What three Summer Olympic sports begin with the letter W?

5. The American Kennel Club recognizes seven breeds of dogs that begin with the letter W. How many can you name?

6. What are the seven interrogatives (words used to ask a question) that begin with the letter W?

7. How many species of animals that begin with the letter W can you come up with?

8. What is Tim Berners-Lee credited with inventing in 1990?

9. Who, along with Francis Crick, discovered the structure of DNA in 1953?

10. Who was the architect who designed St. Paul's Cathedral in London, built from 1675 to 1711?

11. Which Jerusalem landmark is a remnant of the wall that surrounded the Jewish Temple?

12. Which German composer is known for the opera *Tristan and Isolde*?

13. Which thirteenth-century Scottish independence fighter was portrayed in the movie *Braveheart*?

14. What is the British venue for the Grand Slam tennis tournament?

15. What do these acronyms stand for?
WASP
WMD
WTC
WWJD
WHO
WSJ
WWF

Answers on page 395

WORD PARTS

The word *bather* is defined as "a person that takes a bath or goes swimming." In this game, however, we supply the definition not of a word, but of its parts. For example, given the first clue *Louisville Slugger*, plus the second clue *the opposite of him*, the answer is *bather* (*bat* + *her*).

1. Pork provider + a very, very long time

2. Lower part of the digestive tract + a raised subway line or railroad

3. Filling for a Newton + kidney waste product

4. Old Glory + to go on a verbal tirade

5. The basic unit of heredity + all-school gathering before the big game

6. Hard physical work + the first letter of the alphabet + a member of the Conservative Party in the United Kingdom

7. Pa's spouse + a large, domesticated pig + whichever

8. Fancy dock for small yachts and boats + Mr. Koppel

9. A small rug or pad + the bottom of a skirt + the first letter of the alphabet + quick involuntary facial spasms

10. Shortened term for a chemical curl producer + to consume + Mr. Bradley of *60 Minutes*

11. Short for "in regard" + the opposite of private + two-letter indefinite article usually meaning "one"

12. Armed fighting between nations + sprinted + fastens one's shoes

Answers on page 396

WORD PICTURES

Each picture represents one part of a word or common two-word phrase. For example, if you combined a picture of a *worm* and a picture of a *book*, you would get the word *bookworm*. How many of the eight words or two-word phrases can you find?

Answers on page 396

complete the words

long-term memory
executive functioning
multitasking
attention to detail

Complete the words in the grid below using the three-letter words from the list to its left. Each three-letter word will be used once.

List									
AGE	D	O	O				S	A	D
URN	R	A	W				T	L	E
CAN	H	I	S				D	L	E
DAD	O	M	A				H	O	N
VIE	E	R	E				K	S	Y
GUN	P	O	L				T	E	R
HIS	A	M	U				G	R	Y
WIN	S	P	R				L	E	S
LIP	G	O	D				H	E	R
MAR	T	R	E				T	A	L
YES	E	B	B				H	O	L
PET	O	J	O				A	L	L
RAT	B	U	R				D	Y	P
SIN	P	R	E				W	S	H
FAT	P	E	S				E	N	D
BUT	A	V	E				R	L	Y
INK	P	L	A				S	A	R
NET	C	A	R				B	A	G
TIP	V	O	L				O	D	S
ROT	L	O	L				O	P	S

Answers on page 396

odds & ends

long-term memory
working memory

All of the answers in this quiz contain either the consecutive letters ODD or END.

1. Gesturing agreement.

2. The accused party in a lawsuit.

3. The traditional Scottish preparation of this drink involves the mixture of whisky, boiling water, and sugar or honey. Spices, such as cloves or cinnamon, and a lemon slice may be added.

4. A payment made to a stockholder.

5. Thin, slight, svelte.

6. About to happen, imminent.

7. Aphrodite or Nike, for example.

8. Scientists differ about whether this small tube at the end of the large intestine still has a function in the human body.

9. Badly made; sloppy or inferior.

10. This fictional character was known as "The Demon Barber of Fleet Street" both in film and on stage.

11. Dental specialist that deals with the inside of a tooth.

12. This porcelain egg cooker was probably invented by the Royal Worcester Company in the nineteenth century.

Answers on page 396

RIDDLE ME THIS

executive functioning
attention to detail

Riddles often require some unconventional thinking and are a great brain exercise. Think outside the box as you try to solve this classic riddle.

I have towns, but no houses; lakes, but no water; forests, but no trees; and mountains, but no rocks. What am I?

Answer on page 396

QUICK AS A BUNNY ...OR A WINK

Sometimes there are multiple similes (comparative expressions that use the words "like" or "as") that have the same meaning. For example, you could say "quick as a wink" or "quick as a bunny" interchangeably. The number in parentheses indicates how many similes use the same starting words.

1. Clear as (3) _____ _____ _____

2. Old as (3) _____ _____ _____

3. Good as (3) _____ _____ _____

4. Innocent as (2) _____ _____

5. Light as (2) _____ _____

6. Plain as (2) _____ _____

7. Poor as (2) _____ _____

8. Cold as (2) _____ _____

9. Pure as (3) _____ _____ _____

10. Smooth as (5) _____ _____ _____ _____ _____

11. Tough as (2) _____ _____

Answers on page 396

Triplets

Larry, Curly, and Moe. Ready, aim, fire. Those are well-known "triplets." Can you fill in the two missing items that complete each of these triplets?

1. Executive, _____ , and _____

2. Goneril, _____ , and _____

3. Veni, _____ , _____

4. *The Lion,* _____ , *and* _____

5. Gold, _____ , and _____

6. Liberté, _____ , _____

7. The Kentucky Derby, _____ , and _____

8. Alcohol, _____ , and _____

9. Placido Domingo, _____ , and _____

10. Janet, _____ , and _____

11. Bewitched, _____ , and _____

12. Could've, _____ , _____

13. Ear, _____ , and _____

14. Judge, _____ , and _____

15. Lather, _____ , and _____

Answers on page 396

Group Therapy

Group Therapy is the game that proves there is more than one correct answer to a question . . . and we tell you the minimum number of answers you need to come up with. For an extra brain boost, put a one-minute limit on each question.

1. Name six colleges/universities—not including those whose official name begins with the words "The University of . . .".

2. Name six titles for members of the clergy or religious officials.

3. Name six PBS series or programs (past or present).

4. Name five famous cooks/chefs (past or present).

5. Name six countries that border the Pacific Ocean.

6. Name six candidates for president who did NOT win.

7. Name six gemstones.

8. Name five ways to say "thank you" in a language other than English.

Answers on page 397

endings & beginnings

In this game, we provide the first half of a two-word phrase or compound word and the second half of another. For example, given *Credit* _____ *trick*, the one word that completes both clues is *Card*, i.e., *Credit card* and *Card trick*. (If you get stuck, the first letter of the answer is provided in a hint below.)

1. Pine _____ cider

2. Sales _____ fork

3. Office _____ block

4. Pepper _____ muffin

5. Goose _____ shell

6. Salad _____ room

7. Red _____ word

8. Window _____ bag

9. Clock _____ station

10. Post _____ piece

Hints: 1 a; 2 p; 3 b; 4 c; 5 e; 6 d; 7 c; 8 s; 9 r; 10 m

Answers on page 398

MAKING CONNECTIONS

Given nine words or phrases randomly placed in a grid, can you find the three groups of three connected items AND explain why they are connected? Here's a sample grid:

RED	HONEY	BLUE
VIEIRA	HARVEST	PURPLE
FULL	LAUER	COURIC

GROUP 1 WORDS:
Red, Blue, Purple

THEME:
Colors

GROUP 2 WORDS:
Vieira, Lauer, Couric

THEME:
Today show hosts

GROUP 3 WORDS:
Full, Honey, Harvest

THEME:
_____moon

L	E	CP
MS	V	VOICE
BLACK	M	RA

GROUP 1 WORDS

_____ _____ _____

THEME:

_____

GROUP 2 WORDS

_____ _____ _____

THEME:

_____

GROUP 3 WORDS

_____ _____ _____

THEME:

_____

Answers on page 398

WORD TOWER

Every word in a word tower begins with the same two letters. You build the tower by increasing the length of each word by one letter. For example, a five-word tower built on the letters FA could include: FAN, FAST, FABLE, FACTOR, FAILURE.

How far can you go before you get stumped? Using the letters AN, we made a tower seventeen words high! (*Note: Proper nouns are not allowed, and you cannot just add an* s *to make a longer word. For example, if your three-letter word is* ant, *your four-letter word cannot be* ants.) For an extra brain boost, see how tall your tower of words can get in two minutes.

1. AN

2. AN___

3. AN___ ___

4. AN___ ___ ___

5. AN___ ___ ___ ___

6. AN___ ___ ___ ___ ___

7. AN___ ___ ___ ___ ___ ___

8. AN___ ___ ___ ___ ___ ___ ___

9. AN___ ___ ___ ___ ___ ___ ___ ___

10. AN___ ___ ___ ___ ___ ___ ___ ___ ___

11. AN___ ___ ___ ___ ___ ___ ___ ___ ___ ___

12. AN___ ___ ___ ___ ___ ___ ___ ___ ___ ___ ___

13. AN___ ___ ___ ___ ___ ___ ___ ___ ___ ___ ___ ___

14. AN___ ___ ___ ___ ___ ___ ___ ___ ___ ___ ___ ___ ___

15. AN___ ___ ___ ___ ___ ___ ___ ___ ___ ___ ___ ___ ___ ___

16. AN___ ___ ___ ___ ___ ___ ___ ___ ___ ___ ___ ___ ___ ___ ___

17. AN___ ___ ___ ___ ___ ___ ___ ___ ___ ___ ___ ___ ___ ___ ___ ___

Answers on page 398

Common Bonds

long-term memory
executive functioning
attention to detail

The pictures in this puzzle may seem like they have nothing in common. But if you look carefully, you'll see a theme emerge. What is the common bond among these three images?

Answer on page 398

Vivienne's Vowels

executive functioning
long-term memory
attention to detail
processing speed

Vivienne is an odd one. She has an aversion to the letters A, E, I, O, and U. Can you fix her list of geographical locations by putting back the missing vowels? *Note: Any geographical location, from bodies of water and landmarks to cities, states, and countries, is acceptable.* You can make this a more strenuous brain exercise by adding some time pressure: Try to solve this puzzle in three minutes.

1. THP _____

2. SRL _____

3. ND _____

4. CR _____

5. BLV _____

6. STR SLND _____

7. STN _____

8. TH _____

9. MM _____

10. SL _____

Answers on page 398

Anagrams

The letters of each word in this list can be rearranged in multiple ways to form other words. We provide the word and the number of anagrams that are possible to make. (*Remember, you must use ALL the letters in the given word.*) You should give your brain a rest if you can solve all of these anagrams in three minutes.

1. Carets (6) _____ _____

_____ _____

_____ _____

2. Parleys (4) _____ _____

_____ _____

3. Recused (4) _____ _____

_____ _____

4. Rickets (2) _____ _____

5. Spotter (2) _____ _____

6. Bluest (3) _____ _____

_____

7. Carnet (4) _____ _____

_____ _____

8. Parsed (4) _____ _____

_____ _____

Answers on page 398

Letter Play

Complete each word below by filling in the missing letter. Then, unscramble those letters to form the eight-letter word indicated by the given clue. *Note: This game can be quite challenging. Many of the words below can be completed with more than one letter, but only one will work to form the correct eight-letter word.*

COU__T

__ENDER

__INGER

TR__CK

F__RES

G__ANT

__ INER

S__MPLE

_____

(Well acquainted with a person or thing)

Answers on page 398

Whose Biography?

Can you identify the famous subjects from the title of their biographies or autobiographies and the years they lived? If you get stuck, we've provided the years of their lives as a hint.

1. *An Unfinished Life*   (1917–1963)

2. *Angela's Ashes*   (1930–2009)

3. *Hard Drive*   (1955–   )

4. *Dreams from My Father*   (1960–   )

5. *Born Standing Up: A Comic's Life in Show Business*   (1945–   )

6. *Me: Stories of My Life*   (1907–2003)

7. *Team of Rivals*   (1809–1865)

8. *The Agony and the Ecstasy*   (1475–1564)

9. *My Life in France*   (1912–2004)

10. *Get a Life!*   (1931–   )

11. *Lucky Man: A Memoir*   (1961–   )

12. *Walden, or Life in the Woods*   (1817–1862)

13. *Gorillas in the Mist*   (1932–1985)

14. *Seriously . . . I'm Kidding*   (1958–   )

Answers on page 398

Finish the Equation

long-term memory
executive functioning
attention to detail

These brainteasers have been around for decades. Can you complete each equation by replacing the initials with the words that make the saying correct. For example, the answer to 7 = D of the W is 7 = Days of the Week.

1. 3 = B M (S H T R)

2. 3 = S and Y O

3. 6 = S on a G

4. 13 = O C

5. 18 = H on a G C

6. 29 = D in F in a L Y

7. 52 = C in A D (W J)

8. 64 = S on a C B

9. 66 = B of the B

10. 76 = T L the B P

11. 100 = P in a D

12. 206 = B in the H B

Answers on page 398

MILITARY INTELLIGENCE

All of the answers in this game are words and phrases that include a military rank.

1. Peter Pan's nemesis.

2. Freelance crime solver.

3. One of the "Big Three" automobile manufacturers in the United States.

4. Spanking or paddling, for example.

5. Baton twirler in a parade.

6. Wording you might find on a "No Trespassing" sign.

7. This popular children's television program, conceived by and starring Bob Keeshan, debuted in 1955 and ended its run just shy of thirty years later.

8. Thomas Edison was one of the founders of this company that today manufactures appliances, jet engines, etc.

9. One of the four key professional sports leagues in North America.

10. This soap opera, which is set in the fictional city of Port Charles, is the third-longest-running drama in American television history.

11. Term for "unmentionable" human anatomy.

12. Nautical breakfast cereal.

13. Food company that includes brands such as Betty Crocker, Pillsbury, and many more.

Answers on page 399

ALPHABET TRIVIA

The only thing these trivia questions have in common is that all of the answers begin with or contain the letters X, Y, or Z.

1. Which two countries have an X in their name?

2. Name a house cat and a wild cat that both end with the letter X.

3. Which two US-based Fortune 500 companies have two X's in their names?

4. What is the only book of the Old Testament that contains the letter X?

5. What is the Greek mythological river that forms the boundary between the earth and Hades?

6. How many of the six US state names that contain the letter Y can you name?

7. This "Y" river is the third-longest river in the world.

8. Twentieth-century Russian president whose last name begins with the letter Y.

9. The only Canadian territory that begins with the letter Y.

10. A Jewish holy day that begins with the letter Y.

11. Name the two Top Ten Internet sites that begin with the letter Y.

12. What is the only US state whose name contains the letter Z?

13. This other name for a blimp begins with the letter Z.

14. What stringed musical instrument begins with the letter Z?

15. Which actress, whose last name begins with the letter Z, played Bridget Jones?

Answers on page 399

long-term memory
executive functioning

ODD **MAN** OUT

long-term memory
working memory
executive functioning

All of the items in each list have something in common—with one exception. Your job is to find which item doesn't fit and to explain why it is the "odd man out."

1. Paul Newman, Ron Howard, Judy Garland, Patty Duke

2. Ocean, Radio, Heat, Silver

3. Stuart Little, Speedy Gonzales, Winnie-the-Pooh, Topo Gigio

4. New Mexico, Arizona, North Carolina, Oklahoma

5. Tokyo, Madrid, Stockholm, Damascus

6. India, United Kingdom, United States, Israel, Germany

7. Martha Stewart, Carrie Fisher, Dorothy Hamill, Chris Evert

8. Barbara Boxer, Jay Leno, Cybill Shepherd, Mark Spitz

Answers on page 399

Common Bonds

long-term memory
executive functioning
attention to detail

The pictures in this puzzle may seem like they have nothing in common. But if you look carefully, you'll see a theme emerge. What is the common bond among these three images?

 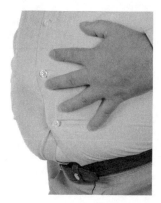 

Answer on page 399

DOUBLE TROUBLE

Can you find the one word that follows each list of words to make a common two-word phrase or compound word? For example, the one word that completes *honey, polar,* and *teddy* is *bear* (*honey bear, polar bear, teddy bear*). If you get stuck, we've provided the first letter of the correct answer as a hint at the bottom of the page.

1. Ghost, type, copy

_____

2. Book, hall, trade

_____

3. Bad, pot, tough

_____

4. Spot, head, sky

_____

5. Sun, wall, wild

_____

6. Pit, rain, water

_____

7. Private, shut, evil

_____

8. Cold, lame, sitting

_____

9. Ice, lock, mail

_____

10. Wish, back, herring

_____

Hints: 1 w; 2 m; 3 l; 4 l; 5 f; 6 f; 7 e; 8 d; 9 b; 10 b

Answers on page 399

SCRAMBLED MOVIES

working memory
executive functioning
processing speed

Unscramble the letters in each clue below to reveal a list of movies with one-word titles. For an even better brain exercise, try to complete this quiz in two minutes.

1. CKORY _____

2. CHOPSY _____

3. ANOPTT _____

4. AABMNT _____

5. AILLOT _____

6. EINSSTW _____

7. EIOOSTT _____

8. AABCERT _____

9. AADEMSU _____

10. EGIORTV _____

11. AACCEFRS _____

12. AACPRSSTU _____

13. ACHINNOTW _____

14. CKMNOORSTU _____

15. ACDEEEILNRV _____

Answers on page 399

Letter Play

long-term memory
executive functioning
multitasking
attention to detail

Complete each word below by filling in the missing letter. Then, unscramble those letters to form the eight-letter word indicated by the given clue. *Note: This game can be quite challenging. Many of the words below can be completed with more than one letter, but only one will work to form the correct eight-letter word.*

GRA__E   SPA__E   LEA__E   __IGHT

B__TTER   __ATCH   __EACH   BL__ND

____ ____ ____ ____ ____ ____ ____ ____

(A precious gem)

Answers on page 399

FIND THE ANACHRONISMS

This is a busy store from the year 1900. Can you identify the 12 anachronisms, i.e., the items that should *not* be in the image because they didn't actually exist in 1900?

ESCALATOR

LINCOLN LOGS

CHICAGO

working memory
executive functioning
attention to detail
multitasking

*Answers
on page 400*

Presidential Anagrams

Unscramble these anagrams and you'll reveal the names of some US presidents.

1. Oh Rot Verb Here _____

2. He Bugs Gore _____

3. China Born Llama _____

4. Jenny Honked _____

5. Ma A Kabob Car _____

6. Hog Growing Senate _____

7. Ma Joins Dames _____

8. A Granola Nerd _____

9. Try Mr Ice Jam _____

10. Ah Run Martyr _____

11. No Irrelevant Folks _____

12. Grovel Rev Candle _____

Answers on page 403

Letter Play

long-term memory
executive functioning
multitasking
attention to detail

Complete each word below by filling in the missing letter. Then, unscramble those letters to form the eight-letter word indicated by the given clue. *Note: This game can be quite challenging. Many of the words below can be completed with more than one letter, but only one will work to form the correct eight-letter word.*

__ANDLE   EXPLO__E   P__AYER   GLO__E

__ARS   P__RCH   PUR__E   M__STER

____ ____ ____ ____ ____ ____ ____ ____

(A "sound" answer)

Answers on page 403

MAKING CONNECTIONS

Given nine words or phrases randomly placed in a grid, can you find the three groups of three connected items AND explain why they are connected? Here's a sample grid:

RED	HONEY	BLUE
VIEIRA	HARVEST	PURPLE
FULL	LAUER	COURIC

GROUP 1 WORDS:
Red, Blue, Purple

THEME:
Colors

GROUP 2 WORDS:
Vieira, Lauer, Couric

THEME:
Today show hosts

GROUP 3 WORDS:
Full, Honey, Harvest

THEME:
_____moon

WORTH	ROSE	GEORGE
MAGIC	KNOX	BURNING
HOWARD	LYNDON	DIX

GROUP 1 WORDS

_____ _____ _____

THEME:

_____

GROUP 2 WORDS

_____ _____ _____

THEME:

_____

GROUP 3 WORDS

_____ _____ _____

THEME:

_____

Answers on page 403

Act Your Age

long-term memory
executive functioning
attention to detail

All of the familiar phrases in this quiz take the same form: *(Blank) your (Blank)*, as in *Act your age* or *Blow your horn*. We provide the last two words and you must give the first word. For each question there will be multiple answers. For example, given the clue: *(blank) your fingers*, your answers might be *cross* and *snap* (*Cross your fingers, Snap your fingers*). The number in parentheses indicates how many correct answers we found for each question.

Important note: For each phrase, only one word is missing. For example, given the clue *(blank) your mouth*, a correct answer would be *shut* (*Shut your mouth*). An incorrect answer would be *melt in* (*Melt in your mouth*) because there are two words in that answer.

1. _____ your lip (3)

2. _____ your feet (4)

3. _____ your hands (3)

4. _____ your heart (4)

5. _____ your back (5)

6. _____ your life (6)

7. _____ your mind (7)

8. _____ your eyes (8)

9. _____ your hair (11)

10. _____ your head (11)

Answers on page 403

SOLUTIONS

CHAPTER ONE

page 1: Run the Alphabet— One-Syllable Words

These are just a few examples of the many correct answers that are possible for this quiz.

A: Add, Aunts
B: Badge, Branch
C: Catch, Chance
D: Dance, Draft
E: Earth, Eight
F: Flank, Fright
G: Glance, Grass
H: Hinge, Hitch
I: Itch, Inched
J: Joust, Judge
K: Knack, Kneel
L: Lance, Laugh
M: Match, Mosque
N: Neigh, Notch
O: Once, Ought
P: Plant, Prank
Q: Queen, Quick
R: Ranch, Rough
S: Scratch, Strength
T: Trash, Twitch
U: Urged, Used
V: Valve, Vault
W: Would, Wreath
X: Xi
Y: Yearn, Youth
Z: Zests, Zilch

page 2: Making Connections

Spring, Tap, Mineral: Types of water
Twist, Jig, Salsa: Types of dances
Fall, Summer, Winter: Seasons

page 3: Group Therapy

Some Group Therapy questions have many possible correct answers. Your answers may differ from ours and still be correct.

1. All-Bran, Alpha-Bits, Apple Jacks, Cap'n Crunch, Cheerios, Chex (Corn, Rice, and/or Wheat), Cocoa Puffs, Corn Flakes, Corn Pops, Crispix, Fiber One, Froot Loops, Frosted Flakes, Frosted Mini-Wheats, Grape-Nuts, Honey Bunches of Oats, Life, Lucky Charms, Nut 'n Honey, Nutri-Grain, Puffed (Rice or Wheat), Quaker Oats, Raisin Bran, Rice Krispies, Shredded Wheat, Special K, Total, Trix, Wheaties

2. Banjo, Bass, Cello, Clavichord, Dulcimer, Fiddle, Guitar, Harp, Harpsichord, Lute, Lyre, Mandolin, Piano, Sitar, Ukulele, Viola, Violin, Zither

3. Advertisements, Clock, Comic books, Contracts, Directions, Essay, Gas/water meters, Instructions, Letters, Lips, Magazines, Manuals, Maps, Music, Newspapers, Poems, Signs, Subtitles, Thermometers, Wills

4. Camay, Dial, Dove, Irish Spring, Ivory, Lava, Lever 2000, Lifebuoy, Lux, Pears, Safeguard, Zest

5. *The $64,000 Question, Are You Smarter Than a 5th Grader?, Beat the Clock, Card Sharks, Cash Cab, College Bowl, Concentration, (The) Dating Game, Deal or No Deal, Family Feud, (The) Gong Show, (The) Hollywood Squares, I've Got a Secret, Jeopardy!, Let's Make a Deal, Match Game, (The) Mole, Name That Tune,*

(The) Newlywed Game, Password, Press Your Luck, (The) Price Is Right, Pyramid, To Tell the Truth, Truth or Consequences, Queen for a Day, The Weakest Link, What's My Line?, Wheel of Fortune, Who Wants to Be a Millionaire?, You Bet Your Life

6. Chad, Cuba, Fiji, Iran, Iraq, Laos, Mali, Oman, Peru, Togo

7. Baseball, Basketball, Billiards, Bowling, Cricket, Croquet, Golf, Ping pong, Polo, Pool, Racquetball, Rugby, Snooker, Soccer, Softball, Squash, Table tennis, Tennis, Volleyball, Water polo

page 3: Vivienne's Vowels
1. Porcupine
2. Cheetah
3. Buffalo
4. Barracuda
5. Cougar
6. Clam
7. Camel
8. Hyena
9. Alligator
10. Aardvark
11. Squid
12. Alpaca

page 4: Word Pictures
1. Carnation (CAR + nation)
2. Columbine (COLUMN + bine)
3. Marigold (Mari + GOLD)
4. Orchid (OAR + chid)
5. Peony (Peo + KNEE)
6. Pansy (PAN + sy)
7. Poppy (PAW + py)
8. Begonia (BEG + onia)

page 5: Ted's Terrible Titles
1. *The Odd Couple*
2. *Sleepless in Seattle*
3. *Mutiny on the Bounty*
4. *Truth or Consequences*
5. *Singin' in the Rain*
6. *Murder, She Wrote*
7. *The Agony and the Ecstasy*
8. *Jaws*
9. *Death of a Salesman*
10. *Barefoot in the Park*
11. *Breakfast at Tiffany's*
12. *Dead Man Walking*

page 5: Fill in the Letters
Other, more obscure correct answers are possible.
1. Jab, Jag, Jam, Jar, Jaw, Jay, Jet, Jib, Jig, Job, Jog, Jot, Joy, Jug, Jus, Jut
2. Ace, Act, Ice, Icy
3. Toe, Tog, Tom, Ton, Too, Top, Tot, Tow, Toy
4. Plan, Play, Plea, Pled, Plod, Plop, Plot, Plow, Ploy, Plug, Plum, Plus
5. Bomb, Comb, Dumb, Jamb, Lamb, Limb, Numb, Tomb, Womb
6. Boil, Coif, Coil, Coin, Foil, Join, Loin, Roil, Soil, Toil
7. Sawn, Scan, Seen, Sewn, Shin, Shun, Sign, Skin, Soon, Sown, Span, Spin, Spun, Stun, Swan

8. Damp, Deep, Drip, Drop, Dump

page 6: Sentence Sleuth
1. Denver
   (. . . forbi<u>dden ver</u>sion. . .)
2. Boston
   (. . . gum<u>bos to n</u>orthern. . .)
3. Juneau
   (. . . <u>June au</u>ction. . .)
4. Chicago
   (. . . <u>chic! A go</u>ld . . .)
5. Omaha
   (. . . <u>Mom, a ha</u>mster. . .)
6. Miami
   (. . . tsuna<u>mi, a mi</u>llion. . .)
7. Buffalo
   (. . . re<u>buff a lo</u>vely. . .)
8. Baltimore
   (. . . <u>Rob, Al, Tim, or Ed</u> . . .)

page 7: Double Trouble
1. Gold
2. Fruit
3. Power
4. Shoe
5. Clothes
6. Check
7. Bed
8. Sun
9. Night
10. Cold

page 8: Mamma Mia!
A. Lasagna
B. Penne
C. Ravioli
D. Farfalle (also Bow-tie)
E. Macaroni (also Elbow)
F. Gnocchi
G. Fettuccine
H. Spaghetti

I. Tortellini
J. Orzo (also Risoni)
K. Manicotti
L. Orecchiette

page 10: One-Minute Madness: Say Cheese

Other correct answers are possible.
American; Asiago; Blue; Brie; Camembert; Cheddar; Colby; Cream cheese; Edam; Emmentaler; Feta; Goat cheese; Gorgonzola; Gouda; Gruyere; Halloumi; Havarti; Manchego; Monterey Jack; Mozzarella; Muenster; Parmesan; Pecorino romano; Provolone; Queso blanco; Ricotta; Roquefort; Stilton; String; Swiss; Velveeta

page 10: It's Just GRAND

1. Grand Old Party
2. Grand Central Terminal
3. Grand Canyon
4. Grand piano
5. Grand Rapids
6. Grand slam
7. Grand finale
8. Grand Ole Opry
9. Grandma Moses
10. Grandiose

page 11: Alphabet Trivia

1. Austin, Texas
2. Houston Astros, Los Angeles Angels, Oakland Athletics
3. Alabama, Alaska, Arizona, Arkansas
4. Alberta
5. John Adams, John Quincy Adams, Chester Alan Arthur
6. Aquarius, Aries
7. Anchors
8. Apostrophe, Asterisk
9. Arthur Ashe or Andre Agassi
10. Jane Austen
11. Albany, Annapolis, Atlanta, Augusta, Austin
12. "A" acronyms:
   American Automobile Association
   Alcoholics Anonymous
   Automated teller machine
   American Civil Liberties Union
   Absent without leave
   As soon as possible
   Also known as
   America Online

page 12: Not Too TAXing

1. Taxi
2. Exact
3. Extra
4. Latex
5. Syntax
6. Anxiety
7. Extract
8. Laxative
9. Matchbox
10. Excavate
11. Exhausted
12. Juxtapose
13. Intoxicated
14. Relaxation

page 12: Scrambled Colors

1. Brown
2. Black
3. Amber
4. Beige
5. Lilac
6. Orange
7. Yellow
8. Purple
9. Violet
10. Crimson
11. Maroon
12. Lavender

page 13: Quotation Station
(see below)

page 14: Initial Quiz

1. Talcum powder
2. Tea Party
3. Teacher's pet
4. Tennis player (also Tennis pro)
5. Test pilot
6. Theme park
7. Trailer park
8. Thomas Paine
9. Totem poles
10. Term paper
11. *Twin Peaks*

---

page 13: Quotation Station

It is easier to build strong children than to repair broken men.
—Frederick Douglass

I	T		I	S		E	A	S	I	E	R		T	O		B	U	I	L	D
S	T	R	O	N	G		C	H	I	L	D	R	E	N		T	H	A	N	
T	O		R	E	P	A	I	R		B	R	O	K	E	N		M	E	N	

page 14: Trivia—Name Their Sport

1. Boxing
2. Basketball
3. Tennis
4. Swimming
5. Gymnastics
6. Golf
7. Auto racing
8. Track and field
9. Soccer
10. Speed skating

page 15: Word Parts

1. Hired (hi + red)
2. Format (for + mat)
3. Season (sea + son)
4. Sewage (sew + age)
5. Ballad (ball + ad)
6. Catcher (cat + Cher)
7. Alone (Al + one)
8. Badminton (bad + mint + on)
9. Bargain (bar + gain)
10. Brain (bra + in)
11. Capacity (cap + a + city)
12. Heathen (heat + hen)

page 16: Find the Words

(see pages 328–329)

page 18: The Top Top

1. A model model
2. A fair fair
3. A private private
4. A fall fall
5. A fast fast
6. A frank frank
7. A fine fine
8. An iron iron
9. A light light
10. A remote remote
11. A swift swift
12. A tart tart
13. Tender tender
14. A grand grand

page 18: Twiddle Your Thumbs

1. Where your mouth is
2. Lip
3. Nerves
4. At the hip
5. In your throat
6. In the knees
7. On the wrist
8. Heart/Ulcer
9. Hand
10. A sore thumb
11. In the teeth/head/butt
12. Arm of the law

page 19: Prime-Time Rhyme

1. Skit; wit; quit
2. Pitch; rich; itch
3. Hummer; drummer; summer
4. Simple; pimple; dimple
5. Carry; harry; marry
6. Funny; money; honey
7. Sack; snack; quack
8. Junk; spunk; bunk
9. Notion; ocean; lotion
10. Zinc; fink; rink
11. Bellow; yellow; Jell-O
12. Flee; brie; bee

page 19: Riddle Me This

A cold

page 20: Secret Word – MARDI GRAS

Note: Other, more obscure correct answers are possible.

4-Letter Words:

1. Agar
2. Aids
3. Aims
4. Airs
5. Amid
6. Aria
7. Arid
8. Arms
9. Dais
10. Dams
11. Digs
12. Dims
13. Drag
14. Dram
15. Gams
16. Gars
17. Gird
18. Grad
19. Gram
20. Grid
21. Grim
22. Magi
23. Mags
24. Maid
25. Mars
26. Rags
27. Raid
28. Rams
29. Rids
30. Rigs
31. Rims
32. Saga
33. Said
34. Sari

5-Letter Words:
1. Agism
2. Arias
3. Drags
4. Drama
5. Drams
6. Girds
7. Grads
8. Grams
9. Grids
10. Maids
11. **Radar (Secret Word)**
12. Raids

page 21: Complete the Words

	K	N	I	F	E			
		I	N	V	I	T	E	
B	L	I	Z	Z	A	R	D	
A	T	T	I	T	U	D	E	
	D	I	S	P	U	T	E	
			R	A	P	I	D	
	N	I	G	H	T			
		E	V	E	N	T		
		V	I	V	I	D		
			S	C	R	A	P	
	A	N	K	L	E			
B	I	O	P	S	Y			
	T	R	Y	S	T			
	F	L	O	U	R			
V	U	L	N	E	R	A	B	L	E
G	A	L	A	X	Y			
			B	L	A	C	K	
			E	B	O	N	Y	
		M	A	N	U	A	L	
B	A	R	B	E	Q	U	E	
			A	W	E	S	O	M	E
S	H	R	E	D	D	I	N	G
		P	A	J	A	M	A	S
		S	Q	U	A	S	H	
		S	U	M	M	E	R	
		D	I	N	G	Y		

page 22: Pump It Up!
1. Grumpy
2. Mumps
3. Pumpernickel
4. Triumph
5. Slump
6. Consumption
7. Trumpet
8. Plump
9. Frumpy
10. Rumplestiltskin
11. Humpback
12. Jumpsuit

page 22: Odd Man Out
1. *Finger* is the odd man out. All of the other answers are types of beans.
2. *Yellort* is the odd man out. It spells "trolley" backward. All the rest spell the name of car manufacturers backward (Ford, Honda, Volvo).
3. *Wilson* is the odd man out. All of the others are people whose first name is Paul.
4. *Marriott* is the odd man out. It is the only item in the list that is not the name of a salad.
5. *Pencil* is the odd man out. All of the others are types of cake.
6. *Platypus* is the odd man out. All of the other animals are extinct.
7. *Telegraph* is the odd man out. All the rest are typefaces (fonts).
8. *The Alamo* is the odd man out. It is located in Texas. All of the other places are located in California.

page 23: Semordnilap
1. Wed/Dew
2. Gem/Meg
3. Peek/Keep
4. Tips/Spit
5. Spoons/Snoops
6. Mad/Dam
7. Devil/Lived
8. Gulp/Plug
9. Pals/Slap
10. Peels/Sleep
11. Ward/Draw

page 23: Trivia—Fruits & Veggies
1. Beets
2. Cabbage and carrots
3. Grapes
4. Figs, Ginger root, Guava, Kiwi, Mango, Papaya, Pineapple

page 24: Wacky Wordies
1. Eggs over easy
2. Foreign language
3. Ten cents a dance
4. The proof is in the pudding
5. Small talk
6. A friend in need is a friend in deed
7. Banana split
8. Three-alarm fire

whale

wall

water

whisk

window

woman

writing

wires

woodp...

wastepaper basket

wheelchair

wedding dress

wrench

wig

wrist

waving

waitress

wax

watermelon

waffles

wine

wedge

weapon

windsock
walrus
wetsuit
wave
wharf
walker
wing
weiner
wallet
wolfman
watch
wood
web
worm
wreath
wink
waterfall
witch
whip
wizard
whiskers
istle

page 26: Vivienne's Vowels
1. Pepper
2. Peanut butter
3. Caesar salad
4. Beef tacos
5. Salmon
6. Cantaloupe
7. Boiled potato
8. Blue cheese
9. Root beer
10. Poached egg
11. Lasagna

page 27: Alphabet Trivia
1. Bahamas, Barbados, Belize, Bermuda, Bolivia, Brazil
2. Barney, Betty, Bamm-Bamm
3. Badminton, Basketball, Beach volleyball, Biathlon, Bobsledding (or Bobsleigh), Boxing
4. Bronx, Brooklyn
5. Baltic Avenue, Boardwalk, B & O Railroad
6. Boston, Baltimore
7. *Beowulf*
8. Balboa
9. James Buchanan, George H. W. Bush, George W. Bush
10. Bogie and Bacall (Humphrey Bogart and Lauren Bacall)
11. Bilbo Baggins
12. Acronyms:
    Bring your own booze (or bottle)
    Better Business Bureau
    Big Man on Campus
    Brigham Young University
    Bacon, lettuce, and tomato
    British Broadcasting Corp.

page 28: Alphabetically Speaking
1. John Adams (*John Quincy Adams is alphabetically second.*)
2. Africa
3. Earth
4. Clubs
5. Friday
6. Chico
7. Vermont
8. Aardvark
9. Bobby
10. Blue (*Black is not on the color spectrum because it is actually the absence of color.*)
11. Niña
12. Erie

page 29: Name Game
1. Caw + broke + tom (Tom Brokaw)
2. Press + hiss + elf + Lee (Elvis Presley)
3. Teas + sock + rat (Socrates)
4. Ball + eel + loose (Lucille Ball)
5. L + van + wink + rip (Rip Van Winkle)
6. Try + bar + sand + bras (Barbra Streisand)
7. Turkey + bus + ton (Buster Keaton)
8. Rosa + frank + felt + clean (Franklin Roosevelt)
9. Dean + hairy + who + knee (Harry Houdini)

page 30: Anagrams
1. Tap, Pat, Apt
2. Arm, Mar, Ram
3. Guts, Gust, Tugs
4. Opts, Post, Pots, Spot, Stop, Tops
5. Mean, Mane, Name, Amen
6. Meats, Mates, Steam, Tames, Teams
7. Voles, Loves, Solve
8. Serve, Verse, Veers, Sever

page 30: Trivia—On Your Mark
1. Mark Spitz
2. Mark Antony
3. Mark Harmon
4. Mark David Chapman

page 31: Triplets
1. Blood, sweat, and tears
2. Lock, stock, and barrel
3. Hop, skip, and a jump
4. The butcher, the baker, the candlestick maker
5. Life, liberty, and the pursuit of happiness
6. *Planes, Trains, and Automobiles*
7. Lather, rinse, repeat
8. Id, ego, and superego
9. Eat, drink, and be merry
10. Cool, calm, and collected
11. Healthy, wealthy, and wise
12. Here, there, and everywhere
13. Hook, line, and sinker
14. Rock, paper, scissors

page 31: What's the Nationality?

1. Swiss
2. Russian
3. Roman
4. Hungarian
5. German
6. English
7. Cuban
8. Canadian
9. Belgian
10. Viennese
11. Mexican
12. Irish
13. Danish (French Pastry is also correct.)
14. Chinese

page 32: Riddle Me This

Envelope (While words such as *eve* and *ewe* are technically correct, they wouldn't make much of a riddle!)

page 32: Word Tower

These answers are just a suggestion; many other correct answers are possible:

1. Me
2. Met
3. Menu
4. Media
5. Member
6. Mermaid
7. Medicine
8. Messenger
9. Medication
10. Metabolized
11. Metropolitan
12. Meteorologist

page 33: Making Connections

Snare, Bass, Kettle: Types of drums
Capri, Staten, Ireland: Islands
Bridge, Spades, Hearts: Card games

page 34: Sharp as a Tack

1. American as apple pie
2. Clean as a whistle
3. Cool as a cucumber
4. Dead as a doornail
5. Dull as dishwater
6. Fit as a fiddle
7. Fresh as a daisy
8. Guilty as sin
9. Hard as a rock
10. High as a kite
11. Pretty as a picture
12. Right as rain

page 34: Group Therapy

Some Group Therapy questions have many possible correct answers. Your answers may differ from ours and still be correct.

1. Kirstie Alley, Marlon Brando, John Candy, Chris Christie, Winston Churchill, Aretha Franklin, Jackie Gleason, John Goodman, Oliver Hardy, Henry VIII, Mike Huckabee, Kevin James, Rush Limbaugh, Rosie O'Donnell, Luciano Pavrotti, Elvis Presley (in later life), Al Roker (in the past), Roseanne (Barr), US President William Howard Taft, Elizabeth Taylor (in later life), Orson Welles, Oprah Winfrey (sometimes)

2. Barbecue sauce, Capers, Chili sauce, Chutney, Cocktail sauce, Horseradish, Hot sauce, Ketchup, Mayonnaise, Mustard, Piccalilli, Relish, Salad dressings, Salsa, Soy sauce, Steak sauce, Teriyaki sauce, Vinegars, Worcestershire sauce

3. Jim Belushi, James Brown, Jimmy Buffett, James Caan, James Cagney, James Cameron, Jim Carrey, Jimmy Carter, James Carville, James Fenimore Cooper, James Darren, James Dean, Jimmy Durante, Jimmy Hoffa, James Earl Jones, James Joyce, Jim Lehrer, James Mason, Jim Morrison, Jim Nabors, James Earl Ray, James Stewart, Jimmy Swaggart, James Taylor

4. Aberdeen (Scotland), Abu Dhabi (United Arab Emirates), Acapulco (Mexico), Addis Ababa (Ethiopia), Adelaide (Australia), Afghanistan, Albania, Algeria, Amsterdam (The Netherlands), Andorra, Angola, Ankara (Turkey), Argentina, Armenia, Aruba, Athens (Greece),

Australia, Austria, Azerbaijan
5. Apples, Asparagus, Avocados, Beans, Boston Celtics uniforms, Broccoli, Brussels sprouts, Celery, Collard greens, Cucumbers, Emeralds, Envy, Frogs, Granny Smith apples, Grapes, Grass, Green beans, Green jade, Green tea, Jolly Green Giant, Honeydew melon, Kermit the Frog, Leaves, Lettuce, Limes, Mint, Moss, Olives, Peas, Pepper, Pesto, Pickles, Pine trees, Pistachio ice cream, Shamrocks, Spinach, The Green Hornet, The Hulk, Trees, US money, Zucchini
6. Acorn, Almond, Beechnut, Brazil nut, Cashew, Chestnut, Coconut, Filbert, Hazelnut, Hickory nut, Kola/Cola nut, Macadamia, Peanut, Pecan, Pine nut, Pistachio, Walnut, Water chestnut
7. Apples to Apples, Backgammon, Balderdash, Boggle, Candyland, Checkers, Chess, Chutes and Ladders, Chinese Checkers, Clue, Cranium, Cribbage, The Game of Life, Jenga, Mah Jongg, Mancala, Mastermind, Monopoly, Operation, Othello, Parcheesi, Pictionary, Risk, Scattergories, Scrabble,

Sorry!, Stratego, Taboo, Tri-Ominoes, Trivial Pursuit, Yahtzee
8. Caleb, Calvin, Cameron, Campbell, Carl, Carlos, Carlton, Carmine, Carter, Casey, Casper, Cedric, Chandler, Charles, Chase, Chester, Christian, Christopher, Clarence, Clark, Clay, Clyde, Colin, Conan, Craig, Cyrus

page 35: Finish the Proverb
1. A fool and his money are soon parted.
2. A picture is worth a thousand words.
3. An army marches on its stomach.
4. The apple never falls far from the tree.
5. The end justifies the means.
6. The grass is always greener on the other fellow's side (*or* in the other fellow's yard).
7. The pen is mightier than the sword.
8. The squeaky wheel gets the grease.
9. Money doesn't grow on trees. (*Money doesn't buy happiness* is also correct.)
10. Make hay while the sun shines.
11. Laughter is the best medicine.
12. Good things come to those who wait.
13. God helps those who help themselves.

page 36: Double Trouble
1. Pan
2. Bag
3. Bar
4. Card
5. House
6. Man
7. Mouth
8. Ball
9. Tooth
10. Cane

page 37: Alphabet Trivia
1. California, Colorado, Connecticut
2. Carson City, NV; Charleston, WV; Cheyenne, WY; Columbia, SC; Columbus, OH; Concord, NH
3. Jimmy Carter, Grover Cleveland, Bill Clinton, Calvin Coolidge
4. Columbia University, Cornell University
5. Cut, Clarity, Color, Carat weight
6. Cambodia, Cameroon, Canada, Cape Verde, Central African Republic, Chad, Chile, China, Colombia, Comoros, Costa Rica, Côte d'Ivoire, Croatia, Cuba, Curaçao, Cyprus, Czech Republic, Democratic Republic of the Congo, and Republic of the Congo

7. Capital cities:
   a. Cairo
   b. Canberra
   c. Caracas
   d. Copenhagen
8. Cancer, Capricorn
9. Catcher, Centerfield
10. Carrots, Celery
11. Movies that begin with the letter C:
    a. *Camelot*
    b. *Casablanca*
    c. *Cabaret*
    d. *Carousel*
12. Acronyms/Abbreviations:
    Curriculum vitae
    Cable News Network
    Central Standard Time
    Chief executive officer
    Centers for Disease Control
    Certified public accountant
    Cardiopulmonary resuscitation
    Central Intelligence Agency (or Culinary Institute of America)

page 38: **Two . . .**
1. To tango
2. Punch (*Three* and *Buckle My Shoe* are also correct answers.)
3. Are better than one
4. Men
5. Garage
6. Worth
7. The story (*The same coin* is also correct.)

8. Of a lamb's tail
9. This (or That) game
10. Suit (or Bathing suit)
11. Price of one (*Show* and *Road* are also correct answers.)
12. Bottle

page 38: **Three . . .**
1. *In the Fountain*
2. Hens
3. *The Condor*
4. To the wind
5. *Of Eve*
6. Island
7. *And a Baby*
8. *Match*
9. *Opera*
10. Salad
11. Turn
12. Monte
13. Sloth
14. Plug
15. Stadium
16. Night

page 39: **Initial Quiz**
1. Razor Blade
2. Richard Burton
3. Root Beer
4. *Raging Bull*
5. Raisin Bran
6. Reference Book
7. Rose Bowl
8. Reset Button
9. Roger Bannister
10. Robert Burns
11. Refried Beans
12. Ray Bradbury
13. Robber Barons

page 40: **Word Rebus**
1. Strawberry (Straw + Bear + E)
2. Tomatoes (Toe + May + Toes)
3. Emergency (E + Merge + N + C)
4. Dinosaur (Die + Nose + Oar)
5. Delivery (D + Liver + E)
6. University (U + Knee + Fur + City)
7. Incubate (Ink + Cube + Eight)
8. Pillowcase (Pill + Yolk – Y + Ace)

CHAPTER TWO

page 42: **Heteronyms**
1. Resume (Re ZOOM/RES oo may)
2. Desert (de ZERT/DEZ ert)
3. Bow (BOH/BAO)
4. Close (CLOSE/CLOZE)
5. Complex (com PLEX/ COM plex)
6. Conduct (CON duct/con DUCT)
7. Contract (CON tract/con TRACT)
8. Dove (DOHV/DUHV)
9. Produce (PRO duce/pro DUCE)
10. Refuse (re FUSE/REF use)

page 43: **Common Bonds**
Rock song title: Shake, Rattle, and Roll

page 43: Trivia—Magazine Matters

1. *Time*
2. *People*
3. *Bon Appetit*
4. Gloria Steinem
5. *Rolling Stone*

page 44: Quotation Station

(see below)

page 45: What a Pair

1. Blood and Gore
2. Bob and Weave
3. Bread and Circus
4. Death and Taxes
5. Down and Dirty
6. Free and Clear
7. Pickles and Ice cream
8. Sick and Tired
9. Skin and Bones
10. Search and Rescue
11. Short and Sweet

page 46: Vivienne's Vowels

1. Barack Obama
2. Woody Allen
3. Orson Welles
4. John Lennon
5. Louis Pasteur
6. Lucille Ball
7. Joe DiMaggio
8. Buddha
9. Napoleon
10. Babe Ruth

11. Conan O'Brien
12. Joan Baez

page 46: Endings & Beginnings

1. Golf
2. Stamp
3. Dance
4. Sand
5. Key
6. Jump
7. Bee
8. Window
9. Paper
10. Neck

page 47: Run the Alphabet—Human Anatomy

Other correct answers are possible.

A: Appendix, Aorta
B: Bladder, Brain
C: Cartilage, Clavicle
D: Dermis, Diaphragm
E: Eyes, Elbow
F: Foot, Fibula
G: Gallbladder, Gums
H: Heart, Hand
I: Intestines, Iris
J: Jugular, Jaw
K: Kidney, Knee
L: Liver, Lungs
M: Mouth, Muscles
N: Nose, Nerves
O: Ovaries, Optic nerve
P: Pancreas, Prostate

Q: Quadriceps
R: Ribs, Retina
S: Spine, Stomach
T: Teeth, Tonsils
U: Uvula, Urinary tract
V: Vertebrae, Veins
W: Windpipe, Wrist
X:
Y:
Z:

page 48: Alma's Shopping List

1. Basil
2. Jelly
3. Cookies
4. Lemons
5. Pot Roast
6. Hot Dog
7. Kale
8. Salmon
9. Pickles
10. Tuna Fish
11. Dental Floss
12. Paper Towels

page 48: Looking for LOVE

1. Olive
2. Solve
3. Vowel
4. Novel (Hovel)
5. Evolve
6. Loaves
7. Grovel (Shovel)
8. Revolt
9. Develop
10. Violent (Violets)
11. Novelty
12. Elevator
13. Loveseat (Lovesick, Lovelorn, Loveless, Lovebird)
14. Boulevard

page 44: Quotation Station

I ask not for a lighter burden, but for broader shoulders.
—Jewish proverb

15. Marvelous
16. Voicemail

page 49: Sentence Sleuth
1. Rose (...he<u>ro seldom</u>...)
2. Snapdragon
   (...baby's <u>nap drag on</u>
   ...)
3. Lily (...<u>Lil, your</u>...)
4. Tulip (...<u>tutu, lipstick</u>...)
5. Iris (...<u>I risked</u>...)
6. Gardenia
   (...<u>garden, I always</u>...)
7. Aster (...<u>as terrifying</u>...)
8. Carnation
   (...vi<u>car, "national</u>...)

page 50: Word Pictures
1. Handshake (Hand + Shake)
2. Eggplant (Egg + Plant)
3. Clothespin (Clothes + Pin)
4. Pineapple (Pine + Apple)
5. Plate Glass (Plate + Glass)
6. Salt Water (Salt + Water)
7. Shortstop (Shorts + Stop)
8. Flag ship (Flag + Ship)

page 52: One-Minute Madness: Two-Letter Words
1. am
2. an
3. as
4. at
5. be
6. by
7. do
8. go
9. he
10. if
11. in
12. is
13. it
14. me
15. my
16. no
17. of
18. on
19. or
20. so
21. to
22. up
23. us
24. we

page 52: HOUSE Work
1. Glass houses
2. White House
3. Greenhouse/Hothouse
4. *This Old House*
5. *House of the Seven Gables*
6. Speaker of the House
7. *Little House on the Prairie*
8. In the doghouse
9. Coffee house
10. House of cards
11. Porterhouse
12. *Lighthouse*

page 53: Alphabet Trivia
1. Delaware
2. Denver, CO; Des Moines, IA; Dover, DE
3. Denmark
4. Dallas
5. Dancer, Dasher, Donner (*or* Donder)
6. Dachshund, Dalmatian, Doberman pinscher, and Dandie Dinmont
7. Authors:
   a. Charles Dickens
   b. Fyodor Dostoevsky
   c. Arthur Conan Doyle
8. Danube
9. Famous people with the initials DD:
   a. Doris Day
   b. Danny DeVito
   c. Don Drysdale
   d. David Duchovny
10. Acronyms and abbreviations:
   a. Date of birth
   b. Doing business as
   c. Do-it-yourself
   d. Deoxyribonucleic acid
   e. Designated hitter
   f Driving under the influence

page 54: Drop a Letter and Scramble
1. Race
2. Meat
3. Rash
4. Bard
5. Star
6. Safe
7. Tale
8. East
9. Thaw
10. Palm
11. Bare
12. Diner
13. Hasty
14. Statue

page 54: Change a Letter
1. C—Cell, Cable, Camper
2. J—Jail, Jingle, Jacket
3. R—Rookie, Reach, Rhyme
4. G—Gnarled, Glue, Germs
5. S—Slight, Sense, Soot
6. Q—Quest, Quite, Quilt

7. T—Timed, Touch, Twine
8. G—Grate, Golf, Goal
9. D—Deaf, Drain, Drafty
10. W—Wasp, Wraps, Whopper

page 55: **Signature Songs**
1. Dean Martin
2. Tammy Wynette
3. Sonny & Cher
4. Bob Hope
5. Frank Sinatra
6. The Rolling Stones
7. Judy Garland
8. Tony Bennett
9. Barbra Streisand
10. Tom Jones
11. Woody Guthrie
12. Louis Armstrong
13. Loretta Lynn
14. Tiny Tim

page 56: **Rivals**
1. Mac (Macintosh)
2. The Jets
3. Abel
4. Chevrolet
5. The Yankees
6. Mr. Hyde
7. The McCoys
8. McDonald's
9. The Joker (*Other correct answers, such as The Penguin, are possible.*)
10. Muhammad Ali
11. Richard Nixon
12. Peter Pan (*The crocodile is also correct.*)

page 56: **Riddle Me This**
The letter E

page 57: **Follow the Rules**
(see below)

page 58: **WhoopEE!**
1. Flee
2. Chimpanzee
3. Frisbee
4. Disagree
5. Bungee
6. Filigree
7. Manatee
8. Sightsee
9. Committee
10. Decree
11. Dungaree
12. Pedigree

page 59: **Alphabetically Speaking**
1. Executive
2. East
3. Dewey
4. Alabama
5. Zucchini
6. Bashful
7. Aaron (Hank)
8. Christmas
9. Aquarius
10. Navy
11. Argentina
12. Venus

page 60: **A Penny for Your Thoughts**
1. A day late and a dollar short.
2. All that glitters is not gold.
3. Penny wise and pound foolish.
4. Worth its weight in gold.
5. You get what you pay for.
6. From rags to riches.
7. You bet your bottom dollar.
8. Don't take any wooden nickels.
9. A dime a dozen.
10. It's not worth a red cent. (*It's not worth a plug nickel is also correct.*)
11. One man's trash is another man's treasure.
12. Two sides of the same coin.
13. You pays your money and you takes your chances.

page 57: **Follow the Rules**
1. B I G G I R L S N E E D
2. B I G G I R L S N E E D **D**
3. B I G G I **A** L S N E E D D
4. B I G G I A **M** L S N E E D D
5. B I G G I A M L S **O** N E E D D
6. B I G **D** I A M L S O N E E D **G**
7. B I G D I A M L __ O N E E D G **S**
8. B I G D I A M __ O N __ __ D __ **S**

(Big girls need) BIG DIAMONDS

1. Offend (off + end)
2. Earnest (ear + nest)
3. Marshall (Mars + hall)
4. Topaz (top + AZ)
5. Cooking (coo + king)
6. Cabinet (cab + I + net)
7. Pageant (page + ant)
8. Announce (Ann + ounce)
9. Banking (ban + king)
10. Betray (bet + ray)
11. Candidate (can + did + ate)
12. Forbidden (for + bid + den)

page 62: Secret Word – BASEBALL GAME

Note: Other, more obscure correct answers are possible.

4-Letter Words:

1. Able
2. Ages
3. Alas
4. Ales
5. Alga
6. Alms
7. Asea
8. Babe
9. Bags
10. Bale
11. Ball
12. Balm
13. Base
14. Beam
15. Bees
16. Begs
17. Bell
18. Blab
19. Blam
20. Ease

21. Ebbs
22. Eels
23. Ells
24. Elms
25. Else
26. Gabs
27. Gala
28. Gale
29. Gall
30. Gals
31. Gams
32. Gels
33. Gems
34. Glee
35. Labs
36. Lags
37. Lamb
38. Lame
39. Legs
40. Male
41. Mall
42. Meal
43. Sage
44. Sale
45. Same
46. Seal
47. Seam
48. Seem
49. Sell
50. Slab
51. Slag
52. Slam

5-Letter Words:

1. Abase
2. Algae
3. Amble
4. Babes
5. Bagel
6. Bales
7. Balls
8. Balms

9. Balsa
10. Beams
11. Belle
12. Bells
13. Blabs
14. Blame
15. Blams
16. Blasé
17. Eagle
18. Easel
19. Gable
20. Galas
21. Gales
22. Games
23. Gleam
24. Label
25. Lambs
26. Lames
27. Lease
28. Legal
29. **Llama (Secret Word)**
30. Males
31. Malls
32. Meals
33. Sable
34. Samba
35. Small
36. Smell

page 63: How Much Is . . .?

1. 1009 (1000 + 9)
2. 48 (12 + 36)
3. 16 (8 + 8)
4. 623 (212 + 411)
5. 5 (3 + 2)
6. 31 (8 + 23)
7. 18 (16 + 2)
8. 224 (200 + 24)
9. 19 (9 + 10)
10. 3 (2 + 1 + 0)

1. Eat, Bud, Fig, Sit
2. Mouse, Turkey, Robin, Shark
3. January, Identical, Utopia, Alabama
4. Brazil, Peru, Chile
5. Extra, Jinx, Maximum, Mexico
6. Ford, Lincoln, Hoover, Monroe
7. Atlantic
8. Coors, Miller, Heineken, Molson
9. Orange

QUOTATION:
Thanksgiving is first thanks, then giving.

page 64: **Trivia— Musical Anatomy**
1. In His hands
2. Cheek to cheek
3. Shoulders
4. Your face

page 65: **Group Therapy**
Some Group Therapy questions have many possible correct answers. Your answers may differ from ours and still be correct.
1. Aer Lingus, Air Canada, Air France, Alaska Airlines, American Airlines, British Airways, Delta Airlines, JetBlue, Lufthansa, Northwest Air, Qantas, Southwest Airlines, Swissair, TWA, United Airlines, USAirways, Virgin

2. Jacqueline/Jackie, Jade, Jane, Janet, Janice, Jean/ Jeanne, Jessica, Jill, Joan, Joann/Joanne, Josephine, Joyce, Judith/Judy, Julia, Julie, June

3. Angel food cake, Blue cheese dressing, Bread, Cannellini beans, Cauliflower, Cheese (various types), Cream (whipping cream, sour cream, cream cheese, etc.), Fish/Shellfish, Flour, Marshmallows, Mayonnaise, Milk, Mushrooms, Onions, Potatoes, Rice, Salt, Sugar, Vanilla ice cream, White asparagus, White wine, Yogurt

4. Barbershop, Bellhop, Bishop, Chop, Clop, Coop, Cop, Crop, Develop, Droop, Drop, Eavesdrop, Flop, Gallop, Gumdrop, Hoop, Hop, Lollipop, Loop, Mop, Pawnshop, Plop, Pop, Prop, Raindrop, Scallop, Scoop, Shop, Shortstop, Slop, Snoop, Stop, Swoop, Top, Troop, Wallop

5. Alberta, British Columbia, Manitoba, New Brunswick, Newfoundland and Labrador, Northwest Territories, Nova Scotia, Nunavut (Territory), Ontario, Prince Edward Island, Quebec, Saskatchewan, Yukon Territory

6. George H. W. Bush, Jimmy Carter, Bill Clinton, Calvin Coolidge, Dwight D. Eisenhower, Gerald Ford, Warren G. Harding, Herbert Hoover, Lyndon B. Johnson, John F. Kennedy, William McKinley, Richard Nixon, Ronald Reagan, Franklin D. Roosevelt, Theodore Roosevelt, William Howard Taft, Harry S. Truman, Woodrow Wilson

7. Butter, Candle, Cheese, Chocolate, Fat, Glaciers, Ice cream, Ice cubes, Metal, Plastic, Popsicles, Snow, Soap, Wax, (The) Wicked Witch of the West

8. Airplane, Ambulance, Bicycle, Bus, Car, Desk chair, Golf cart, Hospital bed, Motorcycle, Roller coaster, Roller skates, Shopping cart, Skateboard, Stroller/ Baby carriage, Train, Truck, Vacuum cleaner, Van, Wagon, Wheelchair, Wheelbarrow

page 65: **Ted's Terrible Titles**
1. *Drugstore Cowboy*
2. *Rain Man*
3. *Torn Curtain*
4. *A Farewell to Arms*
5. *A Raisin in the Sun*
6. *Fear and Loathing in Las Vegas*

7. "Lucy in the Sky with Diamonds"
8. *The Old Man and the Sea*
9. *The Scarlet Letter*
10. *The Sopranos*
11. *Uncle Tom's Cabin*
12. "Thanks for the Memory"

page 66: Vivienne's Vowels
1. Istanbul
2. Panama
3. Spain
4. Rome
5. Toronto
6. Annapolis
7. Paris
8. Athens
9. Missouri
10. Cape Cod
11. Honolulu
12. Colorado
13. Albuquerque

page 66: Common Bonds
Red _____:
Carpet, Tape, Sox

page 67: Alphabet Trivia
1. Earth
2. Ecuador, Egypt, El Salvador, Equatorial Guinea, Eritrea, Estonia, Ethiopia
3. Envy
4. Eagle, Echidna, Eel, Egret, Elephant, Elk, Emu
5. Edmonton (in Alberta)
6. Ecclesiastes, Ephesians, Esther, Exodus, Ezekiel, Ezra,
7. Elaine
8. Emerald

9. Eisenhower
10. People whose last names begin with the letter E:
    a. Amelia Earhart
    b. Wyatt Earp
    c. George Eastman
    d. Roger Ebert
    e. Mary Baker Eddy
    f. Everly Brothers (Don and Phil)
11. Acronyms/Abbreviations: Electrocardiogram (from the German, *elektrokardiogramm*)
    Eastern Standard Time
    Emergency medical technician
    Environmental Protection Agency
    Extrasensory perception (*Other correct answers are possible.*)
    European Union

page 68: Memorable TV Lines
1. *The Jack Benny Program*; Jack Benny
2. *Seinfeld*; The Soup Nazi
3. *The Honeymooners*; Ralph
4. *Lost in Space*; Robot
5. *The Tonight Show*; Ed McMahon
6. *Friends*; Joey
7. *CBS Nightly News*; Walter Cronkite
8. *The Price Is Right*; Announcer (Johnny Olson)
9. *Star Trek*; Dr. McCoy
10. *Rowan & Martin's Laugh-In*; Everyone, including President Nixon.

(*The phrase "sock it to me" was taken from popular 1960s song "Respect" by Aretha Franklin.*)
11. *All in the Family*; Archie Bunker
12. *The Waltons*; The Walton family

page 68: Trivia— Batter Up!
1. A perfect game
2. Turner Field (Atlanta) (*because it is owned by Ted Turner*)
3. A full count is when the player at bat has accrued three balls and two strikes.
4. Earned run average (*The ERA, which defines a pitcher's effectiveness, is obtained by calculating the average number of runs scored against him per full game.*)
5. It allows teams to have one player to bat in place of the pitcher.

page 69: Honorific Titles
1. Miss Piggy
2. Dr. Dolittle
3. Dr. Who
4. Aunt Jemima/ Mrs. Butterworth
5. Dr. Watson
6. Mr. Clean
7. Uncle Ben
8. Mr. Spock
9. Uncle Sam
10. Little Miss Muffet

Other, more obscure correct answers are possible.
1. Bay, Cay, Day, Fay, Gay, Hay, Jay, Lay, May, Nay, Pay, Ray, Say, Way, Yay
2. Ace, Ade, Age, Ale, Ape, Are, Ate, Awe, Axe, Aye
3. Bun, Dun, Fun, Gun, Nun, Pun, Run, Sun
4. Stab, Stag, Star, Stat, Stay, Stem, Step, Stet, Stew, Stir, Stop, Stow, Stub, Stud, Stun
5. Pram, Pray, Prep, Prey, Prig, Prim, Prod, Prof, Prom, Prop, Pros, Prow
6. Arch, Each, Etch, Inch, Itch, Loch, Much, Ouch, Rich, Such, Tech
7. Bibs, Bide, Bids, Bike, Bile, Bilk, Bill, Bind, Bios, Bird, Bite, Bits
8. Peep, Perp, Pimp, Plop, Pomp, Poop, Prep, Prop, Pulp, Pump

page 70: **Making Connections**
Pierogi, Kreplach, Shumai: Dumplings
Clog, Loafer, Pump: Types of shoes
Toast, Fries, Kiss: French _____

page 71: **One-Minute Madness: Water Words**
Other, more obscure correct answers are possible. Aqueduct, Basin, Bay, Bight, Brook, Canal, Channel, Cove, Creek, Delta, Estuary, Falls (Waterfall), Firth, Fjord, Geyser, Gulf, Lagoon, Lake, Loch, Ocean, Pond, Pool, Puddle, Reservoir, River, Sea, Sound, Spring, Strait, Stream, Swamp, Tributary, Well, Wetland

page 72: **Beware of the Dog**
A. Chihuahua
B. Bulldog (English)
C. Basset hound
D. Irish setter
E. Bloodhound
F. Pug
G. Pomeranian
H. Boxer
I. Cocker spaniel
J. Rottweiler
K. Great Dane
L. Malamute (Alaskan)

page 74: **Trimble**
1. Hummingbird
2. Shark
3. Koala
4. Gorilla
5. Dolphin
6. Manatee
Jumble Answer: Caribou

page 75: **Nicknames**
1. Automobile
2. Frank Sinatra
3. New York City
4. Chicken soup
5. Joe Namath
6. Japan
7. Missouri
8. Denver
9. Rome
10. A pair of ones (dice roll)
11. Montana

page 75: **Vivienne's Vowels**
1. *War and Peace*
2. "Hey Jude"
3. *St. Elsewhere*
4. *The Office*
5. *Taxi*
6. *Dracula*
7. *Cheers*
8. *The Wire*
9. *Seinfeld*
10. *Zorro*
11. *The Da Vinci Code*
12. "Let It Be"
13. *Face the Nation*

page 76: **Anagrams**
1. Posh, Hops, Shop
2. Awls, Slaw, Laws
3. Scat, Acts, Cats, Cast
4. Deus, Dues, Sued, Used
5. Fares, Fears, Safer
6. Tarps, Parts, Strap, Traps
7. Coats, Ascot, Coast, Tacos
8. Poser, Pores, Prose, Ropes, Spore

page 76: Riddle Me This
Edam

page 76: Riddle Me This
Your heart

page 77: Word Tower
These answers are just a
suggestion; many other correct
answers are possible:
1. Pa
2. Pad
3. Park
4. Patio
5. Papaya
6. Pajamas
7. Pamphlet
8. Pantyhose
9. Paintbrush
10. Pawnbrokers
11. Particularly
12. Participation
13. Pasteurization
14. Parenthetically

page 78: Word Pictures
1. Elbow (L + Bow)
2. Escape (S + Cape)
3. Empty (M + Tea)
4. Belief (B + Leaf)
5. Tidy (Tie + D)
6. Endive (N + Dive)
7. Copy (Cop + E)
8. Explain (X + Plane)

page 79: Alphabet Trivia
1. Florida
2. Frankfort, Kentucky
3. Fiji, Finland, France
4. Fava bean, Fennel, Fig
5. Millard Fillmore, Gerald
   Ford

6. Falcon, Ferret, Finch,
   Fisher, Flamingo,
   Flounder, Fox, Frog
   (*Other correct answers are
   possible.*)
7. Farrah Fawcett
8. F. Scott Fitzgerald
9. Mia Farrow
10. William Faulkner
11. Sally Field
12. Ian Fleming
13. Robert Frost
14. Acronyms/Initials:
    Frequently asked
       questions
    Federal Bureau of
       Investigation
    Food and Drug
       Administration
    Federal Deposit Insurance
       Corporation
    Franklin Delano Roosevelt
    Federal Emergency
       Management Agency
    Frequency modulation
    For your information

page 80: Scrambled Sports
1. Tennis
2. Hockey
3. Boxing
4. Squash
5. Diving
6. Skiing
7. Bowling
8. Surfing
9. Archery
10. Baseball
11. Swimming
12. Wrestling

page 80: Initial Quiz
1. *Hogan's Heroes*
2. Happy Hour
3. Hula Hoop
4. Head Hunter
5. Hilton Head
6. Hobby Horse
7. His Holiness
8. Helen Hayes
9. Ham Hock
10. Hot-Headed
11. Hip Huggers
12. Henry Hudson
    (*Interesting Fact: Hudson's
    crew mutinied in 1611.
    He was set adrift with his
    son and a handful of crew
    members in Hudson Bay
    and was never heard from
    again.*)

page 81: Prime-Time Rhyme
1. Caesar; tweezer; Ebenezer
2. Lobe; *Globe*; Job
3. Lynx; jinx; sphinx
4. Kelp; yelp; help
5. Crawl; squall; brawl
6. Prawn; yawn; fawn
7. Hacker; slacker; cracker
8. Chisel; drizzle; swizzle
9. Tibet; baguette; brunette
10. Choice; Joyce; voice

**page 81: Trivia—Dandy
Candy**
1. Mr. Goodbar
2. Sugar Daddy
3. Hershey's Bar
4. Good & Plenty
5. Almond Joy and Mounds

page 82: **Quotation Station**

The trouble with the rat race is that even if you win you're still a rat.

—Lily Tomlin

page 83: **One-Minute Madness: Islands**

Other correct answers are possible:

1. Aruba
2. Baffin
3. Bahamas
4. Barbados
5. Bora Bora
6. Borneo
7. Corsica
8. Crete
9. Cuba
10. Cyprus
11. Ellesmere
12. Fiji
13. Formosa
14. Galapagos
15. Great Britain
16. Greenland
17. Grenada
18. Guam
19. Hatteras
20. Hawaii
21. Hispaniola
22. Hokkaido
23. Honshu
24. Iceland
25. Indonesia
26. Ireland
27. Jamaica
28. Japan
29. Java
30. Key West
31. Kodiak, Alaska
32. Long Island, NY
33. Mackinac
34. Madagascar
35. Malaysia
36. Manhattan, NY
37. Martha's Vineyard, MA
38. Mykonos
39. Nantucket, MA
40. New Guinea
41. New Zealand
42. Okinawa
43. Papua New Guinea
44. Philippines
45. Puerto Rico
46. Roanoke
47. Sanibel
48. Sardinia
49. Sicily
50. Sri Lanka
51. Sumatra
52. Trinidad and Tobago
53. Victoria
54. Virgin Islands

page 84: **Common Bonds**

Types of lettuce: Boston, Bibb, Iceberg

page 84: **Raise the BAR**

1. Barracks
2. Baritone
3. Barker
4. Barter
5. Barrymore (Drew)
6. Bartenders
7. Barometer
8. Barber
9. Barley
10. Barracuda
11. Barrister
12. Barnacle

CHAPTER 3

page 85: **Fictional Occupations**

1. Television news reporter (*Murphy Brown*)
2. Physician (*Doogie Howser, M.D.*)
3. Psychiatrist/Radio therapist (*Frasier*)
4. Factory worker (and, later, a bar owner) (*All in the Family*)
5. Dry cleaner (*The Jeffersons*)
6. Paleontologist/College professor (*Friends*)
7. Waitress/Barmaid (*Cheers*)
8. Actress (*Gilligan's Island*)
9. Actor (*Friends*)
10. Interior designer (*Will & Grace*)
11. Policeman (*Everybody Loves Raymond*)
12. Newspaper columnist (*Sex and the City*)
13. Chemistry teacher/Drug lord (*Breaking Bad*)

page 86: **Sentence Sleuth**

1. Carrot
   (. . . told O<u>scar, "rot</u>ate. . .)

2. Radish
   (. . . B<u>rad, I sh</u>elved. . .)
3. Tomato
   (. . . Give it <u>to Ma to</u> fix.)
4. Artichoke
   (. . . sm<u>art, I choke</u>d on. . .)
5. Lentil (. . . husband,
   G<u>len, t</u>iled the kitchen. . .)
6. Spinach
   (. . . Walters<u>, "pin a che</u>ck
   to. . .)
7. Potato
   (. . .tea<u>pot, a to</u>aster, and. . .)
8. Onion
   (. . . admiss<u>ion. I onl</u>y. . .)
9. Kale ("Break <u>a le</u>g")
10. Endive
    (. . .the <u>end, I'v</u>e already. . .)

page 87: **Last Name Please**
1. *Longstocking*
2. *Citizen Kane/*
   Citizen Ruth
3. *Cyrano de Bergerac*
4. *Madame Bovary/*
   Madame X
5. *Moll Flanders*
6. *Mrs. Dalloway*
7. *Johnny Tremain/*
   Johnny Guitar
8. *Silas Marner*
9. *Nicholas Nickleby*
10. *The Brothers Karamazov*
11. *The Secret Life of Walter*
    Mitty
12. *The Prime of Miss Jean*
    Brodie
13. *One Day in the Life of*
    Ivan Denisovich
14. *McCabe and Mrs. Miller*
15. *Who's Afraid of Virginia*
    Woolf?

page 87: **Group Therapy**
Some Group Therapy
questions have many possible
correct answers. Your answers
may differ from ours and still
be correct.
1. Argentina, Bolivia, Brazil,
   Chile, Colombia, Ecuador,
   French Guyana, Guyana,
   Paraguay, Peru, Suriname,
   Uruguay, Venezuela
2. Blackjack, Bridge,
   Canasta, Crazy Eights,
   Cribbage, Euchre, Gin, Go
   Fish, Hearts, Old Maid,
   Pinochle, Poker, Rummy,
   Solitaire, Spades, War,
   Whist
3. Apricots, Avocados,
   Cherries, Dates, Mangoes,
   Nectarines, Olives,
   Peaches, Plums
4. Sacramento, San
   Bernardino, San
   Clemente, San Diego, San
   Francisco, San Jose, San
   Marcos, San Mateo, Santa
   Ana, Santa Barbara, Santa
   Clara, Santa Monica,
   Santa Rosa, Simi Valley,
   Stockton, Sunnyvale
5. *Adaptation, August: Osage*
   County, The Bridges of
   Madison County, Death
   Becomes Her, The Deer
   Hunter, Defending Your
   Life, The Devil Wears
   Prada, Doubt, The French
   Lieutenant's Woman,
   Heartburn, The Hours,
   The House of the Spirits,
   Into the Woods, The Iron
   Lady, Ironweed, Julia,
   Julie & Julia, Kramer
   vs. Kramer, Mamma
   Mia!, The Manchurian
   Candidate, Manhattan,
   Out of Africa, Postcards
   from the Edge, The River
   Wild, The Seduction of Joe
   Tynan, Silkwood, Sophie's
   Choice
6. 5th Avenue, Almond Joy,
   Baby Ruth, Butterfinger,
   Dove, Heath Bar,
   Hershey's Milk Chocolate,
   Kit Kat, Mars, Milky Way,
   Mounds, Mr. Goodbar,
   Nestle's Crunch, Reese's
   Peanut Butter Cup,
   Snickers, Sugar Daddy,
   Three Musketeers,
   Toblerone, Twix, York
   Peppermint Patty
7. Aim, Aquafresh,
   Close-Up, Colgate, Crest,
   Gleem, Ipana, Pepsodent,
   Sensodyne, Tom's of
   Maine, Ultra Brite
8. A&E, AMC, Animal
   Planet, BBC America,
   BET, Bravo, CNBC, CNN,
   Cinemax, Comedy Central,
   Discover Channel, Disney,
   ESPN, Food Network,
   Fox News, HBO, HGTV,
   HSN (Home Shopping
   Network), History
   Channel, Lifetime,
   MSNBC, MTV, National
   Geographic Channel,
   Nickelodeon, Oxygen,
   QVC, Showtime, TLC,
   Univision, Weather
   Channel

page 88: **Odd Man Out**

1. *Wolves* is the odd man out. All of the others are names of NFL teams.
2. *Poplin* is the odd man out. It is the only item in the list that is not a form of cooked potato. (It is a type of cotton fabric.)
3. *Teaspoon* is the odd man out. All of the others are types of beds.
4. *Cheese fondue* is the odd man out. All of the other items are things you tie.
5. *A piano* is the odd man out. All of the other items have rings.
6. *O'Brien* is the odd man out. All the rest are "old" things—Old MacDonald, Old Maid, and Old Faithful.
7. *Garden* is the odd man out. All of the others are units of measurement.

page 88: **Alma's Shopping List**

1. Melon
2. Fish
3. Jam
4. Tea
5. Yeast
6. Rice
7. Candles
8. Chili
9. Bubble Gum
10. Sour Cream
11. Fresh Flowers
12. Pork Chop

page 89: **Run the Alphabet—Birds**

Other correct answers are possible.
A: Albatross, Auk
B: Blackbird, Buzzard
C: Crow, Canary
D: Duck, Dove
E: Eagle, Emu
F: Flamingo, Falcon
G: Goose, Grouse
H: Hummingbird, Hawk
I: Ibis, Ivory-billed woodpecker
J: Jay, Jack snipe
K: Kiwi, Kestrel
L: Lark, Loon
M: Magpie, Mockingbird
N: Nuthatch, Nightingale
O: Ostrich, Owl
P: Pigeon, Parrot
Q: Quail, Quetzal
R: Robin, Roadrunner
S: Stork, Sparrow
T: Turkey, Toucan
U:
V: Vulture, Vireo
W: Woodpecker, Whooping crane
X:
Y: Yellow-bellied sapsucker, Yellowleg
Z: Zebra finch

page 90: **Making Connections**

Pupil, Lash, Lid:
Things associated with the eye
Oil, Latex, Finger:
Types of paint
Tide, All, Cheer:
Brands of detergent

page 91: **Alphabet Trivia**

1. George Washington, Grover Cleveland, Gerald Ford, George H. W. Bush, and George W. Bush
2. Gluttony and Greed
3. Georgia, Germany, Greece
4. Gemini
5. Ganges
6. Movies:
a. *Ghost*
b. *Gladiator*
c. *Grease*
d. *(The) Graduate*
e. *Gandhi*
7. Famous people:
a. Clark Gable
b. Yuri Gagarin
c. James Gandolfini
d. Art Garfunkel
8. Acronyms:
Gross domestic product
General infantry (General/Government issue/Gastrointestinal)
Greenwich Mean Time
Grand Old Party
Global positioning system
Gentlemen's Quarterly

page 92: **In the Middle**

1. Wolfgang Amadeus Mozart
2. Franklin Delano Roosevelt
3. Alexander Graham Bell
4. Francis Ford Coppola
5. Hans Christian Andersen
6. Harriet Beecher Stowe
7. John Fitzgerald Kennedy
8. John Quincy Adams
9. Ralph Waldo Emerson
10. George Bernard Shaw

11. James Earl Jones (James Earl Ray *is also correct*.)
12. Francis Scott Key (F. Scott Fitzgerald *is also correct*.)
13. Lee Harvey Oswald

page 92: Finish the Proverb

1. Every cloud has a silver lining.
2. Absence makes the heart grow fonder.
3. All work and no play makes Jack a dull boy.
4. Strike while the iron is hot.
5. One man's trash is another man's treasure.
6. No good deed goes unpunished.
7. Almost only counts in horseshoes and hand grenades.
8. Quitters never win and winners never quit.
9. If wishes were horses, then beggars would ride.
10. Imitation is the sincerest form of flattery.

page 93: TIME Out

1. Time capsule
2. Time clock (Time card *is also correct*.)
3. Time zones
4. Times Square
5. "Once upon a time . . ."
6. Time lapse
7. Ragtime
8. Time and tide
9. ". . . a time for every purpose under heaven."

10. Two-timer
11. *The Time Machine*
12. "It was the best of times, it was the worst of times."

page 93: Riddle Me This
Mushroom (Elbow room is also a correct answer.)

page 94: A Sheepish Sheep

1. A saucy sauce
2. A catty cat
3. A cheesy cheese
4. A chicken chicken
5. A squashed squash
6. A nutty nut
7. A peachy peach
8. A shrimpy shrimp
9. A hammy ham
10. A fishy fish
11. A mousy mouse
12. A yakking yak
13. A foxy fox

page 94: Common Bonds
Strings: Strings on a tennis racket, Apron strings, Violin strings

page 95: They're Grand!

1. Elvis Presley
2. Sarah Palin
3. Eugene O'Neill
4. Queen Elizabeth II

page 95: Sibling Rivalry

1. Beatty and MacLaine
2. Baldwin
3. Astaire
4. Barrymore
5. Bridges
6. Bush

7. Collins
8. De Havilland and Fontaine
9. James
10. Judd

page 96: Initial Quiz

1. Road Rage
2. Richard Rodgers
3. Relay Race
4. Religious Right
5. Rolls Royce
6. Roof Rack
7. Road Runner
8. Robert Redford
9. Renewable Resource
10. Rumpus Room (Recreation Room *and* Ruckus Room *are also correct*.)
11. Rough Riders
12. Rabble Rouser
13. Rachael Ray

page 96: Riddle Me This
A river

page 97: Complete the Words

		S	C	A	T	T	E	R
		H	A	I	R	P	I	N
I	M	A	G	I	N	E		
	P	Y	R	A	M	I	D	
E	N	G	A	G	E	D		
	B	A	Z	O	O	K	A	
	B	E	W	I	T	C	H	
	C	A	B	O	O	S	E	
		P	R	A	Y	E	R	S
		S	H	E	R	B	E	T
R	E	M	O	D	E	L		
	T	R	I	N	K	E	T	
	I	N	F	A	N	T	S	
T	H	R	I	L	L	S		

page 98: **Wacky Wordies**
1. Too good to be forgotten
2. A cut above average
3. Step up to the plate
4. All over again
5. Split personality
6. Leftovers
7. Take five
8. Be on cloud nine

page 100: **Letter Pairs**
1. Sticky
2. Dinner
3. Answer
4. Coyote
5. Fright
6. Peachy
7. Shrimp
8. Lawyer
9. Rotten
10. Kidney
11. Hectic
12. Bistro

page 100: **Endings & Beginnings**
1. Glass
2. Cash
3. Corn
4. Soda
5. Egg
6. Cross
7. Food
8. Saw
9. Candy
10. Bean

page 101: **The Presidents' Jobs**
1. George W. Bush
2. Barack Obama
3. John F. Kennedy
4. Abraham Lincoln
5. Thomas Jefferson
6. Lyndon Johnson
7. Harry Truman
8. Woodrow Wilson
9. Herbert Hoover

page 102: **Run the Alphabet—On the Map**
These are just a few examples of the many correct answers that are possible for this quiz.
A: Amazon River, Antarctica
B: Baghdad, Bahamas
C: Colorado River, Cuba
D: Denmark, Dallas (Texas)
E: Everest (Mt.), Ethiopia
F: France, Finland
G: Greenland, Guatemala
H: Hudson Bay, Hawaii
I: Istanbul, Ireland
J: Japan, Jamaica
K: Kilimanjaro (Mt.), Kyoto
L: Los Angeles, London
M: Mississippi River, Mediterranean Sea
N: Nile River, Norway
O: Oklahoma, Ontario
P: Peru, Poland
Q: Qatar, Quebec
R: Rio de Janeiro, Rwanda
S: Sydney, Sicily
T: Thames River, Turkey
U: Uganda, United Kingdom
V: Vietnam, Venezuela
W: Wales, West Virginia
X: Xenia, Xingu
Y: Yangtze River, Yemen
Z: Zambezi River, Zaire

page 103: **Group Therapy**
Some Group Therapy questions have many possible correct answers. Your answers may differ from ours and still be correct.
1. Joe Biden, Joey Bishop, Joe Cocker, Joseph Conrad, Joseph Cotten, Joe DiMaggio, Joe Frazier, Joseph Haydn, Joseph P. Kennedy, Joe Lieberman, Joe Louis, Joseph McCarthy, Joe Montana, Joe Namath, Joe Paterno, Josef Stalin, Joe Torre
2. Paella, Pancake, Papaya, Pasta, Pastry, Peach, Peanut butter, Pear, Peas, Pecan, Pickle, Pie, Pineapple, Pine nuts, Pizza, Polenta, Pomegranate, Pork, Potato, Pretzel, Pudding
3. Aggravated, Boiling, Cross, Displeased, Enraged, Fuming, Furious, Ill-tempered, Incensed, Indignant, Infuriated, Irate, Livid, Mad, Outraged, Pissed-off, Riled, Steamed, Vexed
4. Alabama, Arizona, California, Colorado, Connecticut, Indiana, Louisiana, Massachusetts, Minnesota, Mississippi, New Mexico, North Carolina, North Dakota, Oklahoma, Pennsylvania, South Carolina, South Dakota, West Virginia

5. "Away in a Manger,"
   "Deck the Halls,"
   "God Rest Ye Merry,
   Gentlemen," "Good King
   Wenceslas," "Hark! The
   Herald Angels Sing," "It
   Came Upon a Midnight
   Clear," "Jingle Bells,"
   "Joy to the World," "The
   Little Drummer Boy," "O
   Holy Night," "O Little
   Town of Bethlehem,"
   "Silent Night," "Silver
   Bells," "The Twelve
   Days of Christmas,"
   "What Child Is This?,"
   "White Christmas"
6. Aluminum, brass, bronze,
   chrome (chromium),
   copper, gold, iron, lead,
   mercury, nickel, pewter,
   platinum, plutonium,
   silver, solder, steel
   (stainless steel), tin,
   titanium, tungsten,
   uranium, zinc, zirconium
7. Sailor, Salesperson,
   School principal,
   Scientist, Scriptwriter,
   Sculptor, Seamstress,
   Secretary, Set designer,
   Silversmith, Singer,
   Social worker, Software
   developer, Soldier, Speech
   pathologist, Sports
   reporter, Statistician,
   Stockbroker, Stonemason,
   Surgeon, Surveyor,
   Systems analyst
8. Blimp, Camp, Chimp,
   Clamp, Dump, Hump,
   Imp, Lamp, Limp, Lump,
   Plump, Primp, Pump,
   Ramp, Scamp, Shrimp,
   Stamp, Stomp, Swamp,
   Thump, Trump

page 103: Vivienne's Vowels
1. Edgar Allan Poe
2. Pete Seeger
3. Hank Aaron
4. Joe Biden
5. Liberace
6. Laurence Olivier
7. Mamie Eisenhower
8. Tom Cruise
9. Madonna
10. Isaac Asimov
11. Pete Rose
12. Cleopatra

page 104: Alphabet Trivia
1. Haiti, Honduras, Hungary
   (*Note: Holland doesn't
   count because its official
   name is The Netherlands.*)
2. Hanoi, Vietnam; Harare,
   Zimbabwe; Havana,
   Cuba; Helsinki, Finland;
   Honiara, Solomon Islands
3. Harrisburg, PA; Hartford,
   CT; Helena, MT;
   Honolulu, HI
4. Table of Elements
   a. Helium
   b. Hydrogen (*Today
      scientists believe there
      are several other
      possible reasons why
      the Hindenburg caught
      fire and crashed to the
      ground.*)
5. Warren Harding,
   Benjamin Harrison,
   William Henry Harrison,
   Rutherford B. Hayes,
   Herbert Hoover
6. Hand, Head, Health,
   Heart
7. Quick-Question Answers:
   a. Hearing
   b. Huron
   c. Harvard
   d. Hinduism
8. Famous people whose last
   names begin with H:
   a. H. R. Haldeman
   b. Harry Houdini
   c. Hugh Hefner
   d. Alfred Hitchcock
   e. Tom Hanks
9. Acronyms and
   abbreviations:
   Home Box Office
   High definition
   Home & Garden
      Television
   Health maintenance
      organization
   High-occupancy vehicle
      (as in HOV lane on a
      highway)
   Headquarters
   Housing and Urban
      Development
   Heating, ventilation, and
      air conditioning

page 105: Word Pictures
1. Apron (APE + ron)
2. Cardigan (CARD + igan)
3. Jacket (JACK + et)
4. Loafers (LOAF + ers)
5. Mittens (MITT + ens)
6. Pinafore (PIN + afore)
7. Toga (TOE + ga)
8. Lingerie (LAWN + gerie)

page 106: Where's the Suburb?

1. New York City
2. Miami
3. Los Angeles
4. Boston
5. San Francisco
6. Washington, D.C.
7. Chicago
8. New Orleans
9. Houston
10. Denver
11. Philadelphia

page 106: OY!

1. Ann*oy*
2. Empl*oy*ee
3. F*oy*er
4. Garg*oy*le
5. *Oy*ster
6. The Beach B*oy*s
7. Bu*oy*
8. V*oy*age
9. Cordur*oy*
10. C*oy*ote
11. Cl*oy*ing
12. B*oy*cott

page 107: Scrambled Foods

1. Pizza
2. Bacon
3. Lobster
4. Waffles
5. Pretzel
6. Ravioli
7. Pudding
8. Popcorn
9. Chicken
10. Zucchini
11. Lasagna
12. Strawberry

page 107: What's the Weather?

1. Wind
2. Storm
3. Hail
4. Rain
5. Snow
6. Fog
7. Rainbow
8. Cloudy
9. Sunny

page 107: Trivia—PBS

1. *The French Chef*
2. Hyacinth Bucket (Bouquet)
3. *NOVA*
4. Robert MacNeil and Jim Lehrer
5. Steve Allen

page 108: Complete the Words

W	A	T	E	R	M	E	L	O	N	
					L	I	B	R	A	R	Y
	H	A	L	L	W	A	Y			
A	U	T	O	M	O	B	I	L	E	
			L	I	Q	U	O	R		
			V	O	D	K	A			
			R	I	N	K				
		B	A	N	K	R	U	P	T	
		G	A	U	Z	E				
			H	A	M	P	E	R		
F	I	R	E	P	L	A	C	E		
		F	L	A	V	O	R			
			N	I	G	H	T			
	C	R	U	S	T	A	C	E	A	N
		P	R	E	J	U	D	I	C	E
			K	I	S	S	I	N	G	
	P	E	R	O	X	I	D	E		
	R	A	S	P	B	E	R	R	Y	
E	L	E	C	T	R	I	C	I	T	Y
	O	B	J	E	C	T				
			N	E	P	H	E	W		
	F	L	U	F	F	Y				
M	A	N	I	C	U	R	E			
		L	A	T	H	E	R			
			H	Y	D	R	A	N	T	
C	A	N	D	L	E	S	T	I	C	K

page 109: **Alphabet Trivia**
1. Iceland, India, Indonesia, Iran, Iraq, Ireland, Israel, Italy
2. Istanbul (about 14 million population), Izmir (about 4 million)
3. Idaho, Illinois, Indiana, Iowa
4. Indianapolis
5. Indigo, Ivory
6. Iguana
7. Inch
8. Ivan
9. Inca
10. Iris
11. "I" people:
    a. Lee Iacocca
    b. Don Imus
    c. Daniel Inouye
    d. Jeremy Irons
    e. Washington Irving
    f. Lance Ito
12. Acronyms and abbreviations:
    International Brotherhood of Electrical Workers
    International Business Machines
    id est (that is to say)
    Intelligence quotient
    Internal Revenue Service
    In vitro fertilization

page 110: **Find the Words**
(see pages 350–351)

page 112: **Mangled Monograms**
1. FDR (Franklin Delano Roosevelt)
2. DDE (Dwight David Eisenhower)
3. RMN (Richard Milhous Nixon)
4. LBJ (Lyndon Baines Johnson)
5. JQA (John Quincy Adams)
6. USG (Ulysses S. Grant)
7. GWB (George W. Bush)
8. JFK (John Fitzgerald Kennedy)
9. WJC (William Jefferson Clinton)
10. HST (Harry S. Truman)
11. BHO (Barack Hussein Obama)
12. RWR (Ronald Wilson Reagan)
13. HCH (Herbert Clark Hoover)
14. MVB (Martin Van Buren)
15. GRF (Gerald R. Ford)

page 112: **Order, Please!**
Dick Van Dyke (1925)
Queen Elizabeth II (1926)
James Dean (1931)
Elvis Presley (1935)
John Lennon (1940)
Bob Dylan (1941)
Bill Clinton (1946)
Al Gore (1948)
Jay Leno (1950)
Vladimir Putin (1952)
Michael Jackson (1958)
Barack Obama (1961)
Michael Jordan (1963)

page 113: **Trimble**
1. Letterman
2. Frost
3. Nelson
4. Brinkley
5. Garroway
6. Henry David Thoreau
Jumble Answer: *David Niven*

page 114: **Go for It!**
1. Gourmet
2. Goggles
3. Gobble
4. Gossip
5. Goober
6. Gondola
7. Google
8. Gorgeous
9. Goiter
10. Goblin
11. Gobbledygook
12. Gory

page 115: **Finish the Equation**
1. 4 = Quarts in a Gallon
2. 7 = Wonders of the Ancient World
3. 12 = Inches in a Foot
4. 12 = Signs of the Zodiac
5. 26 = Letters of the Alphabet
6. 30 = Days Hath September, April, June, and November
7. 36 = Inches in a Yard
8. 50 = Ways to Leave Your Lover
9. 52 = Weeks in a Year
10. 60 = Minutes in an Hour
11. 90 = Degrees in a Right Angle
12. 20,000 = *Leagues Under the Sea*

latch

lobster

lavatory

ladybug

lantern

light bulb

life preserver

lyre

lamp

lollipop

lapel

leotard

lid

laugh

ladle

lettu

lion

locomotive

log

letters

lamb

llama

landscape

leash

lizard

legs

lilies

leaf

lavender

...ak

leprechaun

lumber

lamp post

ladder

OPEN

DUCE

lemons

loaves

lock

lady

lanyard

lottery ticket

2 for 1 DRAFT MON - THURS

lens

lasagna

lei

license plate

lipstick

lips

laces

luggage

limousine

3. When the cat is away, the mice will play.
4. There's plenty of fish in the sea.
5. There's more than one way to skin a cat.
6. If you lie down with dogs, you'll wake up with fleas.
7. Curiosity killed the cat.
8. Don't count your chickens before they hatch.
9. Don't put the cart before the horse.

---

page 122: Riddle Me This
A breath

page 123: Follow the Rules
(see below)

page 124: Quotation Station
(see below)

page 125: Change a Letter
1. B—Break, Block, Bolder
2. S—Soul, Simple, Sandbag
3. F—Farm, Father, Facial
4. D—Doodle, Dwindle, Dentures

---

page 123: Follow the Rules
1. G O D C R E A T E D L I G H T
2. G O N C R E A T E D L I G H T
3. G O N C R E A T E D L I G H T P
4. G A N C R E A T E D L A G H T P
5. G A N C R E A D E T L A G H T P
6. G A N C R __ A D E T E L A G H T P
7. M G A N C R A D E T E L A G H T P
8. M G A N C R M A D E T E L A M G H T P
9. M G A N C R M A D E T H E L A M G __ T P
10. M __ A N C R M A D E T H E L A M __ T P
11. M A N __ __ M A D E T H E L A M __ P

(God created light.) Man made the lamp.

page 124: Quotation Station
After I was elected president, I had my high school grades classified Top Secret.
—Ronald Reagan

A	F	T	E	R		I		W	A	S		E	L	E	C	T	E	D
	P	R	E	S	I	D	E	N	T		I		H	A	D		M	Y
H	I	G	H		S	C	H	O	O	L		G	R	A	D	E	S		C
L	A	S	S	I	F	I	E	D		T	O	P		S	E	C	R	E	T

---

5. T—Taunt, Touch, Train
6. M—Match, Mighty, Model
7. R—Ragged, Read, Reach
8. W—Water, Weather, Weight
9. N—Never, Naïve, Nerve
10. L—Lace, Loose, Lather

page 125: Group Therapy
Some Group Therapy questions have many possible correct answers. Your answers may differ from ours and still be correct.
1. Binoculars, Boots, Briefs, Chopsticks, Crutches, Earrings, Glasses, Gloves, Handcuffs, Headphones, Jacks, Jeans, Kings, Mittens, Pajamas, Panties, Pants, Pliers, Queens, Scissors, Shoes, Skis, Slippers, Sneakers, Socks, Stockings, Sunglasses, Tens, Trousers, Twins, Windshield wipers
2. Empty, Famished, Peckish, Rapacious, Ravenous, Starved/Starving, Voracious
3. Antigua, Aruba, Bahamas, Barbados, Barbuda, Bonaire, Cayman Islands, Cozumel, Cuba, Curacao, Dominican Republic, Grenada, Guadeloupe, Haiti, Jamaica, Martinique, Puerto Rico, St. Barthelemy, St. Croix,

St. Martin, Trinidad and Tobago, Turks and Caicos, Virgin Islands (British and United States)

4. George Burns, George Bush, George Carlin, George Washington Carver, George Clooney, George Foreman, George Gershwin, George Gobel, George Hamilton, George Harrison, George Jessel, George Lopez, George Orwell, George S. Patton, George Raft, George C. Scott, George Bernard Shaw, George Steinbrenner, George Stephanopoulos, George Wallace, George Washington

5. Bagel, Baguette, Biscuit, Boule, Brioche, Challah, Ciabatta, Cornbread, Croissant, Crumpet, English muffin, Flatbread, Focaccia, Lavash, Matzo, Naan, Oatmeal, Pane, Pita, Pumpernickel, Roll, Rye bread, Sourdough, Tortilla, Wheat (Whole wheat) bread, White bread

6. Bike Route, Do Not Enter, Do Not Pass, Freeway Entrance, Keep Right, Left Lane Must Turn Left, No Parking, No Right on Red, One Way, Railroad Crossing, Right Lane Must Turn Right, Road Closed, Slow, Speed Limit, Stop, U Turn, Yield

7. Peach, Periwinkle (blue), Persimmon, Pine green, Pink, Platinum, Plum, Powder blue, Puce, Pumpkin, Purple

8. Angels, Astros, Athletics, Braves, Brewers, Dodgers, Giants, Indians, Mariners, Mets, Nationals, Padres, Phillies, Pirates, Rangers, Red Sox, Reds, Rockies, Royals, Twins, White Sox, Yankees

page 126: Word Pictures
1. Bottleneck (Bottle + Neck)
2. Box spring (Box + Spring)
3. Party (Part + Tee)
4. Sandwich (Sand + Witch)
5. Sundial (Sun + Dial)
6. Stopwatch (Stop + Watch)
7. Headlock (Head + Lock)
8. Monkey (Monk + Key)

page 128: Alphabet Trivia
1. Andrew Jackson, Thomas Jefferson, Andrew Johnson, and Lyndon Johnson
2. Jackson (MS), Jefferson City (MO), and Juneau (AK)
3. Jamaica, Japan, and Jordan
4. James, Jeremiah, Job, Joel, John (+1, 2, 3), Jonah, Joshua, Jude, Judges
5. Jose, Juan, Juliana, Julio, Jaime, Javier, Jesus, Joaquin, Juanita (*Other, less common answers are possible.*)

6. Jacket, Jeans, Jersey Jumper, Jumpsuit (*Other, less common answers are possible.*)
7. Jack-in-the-box, Jacks, Jenga, Jigsaw puzzle, Jump rope (*Other, less common answers are possible.*)
8. Jack Daniels, Jaguar, Jeep, Jell-O, Jelly Belly, Jenny Craig, Jergens, Jet Blue, Jetta, Jockey, John Deere, Johnnie Walker, Jordache, J. P. Morgan, Jif (peanut butter), Jiffy Pop
9. Janet Jackson, Jesse Jackson, Jesse James, Judith Jamison, James (Earl) Jones, Jim Jones, John Paul Jones, Janis Joplin, James Joyce (*Other answers are possible.*)
10. Film titles that begin with the letter J:
    a. *Jaws*
    b. *Jerry Maguire*
    c. *Judgment at Nuremberg*
    d. *Jurassic Park*

page 129: Secret Word – ENCYCLOPEDIA
Note: Other, more obscure correct answers are possible.
5-Letter Words:
1. Ailed
2. Alien
3. Aline
4. Alone
5. Anode
6. Candy

7. Caned
8. Canoe
9. Caped
10. Capon
11. Clean
12. Clone
13. Colic
14. Copay
15. Coped
16. Cycle
17. Cynic
18. Daily
19. Dance
20. Decal
21. Decay
22. Decoy
23. Deice
24. Delay
25. Dicey
26. Doily
27. Dopey
28. Doyen
29. Eland
30. Elope
31. Ideal
32. Inlay
33. Laced
34. Laden
35. Lance
36. Lined
37. Loped
38. Needy
39. Niece
40. Ocean
41. Oiled
42. Olden
43. Oldie
44. Opine
45. Paced
46. Paled

47. Paned
48. Panel
49. Panic
50. Payee
51. Peace
52. Pecan
53. Pedal
54. Penal
55. Pence
56. Peony
57. **Piano (Secret Word)**
58. Piece
59. Piled
60. Pined
61. Piney
62. Place
63. Plaid
64. Plain
65. Plane
66. Plead
67. Plied
68. Poled
69. Pylon
70. Yield
71. Yodel

page 130: President in Name Only
1. Mr. Wilson
2. Andy Taylor
3. Hawkeye Pierce
4. Lincoln
5. Garfield
6. Harrison Ford
7. Sam Adams
8. Hoover
9. The Jeffersons
10. Lou Grant
11. Magic Johnson
12. Denzel Washington

page 130: Trivia— Gone Fishin'
1. Minnow
2. Stingray
3. Salmon
4. Catfish
5. Piranha

page 131: Sentence Sleuth
1. Plumber (…plum-berry…)
2. Carpenter (…carp enter…)
3. Teacher (…tea, cherry…)
4. Florist (…Flor is the…)
5. Attorney (…defeat—torn eyelid…)
6. Banker (…turban, kerchiefs…)
7. Painter (…Spain, Teri…)
8. Journalist (…Journal is too…)
9. Driver (…drive repaired…)
10. Therapist (…Mother a pistol…)
11. Butcher (…but Cher…)
12. Umpire (…bump, I realized…)

page 132: What's Their Job?
1. Supreme Court Justice
2. Ballet dancer
3. Architect
4. Golfer
5. Hockey player
6. Mayor
7. Dictator
8. Film critic
9. Shoe designer
10. Photographer
11. Journalist
12. Pianist

page 133: Complete the Words

F	I	L	I	B	U	S	T	E	R
	T	R	I	G	G	E	R		
		P	O	L	I	T	E		
C	O	M	F	O	R	T	A	B	L	E
	C	H	E	E	S	E			
		A	D	J	U	S	T	E	D
		S	P	O	O	N			
T	A	P	E	S	T	R	Y		
	H	E	A	V	E	N			
	J	I	N	X	E	D			
	W	I	Z	A	R	D			
C	H	O	C	O	L	A	T	E	
P	A	M	P	H	L	E	T		
	H	A	M	M	E	R			
	M	O	U	T	H				
T	H	E	R	A	P	Y			
	N	O	W	H	E	R	E		
		S	Y	S	T	E	M		
C	A	L	E	N	D	A	R		
O	R	I	G	I	N	A	L		
	P	L	A	Q	U	E			
	S	I	S	T	E	R			
S	P	A	R	K	L	E			
O	C	E	A	N					
	C	A	N	O	E				
	F	I	F	T	E	E	N		

page 134: Anagrams

1. Lake, Kale, Leak
2. Tars, Tsar, Star, Rats, Arts
3. Flow, Fowl, Wolf
4. Wider, Weird, Wired
5. Torso, Roost, Roots
6. Thing, Night
7. Claps, Clasp, Scalp
8. Takers, Skater, Streak

page 134: Riddle Me This

A sponge

page 135: Good Going

1. Good Humor
2. Good & Plenty
3. *Good Housekeeping*
4. Good behavior (*or* Good conduct time)
5. Goodwill Industries
6. *Good Morning, Vietnam*
7. *Goodfellas*
8. Good neighbors
9. Good grief
10. Good riddance (to bad rubbish)
11. Thurgood Marshall
12. Good King Wenceslas
13. Jane Goodall

page 135: Easy as Pie

1. Cute as a button
2. Flat as a pancake
3. Neat as a pin
4. Nutty as a fruitcake
5. Pale as a ghost
6. Pleased as punch
7. Shiny as a new penny
8. Smart as a whip
9. Sober as a judge
10. Sturdy as an oak
11. Thin as a rail (Thin as a rake *is also correct.*)

page 136: Character Study

1. *Gone with the Wind*
   Clark Gable
2. *Funny Girl*
   Barbra Streisand
3. *Star Wars*
   Carrie Fisher
4. *Norma Rae*
   Sally Field
5. *Bonnie and Clyde*
   Warren Beatty
6. *Back to the Future*
   Michael J. Fox
7. *The Graduate*
   Anne Bancroft
8. *The Sound of Music*
   Julie Andrews
9. *All the President's Men*
   Robert Redford
10. *It's a Wonderful Life*
    Jimmy Stewart
11. *Butch Cassidy and the Sundance Kid*
    Paul Newman
12. *Raiders of the Lost Ark*
    Harrison Ford
13. *To Kill a Mockingbird*
    Gregory Peck
14. *Citizen Kane*
    Orson Welles
15. *The Godfather*
    Al Pacino

page 136: Common Bonds

Fast food restaurants: Domino's, Red Lobster, Subway

page 137: State of the Word

Note: Other correct answers are possible.

1. Coral
2. Awake
3. Glaze
4. Diary
5. Vicar
6. Acorn
7. Cactus
8. Model
9. Rifle
10. Cigar
11. Shift
12. Glide
13. Until

14. Twine
15. Phobia
16. Blocks
17. Spooky
18. Plague
19. Cement
20. Gumdrop
21. Formal
22. Domino
23. Chimney
24. Flimsy
25. Kimono
26. Warmth
27. Sneeze
28. Convoy
29. Unhappy
30. Banjo
31. Inmate
32. Balcony
33. Pinch
34. Abandon
35. Alcohol
36. Provoke
37. Comfort
38. Papaya
39. Fabric
40. Escrow
41. Wisdom
42. Catnip
43. Shutter
44. Canvas
45. Forward
46. Drawing
47. Lawyer

page 138: Semordnilap
1. Liar/Rail
2. Gnat/Tang
3. Gums/Smug
4. Macs/Scam
5. Mir/Rim
6. Sports/Strops
7. Yaps/Spay
8. Bard/Drab
9. Nomad/Damon
10. Rats/Star
11. Sloop/Pools

page 138: Trivia—Kitchen Science
1. Salmonella, which was discovered in the laboratory of Dr. Daniel Elmer Salmon.
2. Poppy seeds
3. An artificial sweetener
4. Monosodium glutamate

page 139: How Much Is . . . ?
1. 132 (32 + 100)
2. 3,915 (1941 + 1974)
3. 326 (26 + 300)
4. 64 (40 + 24)
5. 79 (4 + 75)
6. 364 (360 + 4)
7. 44 (10 + 34)
8. 56 (16 + 40)
9. 125 (109 + 16)
10. 64 (57 + 7)

page 140: Alphabet Trivia
1. Kazakhstan, Kenya, Kiribati, Kosovo, Kuwait, Kyrgyzstan (Korea *is also acceptable, although their official names are* Democratic People's Republic of Korea *and* Republic of Korea, *respectively.*)
2. Kansas and Kentucky
3. Kangaroo, Koala
4. Karate, Kung fu, Kickboxing
5. Kimono
6. *Kramer vs. Kramer*
7. Kermit
8. Karaoke
9. Krispy Kreme
10. Kayak
11. Kwanzaa
12. Kilimanjaro
13. Kevin Kline
14. Kato Kaelin

page 141: Vivienne's Vowels
1. Rio de Janeiro
2. Havana
3. Australia
4. Jamaica
5. Ontario, Canada
6. Russia
7. Seattle
8. South Africa
9. Nairobi
10. Seoul (Oslo *is also correct.*)
11. Prague
12. Uruguay
13. Aruba

page 141: Endings & Beginnings
1. Pillow
2. Square
3. Dog
4. Record
5. Bubble
6. Fruit
7. Love
8. Space
9. Bank
10. Work

page 142: Word Tower
These answers are just a suggestion; many other correct answers are possible:
1. H
2. Hi
3. Hip
4. Hide
5. Hinge

6. Hiatus
7. Hideous
8. Historic
9. Hibernate
10. Historical
11. Hitchhiking
12. Hippopotamus
13. Hieroglyphics

page 143: Making Connections

Swiss, Blue, Goat: Types of cheese
Mexico, Jersey, York: US states that start with New
Ford, Crocker, White: Famous people named Betty

page 144: Group Therapy

Some Group Therapy questions have many possible correct answers. Your answers may differ from ours and still be correct.

1. Academic, Anemic, Antiseptic, Arithmetic, Barbaric, Basic, Ceramic, Chronic, Civic, Dynamic, Economic, Electric, Epic, Frantic, Garlic, Heretic, Ironic, Logic, Lunatic, Metric, Music, Organic, Panic, Pathetic, Picnic, Public, Republic, Rustic, Scenic, Tactic, Topic, Toxic, Traffic, Workaholic
2. Airplane tickets, Boat, Car, College/Private school, Computer, Dental work, Formal wear (i.e., wedding dress, tuxedo, evening gown, etc.), Home repair/remodel, House/

Apartment, Insurance (car, home, health, etc.), Jewelry, Kitchen appliances, Medical needs, Vacations
3. Ludwig van Beethoven, Abigail Van Buren, Martin Van Buren, Dick Van Dyke, Vincent van Gogh, Dick Van Patten, Claus von Bülow, Diane von Furstenberg, Max von Sydow, Maria von Trapp
4. Andy Capp Fried, Cape Cod Potato Chips, Cheetos, Cheez Doodles, Doritos, Fritos, Funyuns, Lay's Potato Chips, Pringles, Ruffles, Tostitos, Utz Potato Chips, Wise Potato Chips
5. Arkansas, Brazos, Charles, Colorado, Columbia, Connecticut, Cumberland, Des Moines, East, Green, Hudson, James, Mississippi, Missouri, Ohio, Peace, Pecos, Red, Rio Grande, Schuylkill, St. Lawrence, Snake, Wabash, Yukon
6. Accountant, Actor, Administrative assistant, Aerospace engineer, Airplane mechanic, Anesthesiologist, Animal trainer, Anthropologist, Architect, Artist, Astronaut, Athlete, Attorney, Auctioneer, Auditor, Automobile mechanic

7. Advil, Aleve, Anacin, Bayer, Bufferin, Ecotrin, Excedrin, Midol, Motrin, Naproxen, Nuprin, St. Joseph, Tylenol, Vanquish
8. Argentina, Belize, Bolivia, Chile, Colombia, Costa Rica, Cuba, Dominican Republic, Ecuador, El Salvador, Guatemala, Honduras, Mexico, Nicaragua, Panama, Paraguay, Peru, Spain, Uruguay, Venezuela

page 144: Trivia— Improbable Pairs

1. Yoko Ono Bono (Yoko Ono & Sonny Bono)
2. Dolly Dali (Dolly Parton & Salvador Dali)
3. Bo Ho (Bo Derek & Don Ho)
4. Olivia Newton-John Newton John (Olivia Newton-John & Wayne Newton & Elton John)

page 145: Two-Minute Madness: _____ Book

Note: Other correct answers are possible.

1. Appointment book
2. Bankbook
3. Black book
4. Blue Book
5. Checkbook
6. Children's book
7. Closed book
8. Comic book
9. Cookbook
10. Ebook
11. Facebook

12. Good Book
13. Handbook
14. Library book
15. Log book
16. Matchbook
17. Notebook
18. Passbook
19. Phone book
20. Picture book
21. Playbook
22. Pocketbook
23. Prayer book
24. *Redbook*
25. Reference book
26. Schoolbook
27. Scrapbook
28. Sketchbook
29. Storybook
30. Telephone book
31. Textbook
32. Workbook
33. Yearbook

page 146: Fill in the Letters
Other, more obscure correct answers are possible.

1. Cube, Cure, Cute, Dude, Duke, Dune, Dupe, Fume, Fuse, Huge, Jute, Lube, Luge, Lure, Lute, Mule, Muse, Mute, Nude, Nuke, Puce, Puke, Pure, Rube, Rude, Rule, Rune, Ruse, Sure, Tube, Tune, Yule
2. Bang, Bong, Dang, Ding, Dung, Fang, Gang, Gong, Hang, Hung, King, Long, Lung, Pang, Ping, Rang, Ring, Rung, Sang, Sing, Song, Sung, Tang, Tong, Wing, Zing

3. Bead, Dead, Head, Lead, Mead, Read
4. Tail, Thin, This, Toil, Trig, Trim, Trio, Trip, Twig, Twin, Twit
5. Alas, Blab, Blah, Clad, Clam, Clan, Clap, Claw, Clay, Flab, Flag, Flan, Flap, Flat, Flaw, Flax, Glad, Plan, Play, Slab, Slam, Slap, Slat, Slaw, Slay
6. Mica, Mice, Mien, Mild, Mile, Milk, Mill, Mime, Mind, Mine, Mini, Mink, Mint, Minx, Mire, Miso, Miss, Mist, Mite, Mitt
7. Swift, Swill, Swine, Swing, Swipe, Swirl, Swish
8. Shade, Shake, Shale, Shame, Shape, Share, Shave, Shine, Shire, Shone, Shore, Shove

page 146: What's the Sport?
1. Football (American)
2. Track and field
3. Car racing
4. Baseball
5. Bowling
6. Boxing
7. Pool/Pocket billiards
8. Cycling
9. Soccer
10. Golf
11. Horse racing
12. Hockey
13. Roller derby
14. Rugby
15. Skiing
16. Surfing

page 147: Name That Musical
1. *Annie*
2. *Bye Bye Birdie*
3. *Cats*
4. *The King and I*
5. *Fiddler on the Roof*
6. *Evita*
7. *Hair*
8. *Man of La Mancha*
9. *West Side Story*
10. *Les Misérables*
11. *My Fair Lady*
12. *Jesus Christ Superstar*
13. *The Sound of Music*
14. *Oklahoma!*
15. *Grease*

page 148: Prime-Time Rhyme
1. Humble; stumble; mumble
2. Scatter; flatter; shatter
3. Ditty; city; kitty
4. Ignition; addition; audition
5. Tooth; booth; truth
6. Brace; lace; race
7. Tramp; camp; stamp
8. Clash; trash; splash
9. Spray; stray; neigh
10. Verve; serve; swerve
11. Shackle; tackle; spackle
12. Potpourri; referee; Tennessee
13. Slipper; flipper; zipper

page 149: What a Pair
1. Block and Tackle
2. Pins and Needles
3. Knife and Fork
4. Bait and Switch
5. Ball and Chain

6. *Car and Driver*
7. Franks and Beans
8. Park and Ride
9. Rank and File
10. Cap and Gown
11. Crash and Burn

page 150: It's QUITting Time
1. Quilt
2. Equity
3. Quaint
4. Squint
5. Squirt
6. Antique
7. Tranquil
8. Tequila
9. Liquidate
10. Mosquito
11. Quintet
12. Quieter
13. Quantity
14. Equality
15. Quickest
16. Critique
17. Technique
18. Equestrian

page 150: Trivia—Soup's On
1. Minestrone, which often contains spinach, fennel, cannellini beans, and parmesan cheese (which are not typically used in US vegetable soup)
2. Consommé
3. Bisque
4. Borscht

page 151: Alphabet Trivia
1. Laos, Latvia, Lebanon, Lesotho, Liberia, Libya, Liechtenstein, Lithuania, Luxembourg
2. Louisiana
3. Lincoln
4. Lust
5. Lansing, MI; Lincoln, NE; Little Rock, AR
6. Leo, Libra
7. London
8. Los Angeles
9. Leviticus (Old Testament); Luke (New Testament)
10. Lark, Lemming, Lemur, Leopard, Lion, Lizard, Llama, Loris, Lynx (*Other, less common answers are possible.*)
11. Labor Day
12. Linus (the blanket holder), Lucy (bossy and crabby girl)
13. 50
14. Lois Lane, Lana Lang, Lex Luthor, Linda Lee, Lori Lemaris (*Other correct answers are possible.*)
15. Loretta Lynn

page 152: Alphabetically Speaking
1. Alberta
2. Abdomen
3. Yellow
4. Bronx
5. Zion
6. Eight
7. B & O
8. Yale University

9. Abraham Lincoln
10. Psalms
11. C
12. Rook

page 153: Initial Quiz
1. Advertising Agency
2. Affirmative Action
3. Alcoholics Anonymous
4. Addis Ababa
5. Abstract Art
6. Ann Arbor
7. Andre Agassi (Arthur Ashe *is also correct.*)
8. Adam's Apple
9. Action-Adventure
10. Anaheim Angels (*The team was renamed the Los Angeles Angels of Anaheim in 2005.*)
11. Ansel Adams

page 153: Common Bonds
Rice Krispies cereal sound: Snap, Crackle, Pop

page 154: Odd Man Out
1. *Idiotic* is the odd man out. In all of the other answers, the letter E occurs three times.
2. *Aspirin* is the odd man out. All of the others have (or are) arches.
3. *Radley* is the odd man out. All of the others are words or names preceded by a "bo" sound (Beau, Bo, Bow). (Boo Radley was a character in *To Kill a Mockingbird.*)

4. *Kennedy* is the odd man out. All of the others ran for US vice president and lost.
5. *Telephone* is the odd man out. All of the others are types of chips.
6. Your *tongue* is the odd man out. It is something you bite. The rest are things you cross.
7. *Racer* is the odd man out. It is the only word in the list that is not a palindrome.
8. *Sergeant* is the odd man out. All of the others are "codes."

page 154: "I" Exam
1. Idle (Indolent *is also correct.*)
2. Ibuprofen
3. Infinity
4. Italics
5. Idyllic
6. Isolated
7. Itinerary
8. Ideal
9. Incubator
10. Infatuated
11. Impossible
12. Idiosyncrasy

page 155: Memorable TV Lines
1. *The Flintstones*; Fred
2. *Fantasy Island*; Tattoo
3. *Mork & Mindy*; Mork
4. *Hill Street Blues*; Sgt. Esterhaus
5. *Frasier*; Frasier Crane
6. *Everybody Loves Raymond*; Frank Barone
7. *Emeril Live*; Emeril Lagasse
8. *Who Wants to Be a Millionaire?*; Regis Philbin
9. *The Apprentice*; Donald Trump
10. *Hogan's Heroes*; Sgt. Schultz
11. *Newhart*; Larry
12. *Cheers*; Everyone at the bar

page 155: Riddle Me This
Fire

page 156: One-Minute Madness: Vowel States
1. Alabama
2. Alaska
3. Arizona
4. Arkansas
5. Idaho
6. Illinois
7. Indiana
8. Iowa
9. Ohio
10. Oklahoma
11. Oregon
12. Utah

page 156: Alma's Shopping List
1. Ice Cream
2. Apple
3. Cold Cuts
4. Wheat Bread
5. Bread Crumbs
6. Onion Rings
7. Cake Mix
8. Chili Peppers
9. Pea Soup
10. Radish
11. Wax Paper
12. Light Bulbs

page 157: The Name Game
1. Go + no + O + yolk (Yoko Ono)
2. Kite + wall + Turk + Ron (Walter Cronkite)
3. Gray + peck + gory (Gregory Peck)
4. Ken + carol + Eddie + line (Caroline Kennedy)
5. In + franks + rah + art (Frank Sinatra)
6. War + and + hall + E (Andy Warhol)
7. Ill + bill + leek + wrist (Billy Crystal)
8. Shake + will + spear + yam (William Shakespeare)
9. F + stall + Joes + in (Joseph Stalin)

page 158: Finish the Proverb
1. What goes up must come down (*or* What goes around, comes around).
2. Look before you leap.
3. A journey of a thousand miles begins with a single step.
4. An ounce of prevention is worth a pound of cure.
5. The road to hell is paved with good intentions.

6. Youth is wasted on the young.
7. Those who do not learn from history are doomed to repeat it.
8. Absolute power corrupts absolutely.
9. It's better to have loved and lost than never to have loved at all.
10. If you can't stand the heat, get out of the kitchen.
11. Laugh and the world laughs with you. Cry and you cry alone.

CHAPTER FIVE

page 159: **By the Letter**
1. C (Copenhagen)
2. H (Humans)
3. I (Immune system)
4. C (Cricket)
5. K (Knicks *or* Knickerbockers)
6. E (Éclair)
7. N (Canyon)

CHICKEN

page 160: **Vivienne's Vowels**
1. Seafood salad
2. Salami
3. Bananas
4. Papaya
5. Macaroni
6. Applesauce
7. Pea soup
8. Quiche
9. Cheerios
10. Oranges

---

11. Asparagus
12. Onions

page 160: **Number Please**
1. 2 — bars**too**l
2. 10 — u**ten**sil
3. 4 — be**fore**
4. 6 — phy**sics**
5. 10 — bar**ten**der
6. 8 — prim**ate**
7. 9 — ca**nine**
8. 4 — **fore**st
9. 2 — car**too**n
10. 8 — f**reig**ht
11. 6 — clas**sics**
12. 4 — ef**fort**

page 161: **Heteronyms**
1. Tear (TAIR/TEER)
2. Minute (my NEWT/ MIN it)
3. Lead (LED/LEED)
4. Invalid (in VAL id/ IN va lid)
5. Defect (DEE fect/ dee FECT)
6. Digest (DYE jest/ Dye JEST)
7. Content (CON tent/ con TENT)
8. Contest (con TEST/ CON test)
9. Incense (in SENSE/ IN sense)
10. Intern (IN tern/in TERN)
11. Moderate (MOD er it/ MOD er ATE)
12. Project (pro JEKT/ PROJ ect)
13. Rainier (RAIN i er/ Ra NEER)

---

page 162: **Complete the Words**

A	P	P	E	T	I	T	E	
V	A	C	A	T	I	O	N	
S	A	W	H	O	R	S	E	
P	R	A	C	T	I	C	E	
F	O	R	G	E	T	F	U	L
	S	M	U	G	G	L	E	R
U	N	F	E	E	L	I	N	G
A	V	E	R	A	G	E		
H	U	S	B	A	N	D		
	S	W	O	O	N			
B	E	L	I	E	V	E		
A	R	C	H	E	R	Y		
G	A	R	B	A	G	E		
S	K	I	N	N	Y			

page 163: **Word Parts**
1. Tablet (Tab + let)
2. Perjury (per + jury)
3. Chicken (chic + Ken)
4. Honesty (hone + sty)
5. Mistrust (mist + rust)
6. Administer (ad + minister)
7. Asparagus (asp + A + rag + us)
8. Capillaries (cap + ill + Aries)
9. Dandelion (Dan + deli + on)
10. Diversity (diver + sit + Y)
11. Hammock (ham + mock)
12. Hospital (Ho + spit + Al)
13. Infantry (in + fan + try)
14. Microwave (mi + crow + wave)

page 164: **Alphabet Trivia**
1. Maine, Maryland, Massachusetts, Michigan, Minnesota, Mississippi, Missouri, Montana

2. Manatee, Marmot, Meerkat, Mink, Mole, Mongoose, Monkey, Moose, Mountain goat, Mountain lion, Mouse, Mule deer, Musk ox, Muskrat (*Other, less common answers are possible.*)
3. Mexico
4. Mercury, Mars
5. Manitoba
6. 1,000
7. Mickey Mantle and Roger Maris chased Ruth's record and Maris won.
8. Montague
9. Myanmar
10. Mumbai
11. Margaret Mitchell
12. Marion Morrison
13. Mary Magdalene
14. Marilyn Monroe
15. Acronyms:
   Mothers Against Drunk Driving
   Metro-Goldwyn-Mayer
   Missing in action
   Massachusetts Institute of Technology
   Museum of Modern Art (NYC)
   Miles per gallon
   Magnetic resonance imaging

page 165: What's Their Job?
1. Artist
2. Cartoonist
3. Figure skater
4. Chef
5. Coach
6. Jockey
7. Baseball player
8. Opera singer
9. Playwright
10. Television producer
11. Pilot
12. Police officer

page 165: Trivia— "Ladies" Things
1. Bloody Mary
2. Lazy Susan
3. Tin Lizzy
4. Spinning Jenny
5. Round Robin

page 166: Ted's Terrible Titles
1. *A Chorus Line*
2. *A Tree Grows in Brooklyn*
3. *The Secret Life of Bees*
4. *Little House on the Prairie*
5. *The Sun Also Rises*
6. *The Grapes of Wrath*
7. *Pennies from Heaven*
8. *Much Ado About Nothing*
9. *Lost Weekend*
10. "Happy Days Are Here Again"
11. *Diamonds Are Forever*
12. *Crime and Punishment*

page 166: Riddle Me This
Growing older

page 167: Making Connections
Smokey, Teddy, Black: Names of bears
Rocky, Green, Smoky: North American mountain ranges
Blue, Gray, Right: Types of whales

page 168: Bird Watching
A. Canada goose
B. Mute swan
C. California condor
D. Baltimore oriole
E. Woodpecker (Red-headed)
F. Duck (Mallard)
G. Peacock
H. Crow (American)
I. Great blue heron
J. Flamingo
K. Pelican (Great white)
L. Puffin (Atlantic)
M. Sparrow (House)
N. Hummingbird (Ruby-throated)

page 170: Group Therapy
Some Group Therapy questions have many possible correct answers. Your answers may differ from ours and still be correct.
1. Addis Ababa, British Columbia, Buenos Aires, Des Moines, El Salvador, Fort Wayne, Fort Worth, La Paz, Las Vegas, Little Rock, Los Angeles, Mexico City, New Hampshire, New Jersey, New Mexico, New Orleans, New York, New Zealand, Nova Scotia, Phnom Penh, Puerto Rico, Quebec City, Rhode Island, San Francisco, Saudi Arabia, South Africa, South Korea, United Kingdom, West Virginia

2. Wolf Blitzer, Fidel Castro, Santa Claus, Charlie Chaplin, Salvador Dali, Albert Einstein, Fu Manchu, Clark Gable, Adolf Hitler, Ho Chi Minh, Jesus, Abraham Lincoln, Groucho Marx, Chuck Norris, Pablo Picasso, Burt Reynolds, Tom Selleck, Gene Shalit, Rip Van Winkle

3. Steve Allen, Woody Allen, Roseanne Barr, Jack Benny, Milton Berle, Joey Bishop, Lenny Bruce, George Burns, George Carlin, Johnny Carson, Bill Cosby, Billy Crystal, Rodney Dangerfield, Ellen DeGeneres, Phyllis Diller, Totie Fields, Redd Foxx, Whoopi Goldberg, Shecky Greene, Bob Hope, Jay Leno, David Letterman, Steve Martin, Jackie Mason, Eddie Murphy, Bob Newhart, Rosie O'Donnell, Richard Pryor, Don Rickles, Joan Rivers, Chris Rock, Jerry Seinfeld, Red Skelton, Lily Tomlin, Robin Williams, Jonathan Winters

4. Charles Atlas, Charles Barkley, Charles Bronson, Charlie Chaplin, Charles Darwin, Charles DeGaulle, Charles

Dickens, Charlie Gibson, Charles Kuralt, Charles Laughton, Charles Lindbergh, Charles Manson, Charles Osgood, Prince Charles, Charlie Rose, Charles Schulz, Charlie Sheen

5. Automobile, Binoculars, Calculator, Celebration, Dictionary, Discovery, Elevator, Emergency, February, Graduation, Harmonica, Helicopter, Impossible, Information, Invisible, Invitation, Kilometer, Librarian, Motorcycle, Mysterious, Operation, Participate, Photography, Territory, Watermelon

6. Brennan, Cassidy, Cleary, Clooney, Daly, Delaney, Dempsey, Dolan, Fitzgerald, Fitzpatrick, Flanagan, Flynn, Gallagher, Gilligan, Grady, Healy, Kelly, Kennedy, Leary, McCarthy, McLaughlin, McMahon, Murphy, O'Brien, O'Connor, O'Donnell, O'Hara, O'Malley, O'Neill, O'Reilly, O'Rourke, Regan, Rooney, Shea, Sullivan

7. Cabbage, Cantaloupe, Carrot, Cauliflower, Celery, Cherry, Chickpea, Chicory, Chives, Clementine, Coconut,

Collard Greens, Corn, Cranberry, Cucumber

8. Bee, Beetle, Butterfly, Dragonfly, Firefly, Fly, Gnat, Hornet, Ladybug, Locust, Mosquito, Moth, Wasp

page 170: Trivia—A River Runs Through It
1. The Mississippi River
2. The Rio Grande
3. The Thames River
4. The Seine River
5. The Mekong River

page 171: Oscar Moments
1. Sally Field/*Places in the Heart*
2. James Cameron/*Titanic*
3. A Native American woman (Sacheen Littlefeather) who was asked by Marlon Brando to refuse his Best Actor Award for *The Godfather.*
4. Barbra Streisand/*Funny Girl*
5. Ben Affleck/*Good Will Hunting*
6. Halle Berry/*Monster's Ball*
7. Kevin Spacey/*The Usual Suspects*
8. Angelina Jolie/*Girl, Interrupted*
9. Jeff Bridges/*Crazy Heart*
10. Alfred Hitchcock. It was his entire thank-you speech for the Academy's Lifetime Achievement Award.

11. David Niven, responding to a naked streaker running across the stage.
12. Sandra Bullock/*The Blind Side*

page 172: **Wacky Wordies**
1. Quite right
2. I have no idea
3. All in good time
4. Cut corners
5. Go in all directions
6. *Two and a Half Men*
7. Left holding the bag
8. Down South (Going down South *is also acceptable.*)

page 174: **Rivals**
1. Bobby Riggs
2. The Sheriff of Nottingham
3. The Montagues
4. Stephen Douglas
5. The Wicked Witch of the West
6. Aaron Burr
7. Moby Dick
8. Antonio Salieri
9. Larry Bird
10. Darth Vader
11. The Roadrunner
12. The Crips

page 174: **Busy as a Bee**
1. Eager (or Busy) as a beaver.
2. Gentle as a lamb.
3. Loose as a goose. (Silly as a goose *is also correct.*)
4. Naked as a jaybird.

page 177: **Quotation Station**
Doing what you like is freedom. Liking what you do is happiness.
—Frank Tyger

D	O	I	N	G		W	H	A	T		Y	O	U	
L	I	K	E		I	S		F	R	E	E	D	O	M	.
L	I	K	I	N	G		W	H	A	T		Y	O	U	
D	O		I	S		H	A	P	P	I	N	E	S	S	.

5. Crazy as a loon.
6. Proud as a peacock.
7. Sly as a fox.
8. Happy as a clam.
9. Slippery as an eel.
10. Strong as a bull.
11. Nervous as a cat.
12. Sick as a dog.
13. Free as a bird.
14. Blind as a bat.

page 175: **Trimble**
1. *Oklahoma!*
2. Banjo
3. *Funny Girl*
4. Denver (John Denver)
5. Trumpet
Jumble Answer: *Johnny Cash*

page 176: **It's MADness!**
1. Mademoiselle
2. Madonna
3. Madagascar
4. Madison Avenue
5. Madden
6. Madrid
7. Madras
8. Madcap

9. Madeira
10. Madeleine
11. Madrigal
12. *Mad Max*

page 176: **Vivienne's Vowels**
1. Thomas Edison
2. Aristotle
3. Rudy Giuliani
4. Annie Oakley
5. Marie Antoinette
6. Emily Brontë
7. Al Pacino
8. Joe Montana
9. Sean Penn
10. Desi Arnaz
11. Bobby Orr

page 177: **Quotation Station**
(see above)

page 178: **Word Pictures**
1. Tucson (2 + SON)
2. Portugal (PORCH + ugal)
3. Warsaw (War + SAW)
4. Armenia (ARM + enia)
5. Korea (CORE + ea)
6. Panama (PAN + ama)
7. Haiti (HAY + ti)
8. Finland (FIN + land)

1. Namibia, Nauru, Nepal, Netherlands, New Zealand, Nicaragua, Niger, Nigeria, North Korea, Norway
2. Nebraska, Nevada, New Hampshire, New Jersey, New Mexico, New York, North Carolina, North Dakota
3. New Brunswick, Newfoundland and Labrador, Northwest Territories, Nova Scotia, Nunavut
4. Nashville (Tennessee)
5. Paul Newman, Jack Nicholson, David Niven
6. Neon
7. Neiman Marcus and Nordstrom
8. Nathan, Neal (Neil), Nelson, Newt, Nicholas/Nick, Nigel, Niles, Noah, Noel, Norbert, Norman (*Other, less common correct answers are possible.*)
9. Nutmeg
10. Neptune
11. Nixon
12. Acronyms:
National Assoc. for the Advancement of Colored People
National Aeronautics and Space Administration
North Atlantic Treaty Organization
National Broadcasting Corp.
Not in my backyard
National Organization for Women
National Public Radio
National Rifle Association

page 179: **Trivia—Famous Cars**

1. *The Dukes of Hazzard*
2. Volkswagen Beetle
3. *Thelma & Louise*
4. A Ford Bronco

page 180: **Fictional Occupations**

1. Bus driver (*The Honeymooners*)
2. Window dresser (*The Mary Tyler Moore Show* and *Rhoda*)
3. Hardware store owner (*Happy Days*)
4. Substitute teacher (*Golden Girls*)
5. Architect (*The Brady Bunch*)
6. Auto mechanic (and, later, a Marine) (*The Andy Griffith Show* and *Gomer Pyle, USMC*)
7. Chef (*Three's Company*)
8. Comedy show writer (*The Dick Van Dyke Show*)
9. Boxer (*Taxi*)
10. TV news writer (*The Mary Tyler Moore Show*)
11. Postal carrier (*Seinfeld*)
12. Barber (*The Andy Griffith Show*)

page 180: **Order, Please!**

(Sizes are approximate.)
Canada
(3.8 million sq. mi.)
United States
(3.79 million sq. mi.)
Brazil
(3.2 million sq. mi.)
Australia
(2.9 million sq. mi.)
Argentina
(1.0 million sq. mi.)
Saudi Arabia
(830,000 sq. mi.)
Iran
(636,000 sq. mi.)
France
(247,000 sq. mi.)
Japan
(145,000 sq. mi.)
Germany
(137,000 sq. mi.)

page 181: **Finish the Poetry**

1. ". . . Casey has struck out."
2. ". . . it might have been."
3. ". . . the captain of my soul."
4. ". . . cabbages and kings."
5. ". . . food of love, play on."
6. ". . . only stand and wait."
7. ". . . into that good night."
8. ". . . a dangerous thing."
9. ". . . Death, he kindly stopped for me."
10. ". . . but with a whimper."
11. ". . . we band of brothers."
12. ". . . talking of Michelangelo."

page 182: Complete the Words

- TRAMPOLINE
- CHOWDER
- GARLIC
- AIRPORT
- ASTHMA
- PILLOWCASE
- BANJO
- ALWAYS
- BEHAVIOR
- MIXTURE
- BIOGRAPHY
- COBRA
- FRISKY
- DEODORANT
- GLAUCOMA
- KNITTING
- ANTIQUE
- MEDIUM
- FIGHTER
- BIZARRE
- HANDSOME
- KNUCKLE
- LUMBER
- TANTRUM
- BLINDFOLDED
- TANGO

page 183: Run the Alphabet—Beginnings & Endings

These are just a few examples of the many correct answers that are possible for this quiz.

A: Arena, Anemia
B: Bathtub, Blurb
C: Clinic, Comic
D: Dad, Defend
E: Erase, Explode
F: Fluff, Foolproof
G: Gang, Giving
H: High, Health
I: Illuminati, Iambi
J:
K: Kick, Kayak
L: Liberal, Loyal
M: Madam, Minimum
N: Nation, Nylon
O: Oregano, Overdo
P: Parsnip, Peep
Q:
R: Razor, Refrigerator
S: Success, Surplus
T: Tablet, Ticket
U: Ulu, Unau
V: Vav
W: Widow, Willow
X: Xerox
Y: Yesterday, Yummy
Z:

page 184: Find the Words
(see pages 368–369)

page 186: Odd Man Out

1. *A banana* is the odd man out. All of the other items have pockets.
2. *Skiff* is the odd man out. All of the other items are types of glassware. (Skiff is a boat.)
3. *High School* is the odd man out. All of the others are movies that have the word *dirty* in the title.
4. *Bacon* is the odd man out. All of the others complete the phrase "_____ *fever.*"
5. *Miami* is the odd man out. All of the other answers are the last names of people named John.
6. *A driving instructor* is the odd man out. All of the other items on the list have scales.
7. *Kidney* is the odd man out. It is a human organ. The others complete the phrase "_____ *cap.*"
8. *Roosevelt* is the odd man out. All of the others are place names beginning with the word *Cape* (Cape Kennedy, Cape Fear, Cape May).

page 186: Honorific Titles

1. Parson Brown
2. Major Houlihan
3. Dr. Kildare
4. Mr. Coffee
5. Uncle Milty (Milton Berle)
6. Mr. In-Between
7. Mr. Whipple
8. Uncle Fester
9. Mrs. Fields

buildings

bat

bleachers

baseball

bus

birthday cake

blanket

bush

bird

base

bunting

bicycle

ballerina

bells

bassoon

beggar

bass

bald

badge

beard

rglar/andit

bow

benches

belt

burger

baton

beer

bucket

bikini

barbeque

brim

bracelet

brooch

bangles bangs

baguette/bread

bottle

boots

ball

bottle

basket

bagels

buttons

box

banana

bandaid

baby

barefoot

bib

book

bear

bubbles

beak/bill

blocks

Note: Other correct answers are possible.

1. Blue Angel
2. Blue baby
3. Bluebeard
4. Bluebell
5. Blueberries
6. Bluebird
7. Blue blood
8. Bluebonnet
9. Blue Book
10. Blue cheese
11. Blue chip
12. Blue collar
13. Blue crab
14. Blue Cross
15. Blue Danube
16. Blue Devil
17. Blue eyes
18. Bluefish
19. Blue flu
20. Bluegrass
21. Blue-green
22. Blue heaven
23. Blue jay
24. Blue jeans
25. Blue lagoon
26. Blue Laws
27. Blue marlin
28. Blue Monday
29. Blue moon
30. Blue pencil
31. Blue planet
32. Blue plate
33. Blueprint
34. Blue ribbon
35. Blue sky
36. Blue spruce
37. Blue state
38. Blue streak
39. Blue whale

page 188: **Double Trouble**

1. Wash
2. Storm
3. Bow
4. Chair
5. Face
6. Machine
7. Pin
8. Talk
9. Top
10. Milk

page 189: **Making Connections**

Truman, Hamlin, Houdini: Famous people named Harry
Robinson, Davis, Roosevelt: Maiden names of US First Ladies (Michelle Robinson Obama; Nancy Davis Reagan; Eleanor Roosevelt Roosevelt)
Cutter, Scow, Dory: Types of boats

page 190: **Alphabet Trivia**

1. Barack Obama
2. Oslo, Norway; Ottawa, Canada; Ouagadougou, Burkina Faso
3. Ohio, Oklahoma, Oregon
4. Oboe, Ocarina, Organ (*Other, more obscure correct answers are possible.*)
5. Okra, Olive, Onion, Orange (*Other, more obscure correct answers are possible.*)
6. Othello
7. *(The) Odyssey*
8. Ocelot, Octopus, Okapi, Opossum, Orangutan, Orca, Oryx, Osprey, Ostrich, Otter, Owl, Ox, Oyster (*Other, more obscure correct answers are possible.*)
9. Obsidian, Onyx, Opal
10. Famous folks whose last names begin with the letter O:
    a. Carroll O'Connor
    b. Maureen O'Hara
    c. Robert Oppenheimer
    d. Bobby Orr
    e. George Orwell
11. Acronyms:
    Obstetrics-Gynecology
    Obsessive-compulsive disorder
    Overdose
    Oxford English Dictionary
    Orange juice (Orenthal James [Simpson] *is also correct.*)
    Oh my God
    Organization of Petroleum Exporting Countries
    Operating room

page 191: **President in Name Only**

1. Ford's Theatre
2. June Carter
3. Roosevelt Greer
4. Jackson Pollack
5. Tonya Harding
6. Truman Capote
7. *Arthur*
8. Mt. McKinley
9. Helen Hayes
10. Anne Tyler

page 191: **Riddle Me This**

They weren't single. They were all married.

page 192: **Word Rebus**
1. Pioneer (Pie + N + Ear)
2. Anybody (N + E + Bud + D)
3. Incorporate (N + Core + Pour + 8)
4. Lieutenant (Loop – P + 10 + Ant)
5. Infinity (N + Fin + Knit + Tea)
6. Debatable (D + Bait + A + Bull)
7. Geometry (G + Comet – C + Tree)
8. Taxicab (Tacks + Z + Cabin – In)

page 194: **Anagrams**
1. Dome, Demo, Mode
2. Buts, Bust, Stub, Tubs
3. Meta, Mate, Meat, Tame, Team
4. Scion, Coins, Icons, Sonic
5. Slime, Limes, Smile, Miles
6. Voles, Loves, Solve
7. Palest, Pastel, Petals, Plates, Pleats, Staple
8. Caller, Recall, Cellar

page 194: **Trivia—A Bridge Too Far**
1. Alabama
2. Cape Cod
3. Florida (The Seven Mile Bridge connects the Middle Florida Keys with the Lower Florida Keys.)
4. The Hudson River
5. The Niagara River

page 195: **Water, Water Everywhere**
1. Waterloo
2. Come hell or high water
3. Water closet
4. Watergate
5. Waterfowl
6. Blood is thicker than water
7. Whitewater
8. Hot water
9. Water chestnut
10. Still waters run deep
11. *Watership Down*
12. A fish out of water
13. Water lilies

page 196: **Letter Play**
#1 Draft
Felon
Bravo
Naked
Plant
Bacon
Peach
Caddy
DEADLOCK
#2 Clone
Poach
Manor
Gland
Store
Brown
Found
Least
FOOTBALL
#3 Slight
Renter
Stamp
Sleet

Brawl
Strap
Spark
Sings
SPLINTER

page 197: **Signature Songs**
1. Ray Charles
2. Andy Williams
3. Bobby Darin
4. Peggy Lee
5. Celine Dion
6. Maurice Chevalier
7. Harry Belafonte
8. Ethel Merman
9. Nat "King" Cole
10. Helen Reddy
11. Petula Clark
12. Sammy Davis Jr.
13. Rosemary Clooney
14. Dinah Shore
15. Ella Fitzgerald

CHAPTER SIX

page 198: **Exonyms**
1. Venice
2. Munich
3. Florence
4. Copenhagen
5. Greece
6. Genoa
7. Vienna
8. The French Riviera (The literal translation of *Cote d'Azur* is *Azure* [or *Blue*] *Coast*.)
9. Japan
10. Ireland
11. The Hague
12. Norway
13. Moscow

Secret Word – PSYCHOLOGY

Note: Other, more obscure correct answers are possible.

4-Letter Words:
1. Chop
2. Clog
3. Clop
4. Cloy
5. Cogs
6. Cool
7. Coop
8. Coos
9. Cops
10. Copy
11. Cosy
12. Coys
13. Glop
14. Goop
15. Goos
16. Gosh
17. Hogs
18. Holy
19. Hoop
20. Hops
21. Loch
22. Logo
23. Logs
24. Logy
25. Loop
26. Loos
27. Lops
28. Oops
29. Ploy
30. Polo
31. Pool
32. Posh
33. Posy
34. Shoo
35. Shop
36. Slog
37. Slop
38. Solo

5-Letter Words:
1. Chops
2. Clogs
3. Clops
4. Cloys
5. Cools
6. Cooly
7. Coops
8. Coyly
9. Glops
10. Goops
11. Goopy
12. **Gypsy (Secret Word)**
13. Hoops
14. Lochs
15. Logos
16. Loops
17. Loopy
18. Ploys
19. Polos
20. Pooch
21. Pools
22. Scoop
23. Shyly
24. Sloop
25. Spool

page 200: Word Pictures
1. Backbone (back + BONE)
2. Outskirts (out + SKIRTS)
3. Overbite (over + BITE)
4. Underpants (under + PANTS)
5. Downscale (down + SCALE)
6. Offspring (off + SPRING)
7. Infringe (in + FRINGE)
8. Aftershave (after + SHAVE)
9. Withdraw (with + DRAW)
10. Beforehand (before + HAND)

page 202: Last Name Please
1. *Annie Hall*
2. *Being John Malkovich*
3. *Lorna Doone*
4. *Myra Breckinridge*
5. *Pippi Longstocking*
6. *Pudd'nhead Wilson*
7. *Stuart Little*
8. *The Brothers Karamazov*
9. *The Magnificent Ambersons*
10. *The Talented Mr. Ripley*

page 202: Endings & Beginnings
1. Wood
2. Yard
3. Heart
4. Security
5. Face
6. Cheese
7. Suit
8. Banana
9. Rock
10. Shop

page 203: Follow the Rules
(see next page)

page 204: What a Pair
1. Bells and Whistles
2. Fife and Drum
3. Hard and Fast
4. Horse and Buggy
5. Hunt and Peck
6. P's and Q's (Peas and Queues)
7. Sticks and Stones
8. Tool and Die
9. Touch and Go
10. Woodward and Bernstein

page 205: **What's the Title?**

1. *. . . It Looks Like Up to Me*
2. *. . . to Stop Worrying and Love the Bomb*
3. *. . . at the Whistle Stop Cafe*
4. *. . . of Good and Evil*
5. *. . . the Ya-Ya Sisterhood*
6. *. . . Went Up a Hill and Came Down a Mountain*
7. *. . . the Coward Robert Ford*
8. *. . . Whorehouse in Texas*
9. *. . . Five and Dime, Jimmy Dean, Jimmy Dean*
10. *. . . Thanks for Everything, Julie Newmar*

page 205: **Fill in the Letters**

Other, more obscure correct answers are possible.

1. Fang, Fans, Fend, Fens, Find, Fine, Fink, Fins, Fond, Font, Fund, Funk
2. Gage, Gale, Game, Gape, Gate, Gave, Gaze, Gene, Give, Glee, Glue, Gone, Gore
3. Wash, Wasp, West, Wise, Wish, Wisp
4. Bath, Both, Hath, Kith, Lath, Math, Moth, Myth, Oath, Path, With
5. Cater, Dater, Eater, Hater, Later, Mater, Pater, Rater, Tater, Water
6. Bland, Bleed, Blend, Blind, Blond, Blood, Blued
7. Prate, Price, Pride, Prime, Prize, Probe, Prone, Prose, Prove, Prude, Prune

page 203: **Follow the Rules**

1. N E V E R P U T A N A G E
2. N E **M** E R P U T A N A G E
3. N **I M I** R P U T A N A G E
4. N I M I R P U T N G E **A**
5. N I M I R P U T N G E A **M S**
6. N I M I P U T N **R R** G E A M S
7. N I M I P T N U R R G E A M S
8. N I M I P T **O N O** U R R G E A M S
9. **L** N I M I P T O N **Y** O U R R G E A M S
10. L N I M I P T O N Y O U R **D** R G E A M S
11. L I M I T O N Y O U R D R E A M S

(Never put an age) limit on your dreams.
(Dara Torres, USA Gold Medalist in swimming)

8. Breeze, Cheese, Fleece, Freeze, Sleeve, Sneeze, Tweeze, Wheeze

page 206: **Alphabet Trivia**

1. Pakistan, Palau, Panama, Papua New Guinea, Paraguay, Peru, Philippines, Poland, Portugal, Palestine (*Note: Palestine's nation status is disputed, although it has received diplomatic recognition from 132 states.*)
2. Franklin Pierce, James K. Polk
3. Pearl, Peridot
4. Phoenix, AZ; Pierre, SD; Providence, RI
5. Packers (Green Bay), Panthers (Carolina), Patriots (New England)
6. Peugeot, Plymouth, Pontiac, Porsche
7. Panther, Parakeet, Parrot, Partridge, Peacock, Pelican, Penguin, Peregrine falcon, Pheasant, Pig, Pigeon, Pike, Piranha, Platypus, Plover, Polar bear, Porcupine, Possum, Puffer fish, Puffin, Puma
8. Pavarotti (Luciano)
9. Prancer
10. Pennsylvania
11. Printing press
12. Acronyms:
    Public Broadcasting Service
    People for the Ethical Treatment of Animals
    Parental Guidance
    Personal information number
    Palestine Liberation Organization
    Prisoner of war
    Parent-Teacher Association
    Post-traumatic stress disorder

page 207: **Sentence Sleuth**

1. Canada
   (. . . Ameri<u>can adaptation</u> . . .)
2. Amsterdam
   (. . . <u>hamster dam</u>aged . . .)
3. Calcutta
   (. . . logi<u>cal! Cut taxes</u> . . .)
4. Mumbai
   (. . . <u>mum bai</u>led him . . .)
5. Toronto
   (. . . ac<u>tor onto</u> . . .)
6. London
   (. . . basi<u>l on don</u>uts . . .)
7. Hiroshima
   (. . .<u>Hi Ros, hi Ma</u> . . .)
8. Istanbul
   (<u>Tristan bul</u>lied . . .)

page 208: **Initial Quiz**

1. Camp David
2. Charles Dickens
3. *Carpe Diem*
4. Churchill Downs
5. Charles Darwin
6. Clarence Darrow
7. Cough Drops
8. Cold Duck
9. *Coup D'etat*
10. Cardiovascular Disease
11. Carbon Dioxide

page 208: **Trivia—Infamous Nicknames**

1. The Boston Strangler
2. Scarface
3. The Unabomber, which stood for University and Airline bomber because Kaczynski's early target locations were mainly universities and airlines.
4. Son of Sam. After Berkowitz was captured, he told police that Sam was a neighborhood dog that he believed was possessed by the devil.
5. The Hillside Strangler

page 209: **Word Tower**

These answers are just a suggestion; many other correct answers are possible:

1. Or
2. Orb
3. Ores
4. Orbit
5. Orange
6. Orderly
7. Ordinary
8. Orchestra
9. Originally
10. Orthopedics
11. Orthodontist
12. Ornamentation
13. Organizational

page 210: **Group Therapy**

Some Group Therapy questions have many possible correct answers. Your answers may differ from ours and still be correct.

1. Beet, Carrot, Daikon, Ginger, Jicama, Onion, Parsnip, Potato, Radish, Rutabaga, Shallot, Taro, Turnip, Water chestnut, Yam, Yucca
2. Andre Agassi, Jason Alexander, Ed Asner, Charles Barkley, Yul Brynner, James Carville, Dick Cheney, Winston Churchill, Sean Connery, George Foreman, Mahatma Gandhi, Mikhail Gorbachev, Louis Gossett Jr., Ron Howard, Samuel L. Jackson, Michael Jordan, Howie Mandel, Dr. Phil McGraw, Telly Savalas, Damon Wayans, Bruce Willis
3. No borders: Australia, Bahamas, Bermuda, Cuba, Iceland, Jamaica, Japan, Madagascar, New Zealand, Philippines. One border: Canada, Denmark, Dominican Republic, Haiti, Ireland, Portugal, Qatar, South Korea, United Kingdom
4. Ace bandage, Ammonia inhalant/Smelling salts, Antibiotic cream/First aid cream, Antiseptic towelettes, Aspirin, Band-aids, Blanket (silver rescue), Burn cream, Cold pack (instant), Cotton swabs, Eye wash, Finger splint, First aid booklet, Gauze, Iodine, Plastic/Latex gloves, Scissors, Tape
5. Best Western, Clarion Inn, Comfort Inn, Days Inn, Doubletree, EconoLodge, Embassy Suites, Four Seasons, Hampton Inn, Hilton, Holiday Inn, Howard Johnson, Hyatt, Intercontinental, La Quinta, Marriott (and Courtyard by Marriott),

Motel 6, Omni, Quality Inn, Ramada, Red Roof Inn, Ritz-Carlton, Super 8, Travelodge, Westin

6. Cadillac, Camaro (Chevrolet), Camry (Toyota), Caprice (Chevrolet), Caravan (Dodge), Cavalier (AMC), Challenger (Dodge), Charger (Dodge), Cherokee (Jeep), Chevelle (Chevy), Chevrolet, Chrysler, Citation (Chevrolet), Citroën, Civic (Honda), Comanche (Jeep), Concord (AMC), Continental (Lincoln), Corolla (Toyota), Corona (Toyota), Corvair (Chevrolet), Corvette (Chevrolet), Cougar (Mercury), Coupe DeVille (Cadillac), Crown Victoria (Ford)

7. Affix, Annex, Apex, Ax, Box, Coax, Crucifix, Ex, Fax, Fix, Flax, Flex, Fox, Hex, Hoax, Icebox, Index, Jinx, Lox, Lynx, Mix, Onyx, Ox, Perplex, Pox, Reflex, Relax, Sax, Sex, Six, Smallpox, Soapbox, Tax, Tux, Vex, Wax, Xerox

8. Amsterdam, Athens, Barcelona, Berlin, Bilbao, Bonn, Brussels, Budapest, Cologne, Copenhagen, Dresden, Dublin, Edinburgh, Florence, Glasgow, Helsinki, Lisbon, London, Madrid, Naples, Paris, Prague, Rome, Stockholm, The Hague, Vienna, Warsaw

page 210: Sibling Rivalry
1. Kennedy
2. Magliozzi
3. Van Dyke
4. Quaid
5. Roberts
6. Arness and Graves
7. Kennedy
8. Affleck
9. Carpenter
10. Fonda (Asher *is also correct*)

page 211: Vivienne's Vowels
1. Buenos Aires
2. Tahiti
3. Teheran, Iran
4. Juneau, Alaska
5. Vienna, Austria
6. Puerto Rico
7. Boise, Idaho
8. Maine (Oman *is also correct*)
9. Eugene, Oregon
10. Iceland

page 211: Change a Letter
1. A—Aide, Acorn, Alive
2. N—Naked, Night, Nearly
3. T—Tart, Thick, Treat
4. A—Arid, Aiding, Auction
5. C—Cough, Cover, Crown
6. H—Harm, Heading, Horse
7. K—Knit, Know, Kelp
8. E—Eel, Elastic, Earring
9. V—Vanish, Vase, Vanity
10. O—Oath, Oasis, Ooze

page 212: Pour le "Ban"
1. *Ban*quet
2. *Ban*gle
3. *Ban*ana
4. *Ban*jo
5. Tur*ban*
6. Montal*ban* (Ricardo)
7. *Ban*kruptcy
8. Subur*ban*
9. *Ban*gkok
10. Tali*ban*
11. *Ban*ish
12. *Ban*tamweight

page 212: Odd Man Out
1. *Von Furstenberg* is the odd (wo)man out. She is a woman fashion designer. The rest are all male fashion designers.
2. *Write* is the odd man out. All of the others are anagrams of the letters EIMRT.
3. *Greta Garbo* is the odd (wo)man out. She may have lived a private life and shunned publicity, but she never went missing, as all the others did.
4. *Vinyl* is the odd man out. All of the rest are types of golf clubs.
5. *Baseball gloves* is the odd man out. All of the others have chains.
6. *Gretzky* is the odd man out. All of the others are last names of famous people whose first and last names start with the same letter: Charlie Chaplin,

Alan Alda, Robert Redford, Mickey Mantle. (Gretzky's first name is Wayne.)

7. *Halloween* is the odd man out. It is celebrated in October. All the rest are observed in November.

page 213: Sentence Sleuth

1. Antelope (. . . G<u>rant eloped</u>. . .)
2. Parakeet (. . . Grand<u>pa rake Etta's</u> . . .)
3. Snake (. . . <u>his naked</u> . . .)
4. Beaver (. . . <u>be average</u> . . .)
5. Walrus (. . . withdra<u>wal, Rusty</u>)
6. Otter (. . . can<u>not terminate</u> . . .)
7. Salamander (. . . <u>Sal, a man derailed</u> . . .)
8. Jackal (<u>Jack a lot</u> . . .)

page 214: One-Minute Madness: One-Syllable Anatomy

1. Arch
2. Arm
3. Brain
4. Brow
5. Calf
6. Cheek
7. Chest
8. Chin
9. Ear
10. Eye
11. Face
12. Foot
13. Groin
14. Gum
15. Hair
16. Hand
17. Head
18. Hip
19. Jaw
20. Joint
21. Knee
22. Leg
23. Lip
24. Lung
25. Mouth
26. Nail
27. Nose
28. Palm
29. Rib
30. Shin
31. Skin
32. Spleen
33. Throat
34. Thumb
35. Toe
36. Tongue
37. Vein
38. Waist

page 215: By the Letter

1. B Borax
2. A Appetizers
3. N Naples
4. A Andrew
5. N Neptune
6. A Appalachian

BANANA

page 215: Riddle Me This

Incorrectly

page 216: Complete the Words

			S	Y	N	D	R	O	M	E
	M	O	T	H	E	R				
M	I	C	R	O	P	H	O	N	E	
		J	O	I	N	T				
		I	N	J	U	R	Y			
		L	L	A	M	A				
	C	E	L	E	B	R	A	T	E	
		J	I	G	S	A	W			
	C	R	E	A	T	U	R	E		
	S	E	I	Z	U	R	E			
		O	F	F	I	C	E			
		U	S	U	A	L	L	Y		
		K	A	R	A	T	E			
	S	W	O	O	P					
	L	A	W	Y	E	R				
H	U	R	R	I	C	A	N	E		
		C	L	I	N	I	C			
B	A	P	T	I	Z	E	D			
C	A	R	N	I	V	A	L			
	P	A	R	K	I	N	G			
	H	A	M	M	E	R				
	T	W	I	N	G	E				
	B	I	S	H	O	P				
	A	D	J	U	S	T				
	S	E	Q	U	I	N	S			
C	O	N	T	E	X	T				

page 217: Alphabet Trivia

1. Qatar
2. Quito, Ecuador
3. Quebec
4. Queensland
5. Dan Quayle
6. Quotation marks and Question mark
7. Qantas
8. Quaker State
9. Quiznos
10. Quality Inn

11. Q Foods:
    a. Quiche
    b. Quesadilla
    c. Quahogs (pronounced: CO-hogs)
    d. Quail
    e. Quinine
12. Qaddafi (Muammar)
13. Quisling (Vidkun). He was tried after World War II and executed by firing squad in Oslo in 1945.
14. Quinn (Anthony)

page 218: A Spoonful of Medicine
1. Diabetes
2. Angina
3. Parkinson's disease
4. Attention deficit disorder (ADD)
5. Respiratory conditions such as asthma or COPD
6. Pain
7. High cholesterol
8. Anti-acid, reflux, dyspepsia
9. Depression/Anxiety

page 218: Walk a MILE
1. Smile, Slime
2. Dimple
3. Helium
4. Limber
5. Limped
6. Middle
7. Mildew
8. Mingle
9. Pimple
10. Blemish
11. Climate
12. Decimal
13. Dilemma

14. Himself
15. Melting
16. Mineral
17. Demolish
18. Heirloom
19. Masculine
20. Limousine

page 219: Ted's Terrible Titles
1. *Curious George*
2. "Your Cheating Heart"
3. *Terms of Endearment*
4. *Stranger in a Strange Land*
5. "Sitting On the Dock of the Bay"
6. *One Hundred Years of Solitude*
7. *Jailhouse Rock*
8. *In Cold Blood*
9. *How to Succeed in Business Without Really Trying*
10. "Climb Every Mountain"
11. *Bye Bye Birdie*
12. *All About Eve*

page 219: Sleep Deprived
1. The Brothers Grimm
2. Woody Allen
3. Washington Irving
4. Raymond Chandler

page 220: Word Pictures
1. Dogcatcher (Dog + Catcher)
2. Birdbath (Bird + Bath)
3. Beanbag (Bean + Bag)
4. Forklift (Fork + Lift)
5. Seatbelt (Seat + Belt)
6. Quarterback (Quarter + Back)

7. Eyetooth (Eye + Tooth)
8. Doorbell (Door + Bell)

page 222: POT Head
1. Pot of gold
2. Pot luck
3. Pothole
4. Crock-Pot
5. Chamber pot
6. Pot calling the kettle black
7. Sweeten the pot (*Raise the pot* is also acceptable.)
8. Pot sticker
9. Melting pot
10. Pol Pot
11. Potboiler
12. Potter
13. "A watched pot never boils."

page 222: Where's the Suburb?
1. Seattle
2. Atlanta
3. Minneapolis-St. Paul
4. Dallas
5. Detroit
6. Phoenix
7. Indianapolis
8. Baltimore
9. Pittsburgh
10. Cleveland

page 223: Making Connections
Sure, Secret, Ban: Brands of deodorant
Mint, Lime, Forest: Shades of green
Coal Odor, Old Fair, Land Army: Anagrams of US states (Colorado, Florida, Maryland)

Millie (Barbara Bush's dog), Nana (*Peter Pan*), Odie (*Garfield*), Old Yeller (book and movie), Rin Tin Tin, Scooby Doo, Snoopy, Spuds MacKenzie (Budweiser mascot), Toto (*The Wizard of Oz*), Underdog

4. Castro, Chavez, Cruz, Diaz, Flores, Garcia, Gomez, Gonzalez, Hernandez, Juarez, Lopez, Martinez, Moreno, Ortiz, Perez, Ramirez, Rivera, Rodriguez, Romero, Sanchez, Torres

5. Baby oil, Bath oil, Canola oil, Castor oil, Cod liver oil, Corn oil, Crude oil, Grapeseed oil, Linseed oil, Mineral oil, Motor oil, Olive oil, Peanut oil, Safflower oil, Sesame oil, Vegetable oil

6. Ant, Ape, Bat, Bee, Cat, Cow, Dog, Eel, Elk, Emu, Fox, Gnu, Hen, Jay, Owl, Pig, Rat, Yak

7. Apples, Beef, Beets, Cabbage, Cherries, Cranberries, Grapefruit, Grapes, Ketchup, Kidney beans, Licorice, Onion, Pomegranates, Potatoes, Radishes, Raspberries, Red peppers, Red wine, Rhubarb, Salmon, Salsa, Shrimp cocktail, Strawberries, Tomatoes, Watermelon

8. Christmas, Columbus Day, Independence Day, Labor Day, Martin Luther King Day, Memorial Day, New Year's Day, President's Day, Thanksgiving Day, Veterans Day

page 228: Word Rebus

1. Centimeter (Cent + swim – SW + meter)
2. Catacombs (Cat + jack – J + combs)
3. Identical (Eye + dentist – IST + pickle – P)
4. Mustache (Mustard – ARD + ash)
5. Binoculars (Bicycle – Cycle + Knock + Q + Dollars – Do)
6. Optometrist (Mop – M + Toe + Helmet – Hel + Wrist)
7. Economy (Beak – B + Bacon – Ba + Gnome + E)
8. Superlative (Soup + Pearl + Negative – Neg)

page 230: Eights & Fours

(Other correct answers are possible.)

1. Waitress — Wise/Star
2. Seashore — Shoe/Ears
3. Thankful — Flat/Hunk
4. Election — Cone/Tile
5. Waterbed — Draw/Beet
6. Champion — Main/Chop

page 231: Find the Quotation

1. Peso, Cinco, Agua
2. Ohio, Idaho, Iowa
3. Obesity, Avocado
4. Bed, Doe, Map, Pin

5. Sue, Barb, Flo
6. Sloth, Duck, Panda
7. Brooklyn, Hillside, Sheets
8. Pink, Blue, Cyan, Teal
9. Scratch, Stretch, Twelfth

QUOTATION:
The best things in life aren't things. (Art Buchwald)

page 232: Finish the Poetry

1. "... miles to go before I sleep/And miles to go before I sleep." *Stopping By Woods on a Snowy Evening* by Robert Frost
2. "... is yet to be." *Rabbi Ben Ezra* by Robert Browning
3. "... merely players." *As You Like It* by William Shakespeare
4. "... all ye need to know." *Ode on a Grecian Urn* by John Keats
5. "... buy you a diamond ring." Traditional lullaby
6. "... lovely as a tree." *Trees* by Joyce Kilmer
7. "... a raisin in the sun?" *Dream Deferred* by Langston Hughes
8. "... my soul can reach" *How Do I Love Thee?* (Sonnet 43) by Elizabeth Barrett Browning
9. "... and her eyes" *She Walks in Beauty* by Lord Byron
10. "... more temperate." *Sonnet XVIII* by William Shakespeare

page 233: **Stinky Pinky**
1. Stone Phone
2. Jewel School
3. Fish's Dishes
4. Rookie's Cookies
5. Preacher Teacher
6. Shin Skin
7. Butter Putter
8. Flag Bag
9. "Cheeses, Jesus?"
10. Barbara's Candelabras

page 234: **Alphabetically Speaking**
1. Veterans Day
2. Yorkshire terrier
3. Wrench
4. Archery
5. *Sense and Sensibility*
6. Daisy
7. Honolulu
8. Afghanistan
9. Albany
10. George Harrison
11. Blitzen

page 235: **What's Their Job?**
1. Game show host
2. Author
3. Physician
4. Fashion model
5. Race car driver
6. Attorney
7. Astronaut
8. Fashion designer
9. Drummer
10. Ice cream maker
11. Poet
12. Basketball player

page 236: **Alphabet Trivia**
1. Europe: Romania, Russia
   Africa: Rwanda
2. Theodore Roosevelt, Franklin Roosevelt, Ronald Reagan
3. Raleigh (North Carolina), Richmond (Virginia)
4. Rabat (Morocco), Reykjavik (Iceland), Riga (Latvia), Riyadh (Saudi Arabia), Rome (Italy)
5. Rangers (Texas), Rays (Tampa Bay), Reds (Cincinnati), Red Sox (Boston), Rockies (Colorado), Royals (Kansas City)
6. *Richard II, Richard III, Romeo and Juliet*
7. Rabbit, Raccoon, Rat, Rattlesnake, Raven, Reindeer, Rhea, Rhinoceros, Roadrunner, Robin (*Other correct answers are possible.*)
8. Radicchio, Radish, Raspberry, Rhubarb, Rutabaga
9. Rhine (768 miles), Rio Grande (1,900 miles), Red River (1,360 miles)
10. Rhode Island
11. Acronyms and abbreviations:
    Rhythm and blues
    Runs batted in
    Royal Canadian Mountain Police
    Rural Free Delivery
    Rest in peace (*Requiescat in pace*)
    Reserve Officer Training Corps
    Revolutions per minute
    Rest and relaxation
    Répondez s'il vous plait (Please reply)
    Recreational vehicle

page 237: **Sentence Sleuth**
1. Orange
   (. . . <u>or ange</u>r . . .)
2. Purple
   (. . . s<u>pur ple</u>nty . . .)
3. Magenta
   (. . . cust<u>om agent a</u>llowed . . .)
4. Gray
   (. . . actin<u>g, Ray</u> . . .)
5. Pink
   (. . . s<u>pin K</u>enny's . . .)
6. Scarlet
   (. . . Mateo'<u>s car let</u>hal . . .)
7. Orchid
   (. . . <u>porch, I d</u>ove . . .)
8. Brown
   (. . . Bo<u>b, row now</u> . . .)

page 238: **Flower Power**
A. Lavender
B. Black-eyed Susan
C. Amaryllis
D. Begonia
E. Calla lily
F. Carnation
G. Daisy
H. Hyacinth
I. Buttercup
J. Forget-me-not
K. Fuchsia
L. Bird-of-paradise
M. Dandelion
N. Iris

page 240: Odd Man Out

1. *Jefferson* is the odd man out. Jefferson's first name was Thomas. All of the others are presidents named James.
2. *Bottle* is the odd man out. All of the other words are often preceded by the word "red."
3. *Japan* is the odd man out. All of the others are communist countries.
4. *Star* is the odd man out. All of the others are things you "hit."
5. *Middle* is the odd man out. It is a position relative to other things. The rest are types of tubes.
6. *Drain* is the odd man out. All of the others are people named Oliver.
7. *West Side Story* is the odd man out. It was created by Leonard Bernstein, Arthur Laurents, and Stephen Sondheim. All the rest are musicals by Rodgers and Hammerstein.
8. *Saxophone* is the odd man out. All of the others are fictional Barneys.

page 240: Riddle Me This

The taxi driver was walking.

CHAPTER SEVEN

page 241: The Name Game

1. Ink + hell + her + L (Helen Keller)
2. D + L + lend + generous (Ellen DeGeneres)
3. Meter + gym + ante (Jimmy Durante)
4. A + knee + launch (Lon Chaney)
5. Fat + yes + error + Sir (Yasser Arafat)
6. Anne + cone + O + N + pry (Conan O'Brien)
7. Ink + dens + ton + L + wash (Denzel Washington)
8. Stun + church + win + ill (Winston Churchill)
9. D + E + V + Dan + toe (Danny DeVito)

page 242: Vivienne's Vowels

1. Koala
2. Octopus
3. Goose
4. Lion
5. Anteater
6. Iguana
7. Panda
8. Otter
9. Tortoise
10. Flea
11. Emu
12. Ape

page 242: Order, Please!

Titanic Sinks (1912)
US Women Get the Vote (1920)
Insulin Discovered (1921)
Hindenburg Explodes (1937)
First Polio Vaccine (1952)
Martin Luther King Jr. Shot (1968)
Man Walks on Moon (1969)
Nixon Resigns (1974)
Berlin Wall Falls (1989)
Nelson Mandela Freed (1990)
O.J. Simpson Not Guilty (1995)
Hurricane Katrina (2005)

page 243: What Month Is It?

1. The March of Dimes
2. The Mayo Clinic
3. April Fool's Day
4. *Born on the Fourth of July*
5. Juneau
6. Mayor
7. *The Hunt for Red October*
8. *The Teahouse of the August Moon*

page 243: Trivia— It's Offal Food

1. Liver. The term *foie gras* is French for "fat liver."
2. Brain
3. Sweetbread
4. Tripe
5. Haggis

page 244: Initial Quiz

1. Inauguration Day
2. Italian Dressing
3. Ice Dancing
4. *Il Duce*
5. Infectious Disease
6. Insanity Defense
7. Illegal Drug
8. Independence Day
9. Interior Designer/ Decorator

10. Iron Deficiency
11. Isadora Duncan

page 244: **Riddle Me This**
A towel

page 245: **Trimble**
1. Brazil
2. Madagascar
3. Spain
4. Canada
5. Spanish
6. Argentina
7. Australia
8. Switzerland

Jumble Answer: Jamaica

page 246: **Quotation Station**
(see below)

page 247: **No TriX!**
1. Larynx
2. Hoax
3. Chickenpox
4. Annex
5. Suffix
6. Nix
7. Anticlimax
8. Appendix
9. Smallpox
10. Coax
11. Coccyx
12. Equinox

page 247: **Common Bonds**
Sports Equipment: Stick (hockey), Clubs (golf), Bat (baseball)

page 248: **Alphabet Trivia**
1. San Marino, Serbia, Slovakia, Slovenia, Spain, Sweden, Switzerland
2. Sacramento, CA; St. Paul, MN; Salem, OR; Salt Lake City, UT; Santa Fe, NM; Springfield, IL
3. Sleepy, Sneezy
4. Sight, Smell
5. Sloth
6. Scorpio, Sagittarius
7. Oscar-winning movies:
   a. *(The) Sound of Music*;
   b. *(The) Sting*;
   c. *Schindler's List*
8. Salmon, Sandpiper, Seahorse, Seal, Sea lion, Secretary bird, Shark, Sheep, Shrew, Skunk, Sloth, Snake, Sparrow, Squirrel, Starling, Stork, Swan (*Other correct answers are possible.*)
9. People with the initials SS:
   a. Sally Struthers
   b. Stephen Sondheim
   c. Suzanne Somers
   d. Susan Sarandon
10. Acronyms:
    Strategic Arms Limitation Talks
    Scholastic Aptitude Test
    Supreme Court of the United States
    Situation normal, all "fouled" up
    Saturday Night Live
    Save our souls/ship
    Social security number
    Sealed with a kiss

page 249: **Making Connections**
Silver, Iron, Nickel: Metals
Cabbage, Bread, Dough: Terms for money
Crabs, Snails, Clams: Animals with shells

page 250: **Alma's Shopping List**
1. Beets
2. Hard Candy
3. Corn Chips
4. Cat Food
5. Baked Beans
6. Pie Crust
7. Skim Milk
8. Fish Sticks
9. Bran Flakes

page 246: **Quotation Station**
We don't stop playing because we grow old; we grow old because we stop playing.
—George Bernard Shaw

W	E		D	O	N	T		S	T	O	P		P	L	A	Y	I	N	G	
B	E	C	A	U	S	E		W	E		G	R	O	W		O	L	D		W
E		G	R	O	W		O	L	D		B	E	C	A	U	S	E		W	E
	S	T	O	P		P	L	A	Y	I	N	G								

10. Trash Bags
11. Oven Cleaner
12. Cat Litter

page 250: Fill in the Letters
Other, more obscure correct answers are possible.
1. East, Edit, Emit, Exit
2. Chad, Chap, Char, Chat, Chaw, Shad, Shag, Shah, Sham, Shay, Than, That, Thaw, Wham, What
3. Label, Lapel, Legal, Level, Libel, Local, Loyal
4. Black, Blade, Blame, Bland, Blank, Blare, Blasé, Blast, Blaze
5. Beige, Bribe, Bride, Brine
6. Quick, Quiet, Quill, Quilt, Quint, Quire, Quirk, Quite, Quits
7. Thane, Thank, Theft, Their, Theme, There, These, Thick, Thief, Thigh, Thine, Thing, Think, Third, Thong, Thorn, Those, Three, Threw, Throb, Throw, Thumb, Thump, Thyme
8. Blister, Bristle, Bristly, Glisten, Gristle, Hoisted, Hoister, Keister, Moisten, Thistle, Twisted, Twister, Whistle

page 251: Two Minute Madness: _____ Stick
Note: Other correct answers are possible.
1. Breadstick
2. Broomstick
3. Candlestick
4. Celery stick
5. Chapstick
6. Chopstick
7. Cinnamon stick
8. Cue stick
9. Dipstick
10. Drumstick
11. Fish stick
12. Glue stick
13. Hickory stick
14. Hockey stick
15. Joystick
16. Licorice stick
17. Lipstick
18. Matchstick
19. Nightstick
20. Nonstick
21. Pick-up stick
22. Slapstick
23. Speed Stick
24. Swizzle stick
25. Walking stick
26. Yardstick

page 252: Group Therapy
Some Group Therapy questions have many possible correct answers. Your answers may differ from ours and still be correct.
1. Archimedes, Niels Bohr, George Washington Carver, Copernicus, Francis Crick, Marie Curie, Charles Darwin, Albert Einstein, Richard Feynman, Alexander Fleming, Sigmund Freud, Galileo, Stephen Hawking, Edwin Hubble, Percy Julian, Isaac Newton, Alfred Nobel, Louis Pasteur, Linus Pauling, Max Planck, Carl Sagan, Jonas Salk, Nikola Tesla, Neil deGrasse Tyson, James Watson, E. O. Wilson
2. *A Fistful of Dollars* (1964), *Butch Cassidy and the Sundance Kid* (1969), *The Good, the Bad, and the Ugly* (1966), *Gunfight at the O.K. Corral* (1957), *High Noon* (1952), *How the West Was Won* (1962), *Little Big Man* (1970), *The Magnificent Seven* (1960), *The Man Who Shot Liberty Valance* (1962), *McCabe & Mrs. Miller* (1971), *Rio Bravo* (1959), *The Searchers* (1956), *Shane* (1953), *Silverado* (1985), *The Treasure of the Sierra Madre* (1948), *The Wild Bunch* (1969), *They Died with Their Boots On* (1941), *Unforgiven* (1992)
3. Catacombs, Catalog, Catalyst, Catamaran, Catapult, Cataract, Catastrophe, Catatonic, Catch, Category, Cater, Caterpillar, Catfish, Cathedral, Catnip, Catsup, Cattle, Catwalk
4. Cambodia, Cameroon, Canada, Cape Verde, Central African Republic, Chad, Chile, China, Colombia, Congo, Costa Rica, Croatia, Cuba, Cyprus, Czech Republic,

Cote d'Ivoire (Ivory Coast)

5. Louisa May Alcott, Isabel Allende, Maya Angelou, Margaret Atwood, Jane Austen, Charlotte Brontë, Emily Brontë, Pearl Buck, Agatha Christie, Jackie Collins, Emily Dickinson, Joan Didion, Zora Neale Hurstson, Barbara Kingsolver, Harper Lee, Ursula K. LeGuin, Margaret Mitchell, Toni Morrison, Iris Murdoch, Joyce Carol Oates, Ayn Rand, Anne Rice, Nora Roberts, J. K. Rowling, Mary Shelley, Danielle Steel, Alice Walker, Edith Wharton, Virginia Woolf

6. Cha-Cha, Charleston, Foxtrot, Jitterbug, Jive, Lindy Hop, Mambo, Quickstep, Rumba, Salsa, Samba, Swing, Tango, Waltz

7. Bladder, Brain, Gallbladder, Heart, Kidneys, Large intestine, Liver, Lungs, Pancreas, Skin, Small intestine, Spleen, Stomach, Thyroid

8. Paul Cézanne, Leonardo Da Vinci, Salvador Dali, Paul Gauguin, Winslow Homer, Edward Hopper, Frida Kahlo, Thomas Kinkade, Edouard Manet, Henri Matisse, Michelangelo, Claude Monet, Georgia O'Keefe, Pablo Picasso, Jackson Pollock, Auguste Renoir, Diego Rivera, Norman Rockwell, Vincent van Gogh, Rembrandt van Rijn, Jan Vermeer, Andy Warhol, James Whistler

page 252: Common Bonds
Dog Breeds: Afghan, Boxer, Greyhound

page 253: Ted's Terrible Titles
1. *The Perfect Storm*
2. *The Naked and the Dead*
3. "The Long and Winding Road"
4. *Rebel Without a Cause*
5. *Pride and Prejudice*
6. *I Know Why the Caged Bird Sings*
7. *Good Morning, Vietnam*
8. *Dances with Wolves*
9. "Blue Suede Shoes"
10. *Better Homes and Gardens*
11. *Atlas Shrugged*
12. "Yesterday"

page 253: Trivia—Mind Your Business
1. Napa Valley
2. Decker (Alonzo G. Decker)
3. Blockbuster
4. General Motors
5. Nathan

page 254: In the Middle
1. Arthur Conan Doyle
2. Martin Luther King Jr.
3. John Wilkes Booth
4. Frank Lloyd Wright (Andrew Lloyd Webber, William Lloyd Garrison, and David Lloyd George *are also correct.*)
5. Mary Tyler Moore
6. Johann Sebastian Bach
7. Louisa May Alcott
8. William Makepeace Thackeray
9. Edgar Allan Poe
10. William Jefferson Clinton
11. George Washington Carver
12. Billie Jean King
13. Henry Wadsworth Longfellow

page 254: Character Study
1. *The Silence of the Lambs* Anthony Hopkins
2. *Casablanca* Humphrey Bogart
3. *Sunset Boulevard* Gloria Swanson
4. *The Pride of the Yankees* Gary Cooper
5. *Taxi Driver* Robert De Niro
6. *The African Queen* Katharine Hepburn
7. *Bull Durham* Kevin Costner
8. *Midnight Cowboy* Dustin Hoffman
9. *Psycho* Anthony Perkins
10. *Breakfast at Tiffany's* Audrey Hepburn
11. *The King and I* Yul Brynner

12. *Boys Town*
    Spencer Tracy
13. *My Fair Lady*
    Rex Harrison
14. *Ghost*
    Whoopi Goldberg
15. *Terms of Endearment*
    Shirley MacLaine
16. *The Devil Wears Prada*
    Meryl Streep

page 255: Semordnilap
1. Ante/Etna
2. Moor/Room
3. Denim/Mined
4. Lever/Revel
5. Nori/Iron
6. Regal/Lager
7. Mood/Doom
8. Emit/Time
9. Dual/Laud
10. Suez/Zeus

page 256: CAMP Out
1. Big Man on Campus
2. "Camptown Races"
3. Boot camp
4. "...at Camp Granada."
5. Campaign
6. Campbell's (Soup)
7. Scampi
8. Camphor
9. Campobello (*Note: President Franklin D. Roosevelt was born on Campobello Island.*)
10. Campari
11. Hippocampus

page 256: Odd Man Out
1. *Lisbon* is the odd man out. All of the others are types of cookies.
2. *Saxophone* is the odd man out. All of the others are bonds (of one kind or another).
3. *Fork* is the odd man out. All of the other words complete the phrase "flying _____."
4. *Eclipse* is the odd man out. It is an astronomical phenomenon. The rest are types of tables.
5. *Pelican* is the odd man out. It is a bird. All the rest are types of monkeys.
6. *Phoebe* is the odd man out. All of the others are famous people with the last name of Taylor.
7. *Dorian Gray* is the odd man out. All of the others are characters created by Charles Dickens. Dorian Gray is a character created by Oscar Wilde.
8. *Tim* is the odd man out. All of the others are "great."

page 257: Sentence Sleuth
1. Honda (...dis<u>h on Da</u>vid...)
2. Ford (...<u>for D</u>wight...)
3. Audi (...burea<u>u, diva</u>n...)
4. Fiat (..."I<u>f I ate</u>...)
5. Cadillac (...energeti<u>c ad, I'll a</u>che ...)
6. Mustang (...<u>must, A</u>ngie...)
7. Corolla (...ta<u>co roll a</u>nd...)
8. Subaru (...<u>sub, a ru</u>sh...)

page 258: Word Pictures
1. Python (PIE + thon)
2. Antelope (ANT + elope)
3. Dolphin (DOLL + fin)
4. Chimpanzee (chim + PANSY)
5. Penguin (PEN + guin)
6. Badger (BADGE + er)
7. Cobra (co + BRA)
8. Manatee (mana + TEA)

page 259: Group Therapy
Some Group Therapy questions have many possible correct answers. Your answers may differ from ours and still be correct.
1. F. Lee Bailey, Johnnie Cochran, Clarence Darrow, Alan Dershowitz, Atticus Finch, Nancy Grace, Rudy Giuliani, Caroline Kennedy, Abraham Lincoln, Nelson Mandela, Perry Mason, Thurgood Marshall, Barack Obama, Marco Rubio, Barry Scheck, Jeffrey Toobin
2. Helium, Hydrogen, Nitrogen, Oxygen, Fluorine, Neon, Chlorine, Argon, Krypton, Xenon, Radon

3. Than, Thanks, Thaw, Theater, Their, Theme, Theory, Thermal, Thick, Thief, Thigh, Thin, Think, Thirteen, Thorn, Thought, Thread, Three, Throat, Through, Throw, Thumb, Thwart, Thyme

4. *A Midsummer Night's Dream, All's Well That Ends Well, As You Like It, Hamlet, Henry IV, Henry V, Henry VI, Henry VIII, Julius Caesar, King Lear, Macbeth, Much Ado About Nothing, Othello, Richard II, Richard III, Romeo and Juliet, The Merchant of Venice, The Taming of the Shrew, The Tempest, Twelfth Night, Two Gentlemen of Verona*

5. Balmoral, Beanie, Beret, Boater, Bonnet, Bowler, Cap, Chador, Cloche, Coonskin cap, Cowboy hat, Deerstalker, Fascinator, Fedora, Fez, Headdress, Headgear, Headscarf, Helmet, Homburg, Hood, Nightcap, Panama hat, Pillbox, Porkpie hat, Skimmer, Skullcap, Stocking cap, Tam (Tam o'shanter), Top hat, Turban, Watch cap, Yarmulke

6. Bedroom furniture, Car, Cemetery plot, Clothes dryer, Dining room set, Dishwasher, Hand tools, House, Insurance policy, Living room furniture, Luggage, Mattress, Pet, Pots and pans, Refrigerator, Stove, Washing machine, Wedding gown, Wedding ring

7. *30 Rock; All in the Family; Barney Miller; Car 54, Where Are You?; Friends; Glee; I Love Lucy; Law & Order; Mad About You; Mad Men; Make Room for Daddy; My Little Margie; NYPD Blue; Orange Is the New Black; Rhoda; Seinfeld; Sex and the City; Spin City; Taxi; That Girl; The Cosby Show; The Dick Van Dyke Show; The Honeymooners; The Jeffersons; The King of Queens; The Mindy Project; The Nanny; The Odd Couple; The Patty Duke Show; Welcome Back, Kotter; Will & Grace*

8. Shooting, Shuffleboard, Skateboarding, Skating, Skiing, Skittles, Sledding, Snooker, Snowshoeing, Snowboarding, Soccer, Softball, Squash, Steeplechase, Stickball, Stock car racing, Sumo wrestling, Surfing, Swimming

page 259: Trivia—Harvard Dropouts
1. Bill Gates
2. Pete Seeger
3. Robert Frost
4. Matt Damon
5. Mark Zuckerberg

page 260: Alphabet Trivia
1. Tennessee, Texas
2. Taipei, Taiwan (2.6 million); Tehran, Iran (12.2 million); Tianjin, China (13.55 million); Tokyo, Japan (13.23 million); Toronto, Canada (2.6 million)
3. Tallahassee (FL), Topeka (KS), Trenton (NJ)
4. John Tyler, Zachary Taylor, William Howard Taft, Harry Truman
5. Margaret Thatcher
6. Timpani, Tom tom, Triangle, Trombone, Trumpet, Tuba (*Other correct answers are possible.*)
7. Tamarind, Tangerine, Tomatillo, Tomato, Turnip (*Other correct answers are possible.*)
8. Tadpole, Tapir, Tarantula, Tasmanian devil, Termite, Tern, Terrapin, Terrier, Thomson's gazelle, Thrush, Tick, Tiger, Timber wolf, Tortoise, Toucan, Trout, Tsetse fly, Tuna, Turkey, Turtle, Turtle dove (*Other correct answers are possible.*)

9. Touch and Taste
10. Taurus
11. *Titanic, Tootsie, Troy, Trainspotting*...and other correct answers

page 260: Riddle Me This
A glove

page 261: Trivia— Don't Bug Me
1. Centipede
2. Tick
3. Mosquito
4. June bug

page 261: Anagrams
1. Tush, Huts, Shut, Thus
2. Agree, Eager
3. Steno, Notes, Onset, Stone, Tones
4. Being, Binge, Begin
5. Marines, Remains, Seminar
6. Ranged, Gander, Danger, Garden
7. Ethics, Itches
8. Aspired, Diapers, Praised, Despair

page 262: Vivienne's Vowels
1. *Exodus*
2. *Lolita*
3. *"Imagine"*
4. *Cabaret*
5. *Oklahoma!*
6. *Mamma Mia*
7. *Grease*
8. *Nova*
9. *LA Law*
10. *Lassie*
11. *Jane Eyre*

12. *Roots*
13. *The Sopranos*

page 262: Letter Play
<u>H</u>ead
<u>P</u>arts
<u>F</u>ill
<u>Y</u>ellow
<u>B</u>room
Med<u>a</u>l
St<u>a</u>re
<u>T</u>hick
BIRTHDAY

page 263: Finish the Proverb
1. That which does not kill us makes us stronger.
2. Revenge is a dish best served cold. (Revenge is mine *and* Revenge is sweet *are also correct.*
3. Spare the rod and spoil the child.
4. It's better to light a candle than to curse the darkness.
5. A rising tide lifts all boats.
6. Time and tide wait for no man.
7. A chain is only as strong as its weakest link.
8. There's no such thing as a free lunch.

page 263: Honorific Titles
1. Mrs. Doubtfire
2. Madame Defarge
3. Dr. Bombay
4. Dr. Denton's
5. Doc Holliday
6. Miss Brooks
7. Sir Lancelot
8. Auntie Em

9. Mr. Magoo
10. Miss America

page 264: Name Game
1. Stir + loo + past + E (Louis Pasteur)
2. Knee + and + E + roux (Andy Rooney)
3. Weigh + err + hemming + nest (Ernest Hemingway)
4. Fin + go + van + cent (Vincent Van Gogh)
5. Sap + row + arks (Rosa Parks)
6. Patch + E + Alp + no (Al Pacino)
7. Son + Oz + Z + knell (Ozzie Nelson)
8. Son + jack + key + glee (Jackie Gleason)
9. Word + how + ewes (Howard Hughes)

page 265: Endings & Beginnings
1. Moon
2. Coffee
3. Salt
4. Clothes
5. Paper
6. Tail
7. Lady
8. Rail
9. End
10. Sugar

page 265: Group Therapy
Some Group Therapy questions have many possible correct answers. Your answers may differ from ours and still be correct.

1. Padua, Palm Beach, Pamplona, Paris, Pasadena, Pensacola, Peoria, Perth, Philadelphia, Phoenix, Pittsburgh, Plymouth, Port-au-Prince, Portland, Portsmouth, Prague, Providence

2. Bigelow, Black tea, Celestial, Chai, Chamomile, Constant Comment, Darjeeling, Earl Grey, English Breakfast, Green tea, Herbal tea, Lipton, Oolong, Orange Pekoe, PG, Red Rose, Salada, Stash, Tazo, Tetley, Twinings, Typhoo

3. Acrylic paint; Artificial heart; Astroturf; Automatic teller machine (ATM); Barbie doll; Birth control pill; Cable television; Cell phones; Color television; Credit cards; Diet soda; Disposable cameras; DVDs and CDs; Email; Fax machine; Felt-tip pens; High-definition television; HIV-AIDS; Hula hoop; Internet; Liquid Paper (Wite-Out); McDonald's; Microwave oven; Nondairy creamer; Pacemaker; Permanent press fabric; Personal computers; Plastic wrap; Polio vaccine; Post-it notes; Prozac; Seat belts; Shingles vaccine; Teflon; Telephone answering machine; Transistor radio; Valium; Viagra; Video games

4. Anguilla, Antigua and Barbuda, Australia, Bahamas, Barbados, Belize, Bermuda, Canada, Gibraltar, Grenada, Guam, India, Ireland, Jamaica, Kenya, Liberia, New Zealand, Nigeria, Philippines, Samoa, Singapore, South Africa, The Bahamas, United Kingdom, United States of America, Virgin Islands

5. P. T. Barnum, L. L. Bean, e. e. cummings, W.E.B. Du Bois, Cecil B. De Mille, T. S. Eliot, W. C. Fields, F. Scott Fitzgerald, Michael J. Fox, J. Paul Getty, B. B. King, C. S. Lewis, A. A. Milne, Edward R. Murrow, I. M. Pei, J. C. Penney, J. K. Rowling, J. D. Salinger, George C. Scott, O.J. Simpson, J.R.R. Tolkien, Harry S. Truman, H. G. Wells, E. B. White

6. Beaver, Chinchilla, Chipmunk, Gopher, Guinea pig, Hamster, Mole, Mouse, Porcupine, Prairie dog, Rat, Squirrel, Vole

7. Sarong, Scarf, Shawl, Shirt, Shoes, Shorts, Ski hat, Ski jacket, Skirt, Skort, Slacks, Slicker, Slip, Slippers, Smock, Snowsuit, Socks, Sport coat, Suit, Sweater, Sweatpants, Sweatshirt, Swimsuit (*Other, more obscure answers might be possible.*)

page 266: Wacky Wordies
1. Put in my two cents
2. Cake mix
3. Look high and low
4. The price is right
5. Shut up and sit down
6. Bent over backwards
7. There is nothing on TV
8. Raisin bread

page 268: Word Tower
These answers are just a suggestion; many other correct answers are possible:
1. Go
2. Got
3. Gown
4. Gourd
5. Goblet
6. Golfing
7. Goldfish
8. Gooseneck
9. Government
10. Goalkeepers
11. Gobbledygook
12. Gossipmongers

page 269: Add Some Letters

Note: Other, more obscure correct answers are possible.

1. Miked, Mimed, Mined, Mired, Mixed
Miffed, Milked, Milled, Minced, Minded, Minted, Misled, Missed, Misted

2. Batter, Fatter, Hatter, Latter, Matter, Patter, Ratter, Tatter,
Chatter, Clatter, Flatter, Platter, Scatter, Shatter, Smatter, Spatter, Swatter

3. Being, Bling, Boing, Bring
Baking, Baling, Baring, Basing, Bating, Baying, Biding, Biking, Biting, Bluing, Boding, Boning, Booing, Boring, Bowing, Boxing, Busing, Buying

4. Dipped, Lipped, Nipped, Ripped, Sipped, Tipped, Yipped, Zipped
Blipped, Chipped, Clipped, Dripped, Flipped, Gripped, Quipped, Shipped, Skipped, Slipped, Snipped, Tripped, Whipped

5. Lacer, Lager, Lamer, Laser, Later, Laxer, Layer
Lacier, Ladder, Lagger, Lancer, Lander, Lanker, Lapper, Larder, Larger, Lasher, Lather, Latter, Lawyer, Lazier

page 269: Riddle Me This
A secret

page 270: Find the Words
(see pages 390–391)

page 272: Memorable TV Lines

1. *Mission: Impossible*; Recorded voice on tape
2. *Columbo*; Columbo
3. *Sanford and Son*; Fred Sanford
4. *The Addams Family*; Lurch
5. *Wide World of Sports*; Jim McKay
6. *Maude*; Maude Findlay
7. *Saturday Night Live*; Dan Aykroyd (to Jane Curtin)
8. *Kojak*; Kojak
9. *Alice*; Flo Castleberry
10. *Good Times*; J.J. Evans
11. *Welcome Back, Kotter*; Vinnie Barbarino
12. *Diff'rent Strokes*; Arnold

page 272: Letter Play
Eager
Snack
Wing
Nation
Stung
Dump
Scale
Mania
LANGUAGE

page 273: Making Connections
Go, Sorry, Life: Classic board games
Pepper, York, Shriver: Sergeants
Britain, Dane, Lakes: Great

page 274: Alphabet Trivia

1. Uganda, Ukraine, United Arab Emirates, United Kingdom, United States of America, Uruguay, Uzbekistan
2. Unicorn
3. Ugh, Ump, Urn, Use (*Note: according to two dictionaries, "ump" is a word!*)
4. Utah, which comes from the Ute language
5. Uranus
6. Uranium
7. Union of Soviet Socialist Republics (USSR)
8. Uzi
9. Johnny Unitas
10. Ulna
11. Uhura
12. Acronyms:
University of California at Los Angeles
Unidentified flying object
Ultra-high frequency
United Nations
United Negro College Fund
United Press International
United Parcel Service
United States Air Force

page 275: Letter Play
Down
Toffee
Meaner
Donkey
Rock
Sleep
Doily
Pasta
ADOPTION

CHAPTER EIGHT

page 276: Run the Alphabet—Cars

Other correct answers are possible.

A: Audi, Accord (Honda)
B: BMW, Buick
C: Chevrolet, Cadillac
D: Dodge, Duesenberg
E: Explorer (Ford), Escort (Ford)
F: Ford, Fiat
G: GMC, GTO (Pontiac)
H: Honda, Hyundai
I: Isuzu, Infinity
J: Jaguar, Jeep
K: Kia, Karmann Ghia (VW)
L: Lincoln, Lamborghini
M: Mercedes, Mazda
N: Nissan, Nova (Chevrolet)
O: Oldsmobile, Odyssey (Honda)
P: Pontiac, Prius (Toyota)
Q:
R: Rolls Royce, Renault
S: Subaru, Saab
T: Taurus, Toyota
U: Uno (Fiat)
V: Volkswagen, Volvo
W: Wagoneer (Jeep), Wrangler (Jeep)
X:
Y: Yaris (Toyota)
Z: Zephyr (Mercury), Z (Datsun)

page 277: Trimble

1. Shirley
2. Phoebe
3. Frasier
4. Pebbles
5. Buddy
6. Rhoda
7. Ed Norton
8. Muldoon

Jumble Answer: Cosmo Kramer

page 278: Word Pictures

1. Kayak (Ka + YAK)
2. Category (CAT + egory)
3. Coward (COW + ard)
4. Battery (BAT + tery)
5. Foxtrot (FOX + trot)
6. Genteel (Gent + EEL)
7. Pigment (PIG + ment)
8. Selfish (Sel + FISH)

page 279: Initial Quiz

1. Punctuation Mark
2. Adding Machine
3. Priority Mail
4. Air Marshals
5. Alaskan Malamute
6. Paul McCartney
7. Alma Mater
8. Answering Machine
9. Patent Medicine
10. Peat Moss
11. Pinball Machine
12. Praying Mantis

page 279: Trivia—Body of Evidence

1. Umbilical cord
2. Cornea
3. Follicles
4. Jugular

page 280: Prime-Time Rhyme

1. Cooper; trooper; blooper;
2. Chinchilla; gorilla; Manila
3. Quibble; scribble; kibble
4. Clarinet; marionette; suffragette
5. Query; merry; cherry
6. Spawn; yawn; pawn
7. Cloud; loud; crowd
8. Brunch; hunch; punch
9. Go-go; dodo; yo-yo
10. Spunky; junkie; monkey
11. Queasy; sleazy; easy
12. Afraid; betrayed; parade
13. Liberate; suffocate; decorate

page 281: Alphabetically Speaking

1. Brown University
2. LaVerne
3. Atlantic Avenue
4. *All's Well That Ends Well*
5. Argon
6. Zimbabwe
7. Trenton
8. Zachary Taylor
9. United Kingdom
10. Acadia

page 282: Nicknames

1. Wayne Gretzky *or* Jackie Gleason
2. Muhammad Ali
3. Perle Mesta
4. Florence Nightingale
5. Pete Rose
6. Alaska
7. New Mexico
8. Jenny Lind
9. Amelia Earhart
10. New Hampshire
11. The Department of State (*or its location in Washington, DC*)
12. The media

page 282: Common Bonds
World Rivers: Snake (River), Flag of Jordan (Jordan River), Columbia University (Columbia River)

page 283: Two-Minute Madness: _____ Number
Note: Other correct answers are possible.
1. Account number
2. Atomic number
3. Binary number
4. Call number
5. Cardinal number
6. Decimal number
7. Emergency number
8. Even number
9. File number
10. Finite/Infinite number
11. Flight number
12. Identification number
13. Irrational number
14. License number
15. Lucky/Unlucky number
16. Magic number
17. Odd number
18. Ordinal number
19. Page number
20. Part number
21. Phone/Telephone number
22. PIN number
23. Plate number
24. Prime number
25. Random number
26. Rational number
27. Registration number
28. Room number
29. Round number
30. Serial number
31. Whole number
32. Wrong number

page 284: Double Trouble
1. After
2. Bread
3. Counter
4. Dead
5. Love
6. Master
7. Pillow
8. Snake
9. Up
10. Belly

page 285: What's Their Job?
1. Teacher
2. British Prime Minister
3. Magician
4. Anthropologist
5. US Senator
6. Economist
7. Historian
8. Mathematician
9. Jeweler
10. Environmentalist
11. Secretary
12. Psychologist/Psychiatrist

page 286: Alphabet Trivia
1. Venezuela
2. Vietnam
3. Martin Van Buren
4. Vermont and Virginia
5. Verb
6. Vixen
7. Violin and Viola
8. Virgo
9. Volkswagen and Volvo
10. Venus
11. Vermouth and Vodka (Vinsanto *is also correct, though it is not common.*)
12. Ventricle

13. Vertebrae
14. Veins

page 286: Trivia—Title Translations
1. *Uncle Tom's Cabin*
2. "The Fall of the House of Usher"
3. *The Red Badge of Courage*
4. *The Sun Also Rises*

page 287: By the Letter
1. L   Landon (Michael)
2. A   Argentina
3. D   Digestive
4. Y   Yellowstone
5. B   Ball (Lucille)
6. U   Haiku
7. G   Gerontology
LADYBUG

page 288: Follow the Rules
(see next page)

page 289: Out of This WORLD
1. "Laugh and the world laughs with you, . . ."
2. *World Book Encyclopedia*
3. *The New World Symphony*
4. "What a Wonderful World"
5. Carry the weight of the world on his shoulders
6. "I'm the king of the world!"
7. World Wide Web
8. ". . . rules the world."
9. Seven Wonders of the Ancient World
10. "We Are the World"

page 288: Follow the Rules

1. S C I E N C E I S T R U E E V E N I F
2. S **O** I E N **O** E I S T R U E E V E N I F
3. **Y** O I E N O E I **D** T R U E E V E N I F
4. **Y** O I _ N O _ I D T R U E E V E N I F
5. Y O I N O I D T R U E **L** E V E N I F
6. Y O I N O _ D T R U E **L** I E V E N I F
7. Y O I _ _ D O N T R U E L I E V E N I F
8. Y O I D O N T R U E L I E V E N I **T**
9. Y O I U D O N T R _ E L I E V E N I **T**
10. Y O I U D O N T **B** E L I E V E N I T
11. Y O _ U D O N T B E L I E V E _ I T

(Science is true even if) you don't believe it.
Neil deGrasse Tyson (Note: Tyson's precise quote is "The good thing about science is that it is true, even if you don't believe it.")

---

page 289: Riddle Me This
A hole

page 290: Word Pictures
1. S + Choir = Esquire
2. Can + D = Candy
3. Pill + O = Pillow
4. M + Braces = Embraces
5. B + Tray = Betray
6. A + Corn = Acorn
7. F + Fort = Effort
8. N + V = Envy

page 291: Vivienne's Vowels
1. Motorola
2. American Airlines
3. Facebook
4. Radio Shack
5. Volvo
6. Coca-Cola
7. Boeing
8. Google
9. Sears
10. Nike
11. Visa
12. Yahoo

page 291: BravO!
1. Kimono
2. Calico
3. Apollo
4. Flamingo
5. Gizmo
6. Falsetto
7. Fiasco
8. Inferno
9. Buffalo
10. Disco
11. Echo
12. Gazpacho

page 292: Ted's Terrible Titles
1. *Little Women*
2. *A Man for All Seasons*
3. *Animal Farm*
4. *Everybody Loves Raymond*
5. *Family Feud*
6. *Go Tell It on the Mountain*
7. "Let the Good Times Roll"
8. "Life Is a Bowl of Cherries"
9. "Stormy Weather"
10. *Sports Illustrated*
11. *Bury My Heart at Wounded Knee*
12. *Brave New World*

page 292: Fill in the Letters
Other, more obscure correct answers are possible.

1. Anew, Gnaw, Knew, Know, Snow
2. Aeon, Bean, Been, Dean, Fern, Hewn, Jean, Keen, Kern, Lean, Mean, Neon, Peon, Rein, Seen, Sewn, Teen, Tern, Vein, Wean
3. Alive, Chive, Drive, Naïve, Olive, Waive
4. Tract, Trait, Treat, Trout, Trust, Tryst
5. Digit, Licit, Limit, Visit
6. Scale, Scare, Shade, Shake, Shale, Shame, Shape, Share, Shave, Skate, Slade, Slake, Slate, Slave, Snake, Snare, Space, Spade, Spare, Spate, Stage, Stake, Stale, State, Suave
7. Boast, Boost, Coast, Foist, Hoist, Joist, Joust, Moist, Roast, Roost, Toast, Worst
8. Endive, Engine, Entice, Entire, Incise, Incite, Inside, Invite, Online, Unlike, Unripe

page 293: Making Connections

States, Airlines, Nations: United _____

Earl, Hussein, S.: Middle names of US Presidents

XII, Boxcars, $2^2 \times 3$: Twelve

page 294: How Much Is . . .?

1. 1447 (7 + 1440)
2. 220 (20 + 200)
3. 11 (3 + 8)
4. 13 (6 + 7) (*Because she married Richard Burton twice, Ms. Taylor had 8 marriages but 7 husbands.*)
5. 43 (40 + 3)
6. 1980 (1969 + 11)
7. 25 (12 + 13). (*Canada has 10 provinces and 3 territories.*)
8. 9 (7 + 2)
9. 1628 (1616 + 12)
10. 155 (55 + 100)

page 295: Complete the Words

		B	U	B	B	L	E		
		B	U	R	G	L	A	R	Y
R	E	C	O	G	N	I	Z	E	
S	W	E	E	P	S	T	A	K	E	S
		C	R	I	S	P	Y		
		B	L	A	D	E	S		
			Y	E	L	L	O	W	
			A	D	J	A	C	E	N	T
				S	Q	U	A	L	L
		A	L	O	U	D			
M	O	U	T	H	W	A	S	H	
W	O	N	D	E	R				
		A	P	R	O	N			
			S	W	A	M	P		
A	N	O	N	Y	M	O	U	S	
A	C	C	O	M	M	O	D	A	T	E

		C	R	A	Z	I	E	S	T
		D	E	V	I	L			
E	D	U	C	A	T	E			
		P	I	C	K	L	E		
V	I	L	L	A	I	N			
		P	A	J	A	M	A	S	
		C	H	I	R	P			
C	H	A	R	C	O	A	L		
		V	I	X	E	N			
D	A	F	F	O	D	I	L		

page 296: The Name Game

1. Owe + rob + hurt + din + ear (Robert DeNiro)
2. Ah + sew + lore + fee + in (Sophia Loren)
3. Ray + bill + ham + league (Billy Graham)
4. Don + land + my + call (Michael Landon)
5. O + ah + shell + me + bomb (Michelle Obama)
6. High + Lassie + lease + sell (Haile Selassie)
7. Blow + Pa + ahs + O + pick (Pablo Picasso)
8. Home + I + toll + yah + luck + knee + A (Ayatollah Khomeini)
9. Niece + toe + Oprah + no (Tony Soprano)

page 297: Heteronyms

1. Bass (BASS/BASE)
2. Row (ROE/RAO)
3. Release
4. Object (OB ject/ob JECT)
5. Deliberate (de LIB er it/de lib er ATE)
6. Console (CON sole/con SOLE)
7. Excuse (Ex SKYOOSE/ Ex KEWZ)
8. Last
9. Recreation (WRECK re a shun/REE cree a shun)
10. Reservations
11. Sewer (SUE wer/SO wer)
12. Buffet (BUFF et/bu FAY)

page 298: Alphabet Trivia

1. Warsaw, Poland; Washington, DC; Wellington, New Zealand; Windhoek, Namibia
2. Washington; West Virginia; Wisconsin; Wyoming
3. George Washington; Woodrow Wilson
4. Water polo; Weightlifting; Wrestling (freestyle and Greco-Roman)
5. Weimaraner; Welsh corgi; Welsh terrier; West Highland terrier; Wheaten terrier; Whippet; Wirehaired fox terrier
6. What; When; Where; Who; Why; Which; Whose
7. Wallaby, Walrus, Wapiti, Warthog, Water buffalo, Water moccasin, Waterbuck, Weasel, Whale, Wildebeest, Wolf, Wolverine, Wombat, Woodchuck, Woodpecker (*Other correct answers are possible.*)
8. World Wide Web
9. James Watson
10. Christopher Wren
11. Western Wall (Wailing Wall)
12. Richard Wagner
13. William Wallace

14. Wimbledon
15. Acronyms:
    White Anglo-Saxon
    Protestant
    Weapons of mass
    destruction
    World Trade Center
    What would Jesus do?
    World Health
    Organization
    Wall Street Journal
    World Wildlife Fund
    (*or* World Wrestling
    Federation)

page 299: **Word Parts**
1. Pigeon (pig + eon)
2. Colonel (colon + el)
3. Figurine (fig + urine)
4. Flagrant (flag + rant)
5. Generally (Gene + rally)
6. Laboratory (Labor + A + Tory)
7. Mahogany (ma + hog + any)
8. Marinated (marina + Ted)
9. Mathematics (mat + hem + A + tics)
10. Permeated (perm + eat + Ed)
11. Republican (re + public + an)
12. Warranties (war + ran + ties)

page 300: **Word Pictures**
1. Pickpocket (Pick + Pocket)
2. Tongue twister (Tongue + Twister)
3. Mousetrap (Mouse + Trap)
4. Finger bowl (Finger + Bowl)

5. Dragonfly (Dragon + Fly)
6. Buttonhole (Button + Hole)
7. Forecast (Four + Cast)
8. Piecemeal (Peace + Meal)

page 302: **Complete the Words**

D	O	O	D	A	D	S		
	W	H	I	S	T	L	E	
	S	W	I	N	D	L	E	
	M	A	R	A	T	H	O	N
	R	E	M	A	R	K	S	
P	O	L	Y	E	S	T	E	R
A	M	U	S	I	N	G		
S	P	R	I	N	K	L	E	S
G	O	D	F	A	T	H	E	R
	R	E	B	U	T	T	A	L
	B	R	O	T	H			
	J	O	U	R	N	A	L	
B	U	R	G	U	N	D	Y	
P	R	E	V	I	E	W	S	
	S	T	I	P	E	N	D	
	E	A	G	E	R	L	Y	
P	L	A	N	E	T	S		
C	A	R	P	E	T	B	A	G
V	O	L	C	A	N	O		
L	O	L	L	I	P	O	P	S

page 303: **Odds & Ends**
1. Nodding
2. Defendant
3. Hot toddy
4. Dividend
5. Slender
6. Impending
7. Goddess
8. Appendix
9. Shoddy
10. Sweeney Todd
11. Endodontist
12. Coddler

page 303: **Riddle Me This**
A map

page 304: **Quick as a Bunny . . . or a Wink**
Other, more obscure answers are possible.
1. A bell; Day; Mud
2. Dirt; Methuselah; The hills
3. Gold; New; It gets
4. A newborn babe; A lamb
5. Air; A feather
6. Day; The nose on your face
7. Dirt; A church mouse
8. Ice; a witch's teat
9. Gold; Ivory Soap; The driven snow
10. A baby's bottom/ behind; Glass; Ice; Satin; Silk
11. Leather; Nails

page 305: **Triplets**
1. Executive, legislative, and judicial
2. Goneril, Regan, and Cordelia
3. Veni, vidi, vici
4. *The Lion, the Witch, and the Wardrobe*
5. Gold, frankincense, and myrrh
6. Liberté, egalité, fraternité
7. The Kentucky Derby, the Preakness, and the Belmont Stakes
8. Alcohol, Tobacco, and Firearms
9. Placido Domingo, Jose Carreras, and Luciano Pavarotti

10. Janet, Chrissy, and Jack
11. Bewitched, bothered, and bewildered
12. Could've, would've, should've
13. Ears, nose, and throat
14. Judge, jury, and executioner
15. Lather, rinse, and repeat

page 306: Group Therapy
Some Group Therapy questions have many possible correct answers. Your answers may differ from ours and still be correct.

1. Brown, Columbia, Dartmouth, Emory, Florida State, Georgia Institute of Technology (Georgia Tech), Grinnell, Harvard, Howard, Iowa State, Loyola, New York University, Northwestern, Notre Dame, Pepperdine, Rice, Stanford, Trinity, Tufts, Tuskegee, Wheaton, Yale

2. Abbot, Archbishop, Bishop, Cantor, Cardinal, Chaplain, Dalai Lama, Deacon, Elder, Father, Imam, Minister, Mother Superior, Nun, Pastor, Patriarch, Pope, Preacher, Priest, Rabbi, Reverend, Sister, Vicar

3. *3-2-1- Contact, American Experience, American Masters, Antiques Roadshow, Arthur, Austin City Limits, Barney, Cosmos, Curious George, Electric Company, Eyes on the Prize, Frontline, Masterpiece Theatre, Mr. Rogers' Neighborhood, Mystery, Nature, NOVA, PBS NewsHour, POV, Reading Rainbow, Sesame Street, The Civil War, This Old House, Vietnam, Where in the World Is Carmen Sandiego?, ZOOM*

4. Mario Batali, James Beard, Anthony Bourdain, Joyce Chen, Julia Child, Paula Deen, Auguste Escoffier, Fanny Farmer, Bobby Flay, Ina Garten, Graham Kerr, Emeril Lagasse, Jacques Pepin, Paul Prudhomme, Wolfgang Puck, Gordon Ramsay, Rachael Ray, Martha Stewart

5. Australia, Brunei, Cambodia, Canada, Chile, China, Colombia, Costa Rica, Ecuador, El Salvador, Guatemala, Honduras, Indonesia, Japan, Malaysia, Mexico, New Zealand, Nicaragua, North Korea, Panama, Papua New Guinea, Peru, Philippines, Russia, Singapore, South Korea, Taiwan, Thailand, United States of America, Vietnam (*and the many small island countries in the Pacific*)

6. Thomas Dewey, Bob Dole, Stephen Douglas, Michael Dukakis, Barry Goldwater, Al Gore, Hubert Humphrey, Jesse Jackson, John Kerry, Alf Landon, John McCain, George McGovern, Walter Mondale, Ralph Nader, Mitt Romney, Adlai Stevenson, Wendell Willkie

7. Agate, Amber, Amethyst, Aquamarine, Citrine, Coral, Diamond, Emerald, Garnet, Iolite, Jasper, Lapis lazuli, Onyx, Opal, Pearl, Quartz, Ruby, Sapphire, Tanzanite, Topaz, Turquoise

8. *Merci*/French; *Gracias*/Spanish; *Danke*/German; *Grazie*/Italian; *Obrigado*/Portuguese; *Spasibo*/Russian; *Shukran*/Arabic; *Arigato*/Japanese; *Xie Xie*/Mandarin Chinese; *Efharisto*/Greek; *Mahalo*/Hawaiian; *Toda*/Hebrew

page 306: Endings & Beginnings
1. Apple
2. Pitch
3. Building
4. Corn
5. Egg
6. Dressing
7. Cross
8. Shopping
9. Radio
10. Master

page 307: Making Connections
V, L, M: Roman numerals
Voice, E, Black: _____ Mail
CP, MS, RA: Diseases known by two letters (cerebral palsy, multiple sclerosis, rheumatoid arthritis)

page 308: Word Tower
These answers are just a suggestion; many other correct answers are possible:
1. An
2. Ant
3. Ante
4. Angel
5. Animal
6. Anatomy
7. Animator
8. Anarchist
9. Antiseptic
10. Anniversary
11. Anticipation
12. Announcements
13. Anesthesiology
14. Anthropologists
15. Anthropomorphism
16. Antirevolutionary
17. Antivivisectionist

page 309: Common Bonds
Nut, Ritz, Fire : _____ Cracker

page 309: Vivienne's Vowels
1. Ethiopia
2. Israel
3. India
4. Cairo
5. Bolivia
6. Easter Island
7. Austin
8. Utah
9. Miami
10. Oslo

page 310: Anagrams
1. Carets, Caster, Caters, Crates, Reacts, Recast, Traces
2. Parleys, Parsley, Players, Replays, Sparely
3. Recused, Reduces, Rescued, Secured, Seducer
4. Rickets, Sticker, Tickers
5. Spotter, Potters, Protest
6. Bluest, Bustle, Sublet, Subtle
7. Carnet, Canter, Nectar, Recant, Trance
8. Parsed, Drapes, Rasped, Spared, Spread

page 310: Letter Play
Cou<u>r</u>t
<u>L</u>ender
<u>F</u>inger
Tri<u>c</u>k
F<u>a</u>res
G<u>i</u>ant
<u>M</u>iner
<u>S</u>ample
FAMILIAR

page 311: Whose Biography?
1. John F. Kennedy
2. Frank McCourt
3. Bill Gates
4. Barack Obama
5. Steve Martin
6. Katharine Hepburn
7. Abraham Lincoln
8. Michelangelo
9. Julia Child
10. William Shatner
11. Michael J. Fox
12. Henry David Thoreau
13. Dian Fossey
14. Ellen DeGeneres

page 312: Finish the Equation
1. 3 = Blind Mice (See How They Run)
2. 3 = Strikes and You're Out
3. 6 = Strings on a Guitar
4. 13 = Original Colonies
5. 18 = Holes on a Golf Course
6. 29 = Days in February in a Leap Year
7. 52 = Cards in a Deck (Without Jokers)
8. 64 = Squares on a Checker/Chess Board
9. 66 = Books of the Bible
10. 76 = Trombones Led the Big Parade
11. 100 = Pennies in a Dollar
12. 206 = Bones in the Human Body

1. Captain Hook
2. Private detective (Private eye *is also correct.*)
3. General Motors
4. Corporal punishment
5. Majorette
6. Private property
7. Captain Kangaroo
8. General Electric
9. Major League Baseball
10. *General Hospital*
11. Private parts
12. Cap'n Crunch
13. General Mills

page 314: **Alphabet Trivia**
1. Mexico, Luxembourg
2. Manx and Lynx
3. ExxonMobil and Xerox
4. Exodus
5. Styx
6. Kentucky, Maryland, New Jersey, New York, Pennsylvania, Wyoming
7. Yangtze
8. Yeltsin (Boris)
9. Yukon
10. Yom Kippur
11. Yahoo! and YouTube
12. Arizona
13. Zeppelin
14. Zither
15. Zellweger (Renée)

page 315: **Odd Man Out**
1. *Paul Newman* is the odd man out. All of the others started acting when they were children.
2. *Silver* is the odd man out. All of the others are types of waves.
3. *Winnie-the-Pooh* is the odd man out. He is a fictional bear. The rest are fictional mice.
4. *North Carolina* is the odd man out. It is the only state in the list that was not admitted to the Union in the twentieth century. (North Carolina was one of the original thirteen colonies. It gained its statehood in November of 1789.)
5. *Tokyo* is the odd man out. All of the others are capitals of countries that start with the letter S (Spain, Sweden, Syria).
6. *The United States* is the odd man out. All of the other countries have had a woman president/prime minister.
7. *Chris Evert* is the odd (wo) man out. All of the others have the name of a food in their last names: STEWart, FISHer, and HAMill.
8. *Jay Leno* is the odd man out. All of the others have last names that are also breeds of dogs.

page 315: **Common Bonds**
Types of dances: Square, Belly, Tap

page 316: **Double Trouble**
1. Writer
2. Mark
3. Luck
4. Light
5. Flower
6. Fall
7. Eye
8. Duck
9. Box
10. Bone

page 317: **Scrambled Movies**
1. *Rocky*
2. *Psycho*
3. *Patton*
4. *Batman*
5. *Lolita*
6. *Witness*
7. *Tootsie*
8. *Cabaret*
9. *Amadeus*
10. *Vertigo*
11. *Scarface*
12. *Spartacus*
13. *Chinatown*
14. *Moonstruck*
15. *Deliverance*

page 317: **Letter Play**
Grape
Spare
Lease
Eight
Bitter
Hatch
Peach
Bland
SAPPHIRE

page 318: **Find the Anachronisms**
(see pages 400–402)

page 318: Find the Anachronisms

(see explanatory notes on page 402)

windshield wipers

parking meter

model t

popsicle

Coca-Cola

bandaid

polaroid camera

crossword puzzle

scrabble

aerosol spray
The first patent for an aerosol spray can was granted in Oslo, Norway, in 1927 to Erik Rotheim, a chemical engineer. He was granted a US patent in 1931. The disposable spray can was invented even later.

Band-Aid
The Band-Aid was invented in 1920 by Thomas Anderson and Earle Dickson. Dickson, who came up with the idea because his wife frequently cut and burned herself while cooking, was an employee of Johnson & Johnson. He later rose to become a company vice president.

bubble gum
While gum has been around for millennia, bubble gum, which is less sticky and more "stretchy" than standard chewing gum, was invented in 1928 by Walter E. Diemer, who worked for the Fleer Chewing Gum Company.

crossword puzzle
Although there were puzzles called "cross words" before 1900, they were very different in look and form from today's modern crossword puzzles. By most accounts, Arthur Wynne published a "Word Cross" puzzle that embodied most of the features of the puzzle as we know it today in the *New York World* on December 21, 1913.

Lincoln Logs
Lincoln Logs were invented in 1916–17 by John Lloyd Wright, son of the famous architect Frank Lloyd Wright.

Model T
Considered the first affordable automobile, the Ford Model T debuted in 1908.

parking meter
We have Roger W. Babson to thank for the parking meter, which was patented in 1928.

Polaroid instant camera
While the history of the camera goes back centuries to the camera obscura, the hand-held instant camera was conceived by Edward Land, the founder of Polaroid, in 1943, when his 3-year-old daughter asked why she couldn't see the picture he had just taken of her. On November 26, 1948, the first Land camera was sold for $89.95 at Jordan Marsh department store in Boston.

Popsicle
Eleven-year-old William "Frank" Epperson inadvertently invented the first popsicle in 1905 when he left a sweet drink outside on a freezing night. He introduced the fruit-flavored "Popsicle" as a product in 1922.

rotary dial candlestick phone
While the rotary dial phone was invented in 1889, it wasn't until 1919 that the first rotary dial was used in a telephone.

Scrabble
Alfred Mosher Butts, an American architect, created a game called "Criss-Crosswords" in 1938. After failing to interest a game manufacturer in his invention, Butts sold the rights to James Brunot, who simplified the rules and changed the name to Scrabble. But the game still didn't sell well until 1952 when Jack Straus, then president of Macy's department store, played Scrabble while he was on vacation. Surprised to discover that his store didn't carry the game, Macy's placed a large order, and the success of this now iconic game was secured.

windshield wipers
Invented in 1903 by Mary Anderson, windshield wipers began to appear in cars after 1905.

page 320: Presidential Anagrams

1. Herbert Hoover
2. George Bush
3. Abraham Lincoln
4. John Kennedy
5. Barack Obama
6. George Washington
7. James Madison
8. Ronald Reagan
9. Jimmy Carter
10. Harry Truman
11. Franklin Roosevelt
12. Grover Cleveland

page 320: Letter Play

Candle
Explode
Player
Globe
Ears
Perch
Purse
Mister
DECIBELS

page 321: Making Connections

Worth, Dix, Knox: Fort

_____

Magic, Lyndon, Howard: People named Johnson
Rose, George, Burning: Words with "Bush"

page 322: Act Your Age

Other, more obscure correct answers are possible.

1. Bite your lip, Button your lip, Zip your lip
2. Move your feet, Shuffle your feet, Stamp your feet, Wipe your feet
3. Clap your hands, Raise your hands, Wash your hands
4. Bless your heart, Break your heart, Cross your heart, Follow your heart
5. Arch your back, Behind your back, Break your back, Turn your back, Watch your back
6. All your life, Bet your life, Change your life, Live your life, Risk your life, Ruin your life
7. Blow your mind, Broaden your mind, Change your mind, Free your mind, Lose your mind, Open your mind, Speak your mind
8. Blink your eyes, Close your eyes, Cover your eyes, Dry your eyes, Open your eyes, Rest your eyes, Roll your eyes, Shut your eyes
9. Brush your hair, Comb your hair, Curl your hair, Cut your hair, Dye your hair, Lose your hair, Part your hair, Shampoo your hair, Straighten your hair, Toss your hair, Wash your hair
10. Bang your head, Bury your head, Hang your head, Lose your head, Nod your head, Over your head, Shake your head, Shave your head, Upside your head, Use your head, Watch your head

photo credits

Imran Khan p. 41 (number 8); Ashley Kirk p. 315 (bottom left); KirsanovV p. 278 (center right); kojihirano p. 168 (middle left); iurii Konoval p. 239 (buttercup); koosen p. 301 (button); korionov p. 94 (bottom right); kornnphoto p. 153 (bottom right); Maya Kovacheva p. 105 (bottom right); koya79 p. 51 (top center), p. 192 (letter D block); Laures p. 73 (top left); Olivier Le Moal p. 40 (May 1st); lenta p. 239 (forget-me-not); lepas2004 p. 66 (bottom left); lexaarts p. 78 (center right); lisafx p. 78 (center left); Valerie Loiseleux p. 258 (center right); LorenzoPatoia p. 51 (center left); LotusInteractive p. 192 (bud); lucielang p. 178 (top center), p. 192 (apple core); luiscarlosjimenez p. 66 (bottom right); LUTFI_URE p. 4 (top center), p. 41 (knee); mantonino p. 8 (top right); MargoeEdwards p. 229 (bacon); MariaBrzostowska p. 238 (center right); Maridav p. 127 (top right); marilyna p. 8 (center left); DAVID MARIUZ p. 228 (meter); masta4650 p. 178 (top left); matka_Wariatka p. 239 (hyacinth); matthiashaas p. 300 (bear trap); maxuser p. 193 (letter P); maxvuer p. 238 (bottom left); mbudley p. 193 (letter C); Brian McEntire p. 220 (catcher); melking p. 300 (tongue); michaeljung p. 290 (choir); MichaelNivelet p. 193 (knitting); mikdam p. 136 (bottom center); mikewesson p. 50 (top left), p. 201 (hand); milanvachal p. 73 (center right); mimic51 p. 4 (top left); mishooo p. 238 (bottom right); morenina p. 178 (center); moorlands p. 8 (top left); Naddiya p. 126 (bottom left); naqiewei p. 229 (negatives); Nasared p. 126 (center right); Nerthuz p. 229 (wrist); Newnow p. 126 (top right); NiDerLander p. 221 (child in bath); Kary Nieuwenhuis p. 117 (bottom right), p. 221 (quarter); nito100 p. 238 (top left); noegruts p. 168 (top left); Noraluca013 p. 8 (center right); nssrw1 p. 41 (letter U); nuiiun p. 41 (cube); olgaman p. 8 (bottom left); OlgaMiltsova p. 51 (bottom left), p. 290 (braces); Olmarmar p. 229 (mop); tyler olson p. 228 (dentist); Ozanbulbul p. 201 (kid drawing); Paffy69 p. 228 (eye); paleka19 p. 40 (glove); papparaffie p. 193 (number 10); PaulReevesPhotography p. 168 (middle right); PChStudios p. 126 (center); PeJo29 p. 315 (bottom center); Perseomed p. 300 (Roman numeral 4); petecripps p. 169 (pelican); photobac p. 72 (top left); PhotoEuphoria p. 221 (father lifting son); Photography1971 p. 40 (toe), p. 105 (bottom left); PicturePartners p. 278 (center left), p. 278 (bottom right); Pixel_Pig p. 4 (bottom left), p. 41 (oar); PixelEmbargo p. 127 (center left); post424 p. 290 (pill); Warren Price p. 9 (bottom left); Radist p. 136 (bottom right); RakicN p. 40 (straw); Rawpixel Ltd p. 4 (bottom right); riedochse p. 41 (egg yolk); robynmac p. 8 (bottom right); ronen p. 105 (top right); rosendo p. 301 (peace sign); RTimages p. 127 (center); RuslanOmega p. 258 (bottom left); RuthBlack p. 192 (letter M), p. 229 (letter Q); Santiaga p. 193 (tea); Sazonoff p. 229 (pearl); scanrail p. 220 (bell); SergioZacchi p. 220 (bean); setixela p. 84 (top left); sgame p. 220 (tooth); sil63 p. 9 (bottom right); Sergey Skleznev p. 300 (wooden bowl); Skystorm p. 220 (fork); Smileus p. 193 (tree); snokid p. 290 (tray); somkcr p. 40 (letter N); sphoom p. 40 (merge sign); SSSCCC p. 178 (bottom left), p. 193 (fin); Stephen_Edwards p. 127 (top middle); stevanovicigor p. 229 (knock); SteveByland p. 168 (top right), p. 168 (bottom left); STILLFX p. 41 (fur coat); studiof22byricardorocha p. 9 (top left); svanhorn p. 84 (top right); Taily p. 300 (dragon); tamara_kulikova p. 239 (iris); TAnutka p. 9 (center left); tatniz p. 84 (top center); terex p. 78 (center); the-lightwriter p. 201 (pants); Cory Thoman p. 193 (worm on hook); Tomo75 p. 278 (top left); Tribalium p. 247 (bottom right); Tsekhmister p. 278 (bottom left); turtix p. 51 (top right); Ukususha p. 193 (letter Z), p. 228 (letter J), p. 229 (letter M); Ulga p. 200 (board); ulkan p. 220 (pug); vadimrysev p. 220 (back); ValuaVitaly p. 40 (foot), p. 201 (shave); VikaSuh p. 201 (scale); Vjom p. 193 (comet); VladimirFLoyd p. 192 (ear); vnlit p. 238 (center left); volgariver p. 229 (soup); vtls p. 73 (bottom left); massimiliano vuerich p. 238 (bottom left); Craig Wactor p. 229 (mustard), p. 229 (ash); WellfordT p. 105 (top center); WestLight p. 258 (center); Willard p. 229 (helmet); WilleeCole p. 72 (top right); wissanu99 p. 153 (top right); witoldkr1 p. 300 (pick); Yulia-Images p. 127 (center right); yvdavyd p. 309 (top center); zentilia p. 51 (center right); zimindmitry p. 94 (bottom center); Zwilling330 p. 229 (toucan).

about the author

Nancy Linde created and runs Never2Old4Games.com, an online subscription service for activities professionals working with senior citizens at assisted living residences, retirement communities, senior centers, and other senior-serving organizations. She is also the author of *399 Games, Puzzles & Trivia Challenges Specially Designed to Keep Your Brain Young*. Prior to her work with seniors and games, she was a filmmaker who produced, wrote, and directed more than a dozen documentary films, including the PBS series *NOVA*. She lives in Massachusetts.